Petals of the Lotus

108 Inspirations to Awaken, Blossom and Bloom

Elise Cantrell

Shining Lotus Publishing

Library of Congress Cataloging-in-Publication
Data available upon request.

Shining Lotus Publishing books may be
ordered through booksellers or by contacting:

Shining Lotus Publishing
524 Sir Howard Circle
Kohler, WI 53044
www.40DaystoEnlightenedEating.com
1(920)917-8562

ISBN-13: 978-0-692-27794-2
ISBN-10: 0692277943

Printed in the United States of America.

First Edition

The author of this book does not prescribe the use of any technique as a form of treatment for physical, medical, emotional or relationship problems without the advice of a physician, either directly or indirectly. The intent of the author is only to offer information of a general nature to help you in your quest for body, mind and spirit wellness. In the event that you use the contents and information of the book for yourself, which is your constitutional right, the author and the publisher assume no responsibility for your actions.

About the front cover artist:

Each Cassy Tully original painting is meticulously created using Cassy's signature relief-painting technique. Based on extensive research of relief sculpting in Italy, Cassy uniquely blends traditional sculpting techniques with modern acrylic painting methods. This increases the level of relief and illusion of perspective in her paintings. Hints of iridescent paint provide subtle plays of light. Cassy's signature style is easily recognizable and each painting is a magnificent masterpiece.

As Cassy Tully original and commissioned artwork grows in value and prestige, it is Cassy's goal to give back and make a difference in the lives of others in honor of all those who have supported her passion for art. Cassy strives to serve as a model of success for other artists and women-business owners. In addition to contributing to charitable organizations and fund-raising auctions, Cassy has established the Cassy Tully - Heritage Scholarship for Young Artists to preserve her legacy and contribute to talented young artists.

"Cassy Tully - Fine Art" is located in the heart of historic Plymouth, Wisconsin. For more information on Cassy's original and commissioned artwork, visit www.cassytully.com.

Acknowledgements

I would like to express my heartfelt gratitude and appreciation to Lorrie Ransome, my editor, for her sharp eye for detail and going through the manuscript with a fine tooth comb! I deeply thank artist Cassy Tully for sharing the beautiful artwork that graces the front cover so perfectly. Thank you to my mom, Billie Edmonds, for being a second set of eyes and carefully reading through all 108 inspirations! Thank you to talented graphic designer, Christine Hitchcock for creating an exceptional book cover design and inspiring book interior. Thank you to my husband Mark Cantrell for patiently listening to me read each and every blog through to you, and for your insights and suggestions. Thank you to my students and friends for your inspiration and excitement that gave me an extra boost of perseverance and enthusiasm to bring this project from idea to fruition. I want to thank my precious family for their support, sacrifice and patience during the writing and publishing process. With your love and encouragement, I am sharing my passion for mind, body and spirit wellness with everyone! I want to thank God for writing this book through me, for the credit belongs to God alone! Thank you to the masters, *gurus*, teachers, scientists, philosophers and dreamers who passed along timeless wisdom and changeless truth so that we can all continue to rise towards our highest selves now and forever.

Namaste,

Elise Cantrell

Introduction

Awakening is like the opening of a lotus flower. The petals begin to soften their tight grip on the center and slowly peel away from the known until they blissfully and brilliantly open into their own magnificence. A flower's full beauty is only beheld when it is fully open, exposed and vulnerable. We as human beings awaken like the petals of a lotus over time through a succession of "ahas" interspersed with a progression of letting go. The lotus flower is said to rise up from the mud and murk beneath it and float above the dark depths it was born into. Although it took root in muddy waters, the lotus is able to make it to the light and fully bloom sharing its beauty and splendor.

Don't be afraid to open slowly; fear only staying closed. Chinese sage, Lao Tzu once said, "When I let go of who I am, I become who I might be." Many of us stand in those murky waters and remain in a tight bud awaiting our own opening. It is my intention that this string of 108 inspirations will light the way for you to ascend and open to a new way of life centered in love, joy, contentment and bliss. Now is the time to rise above the mud and murk of human experience and become who you were meant to be in beauty, majesty and splendor. I invite you to awaken, blossom and bloom . . .

Contents

Acknowledgements 6

Introduction 7

Awaken, Blossom and Bloom 11

What is the Significance of 108? 14

Are You Awakening?. .16

Finding Your Tribe 20

Are You Addicted to "Busy?" 22

What is Coming between YOU and JOY? 24

Are You Listening to Your Intuition? 27

Simplify Your Life 29

Life Lessons I Wish I Could Go Back 32

Unwrap Your Spiritual Gifts. 34

Affirmations to Heal and Harmonize the *Chakras* 37

Letting Go to Set Yourself Free 40

Am I on the Right Path? 44

Seven Things Thriving People Do Differently 46

A Prescription for Self-Care. 49

Step into Your Light and Shine 53

Don't Do Yoga, BE Yoga 56

What is Your Personal Mission Statement? 58

Trying vs. Being 60

What Can Dogs Teach Us about Stress? 62

Flowing Water Never Decays 64

The Seven Doors 66

Packing Guide for the Journey of Life 69

Paradise 73

Experiments in Love. .74

Life is a Playground 76

Taking Your Vacation Back with You into Your Life 78

Are you Being Kind Enough to Yourself? 81

Let the Real You Come Out to Play. 84

Weekend Review. 89

Creating Space for Grace 91

Sacred Geometry: The Power of the Triangle 95

How to Do What You Love, Succeed and Thrive! 97

Free Yourself 100

Living with Paradox 103
Staying Balanced and Grounded 106
Life Lessons I Learned from Writing a Book 110
A Walk Among the Dead 114
Unplugged!. 117
The Law of Expansion and Contraction 118
Enough. 120
Non-Striving: Life is Like a Cat 122
Turning Your Thinking Upside Down 125
Uncloaking Joy. 127
Balancing Life 130
Eight Ways to Refill Your Tank 132
The Art of Balancing Effort with Surrender 136
Life is Like a Yellow Brick Road. 140
Hidden Treasure 144
Conversation: Speaking Skillfully 145
Christmas in July? 149
Cultivating Courage 151
What Stands between You and Feeling Free? 154
The Sound of Silence 156
Be Kinder . . . to You 159
Transformation 161
Flowing in the Current of Grace 163
You're Not Full of Holes, You Are Whole 165
New Moon, New You. 167
The Ebb and Flow 169
WHO? 171
Spring Back to Life 174
Inquiring Minds 176
The Path 178
Sweetness 181
Without Space, There is No Room for Grace! 183
Is Yoga Evil??? 185
Releasing the "Should" Out of the Shoulders 187
Pressing the "Pause Button" in Your Life. 189
Blissed Out. 191
Yoga is Unity. 192
Get Unstuck 195
Starting Over. 200

Eight Stepping Stones to Manifesting Your Intentions 202
My Year of *Karma* and "CAR-ma" 206
Is Exploring Your Lunar Side Lunacy??? 208
Weeding Out Your Life 210
Returning Home to Yourself 212
Shape Shifting 214
Come on to Your Mat as Little Children 216
Peeling Away the Layers 218
The Remover of Obstacles 221
Riding the Winds of Change 224
"Bee" Inspired! 226
Polishing Your Inner Jewel 228
Stillness amidst the Storm 230
Letter from an Open Soul 232
Pancha Mahabhutani 235
Knowing When to Cry Uncle 238
Free To Be You 240
Repair, Rebuild, Restore, Renew 242
Aparigraha: The Art of Letting Go 243
Beat to Your Own Drum 245
The Power of Words 247
Thawing Out Your Mind, Body, and Spirit 249
Shine Your Light 251
Sacred Rest 253
The Healing Power of Beauty 256
The Message of the Snow 259
Letting Go 260
Inner Strength for Life's Obstacles 262
Are You Breaking Your Own Heart? 267
Make Your Yoga Practice a Mini-Vacation 269
Shifting Momentum in Your Life 271
Relaxing the Grasp 277
Unwrap Your Radiance 279

Awaken, Blossom and Bloom

Sooner or later everything awakens, at its own pace, in its own time. In spring nature awakens. The ice melts, and the bulbs burst through the earth! The birds come alive singing their songs. The grass greens and grows, and the trees bud, blossom and bloom. As we witness this sacred act of awakening in nature, we recognize that humans have the capacity to awaken too. The difference, however, is that humans can choose to stay in the dark and "sleep walk" through life, or we can consciously decide to wake up. What does it mean for humans to awaken?

Awakening begins when we start to *pay attention*. We awaken when we choose to fully participate in life and stop allowing ourselves to be distracted from what is really there. Our culture is constantly preoccupied by phone calls, text messages, emails, over-booked schedules, acquiring money and things, and all the other noise around us. When we aren't engrossed in all of those things, we often resort to "numbing out," with TV, alcohol, or other more dangerous addictions. Most of us are so preoccupied with distractions that we fail to see, experience and know reality as it is. We have become desensitized to what is *really* going on, both within ourselves and in the outside world. We have lost touch with who we really are, what we really want, and who we are to become.

To awaken, it is necessary to become *present* to life. We must be conscious, awake, and aware of each moment just as it is, without the need to divert our minds with business, detachment, delusion, or numbing. Although it would be impossible to get rid of every distraction (lest one become a hermit), it is important to recognize that all of these *are* distractions, keeping us at arm's length from the beauty of awakening and new growth reflected in nature. When we keep ourselves in the dark, we can't bud, blossom or bloom!

Awakening is *feeling*! We spend a lot of time trying not to feel. We have become masters at anesthetizing ourselves from our emotions. We have distanced ourselves so far from our own emotions that we have no idea how we feel about anything. Awakening is about opening up to your own emotions, recognizing them, *feeling* them, *trusting* them, and allowing them to become the guidance system they were intended to be. Emotions contain volumes of helpful information about ourselves, the people around us, the world, decision making, and guidance which way to go next. When we lose touch with our emotions, we lose touch with reality and with ourselves. When we delete our emotions we are deleting our innermost wisdom!

Awakening involves recognizing your *intuition*. Tuning in to your "gut" feelings, instincts, hunches, and vibes. When you get a negative "vibe" from someone, trust it! Awakening involves allowing yourself to see and hear the *truth*, your own truth, truth about the world around you, and universal truth. We all have inner truth-sensors, but over generations we have allowed reason and logic to overtake our innate intuitive sense. This has caused intuition to atrophy. Reason and logic are equally important, but they were not created to stand alone. Employing both your intuition and your intellect jointly is awakening! When you begin to awaken, you begin to know the truth. You recognize that truth is not something you are told; it is something you know.

We are spoon-fed many false truths by the mass media, politicians, the food industry, the pharmaceutical industry, and other institutions, which have their own agendas. Often this information is skewed towards their best interest, and not in our own. We have been conditioned to blindly trust and believe. Awakening is about discerning the truth for yourself. Truth can only be discovered through direct perception, direct knowledge. Because we have been so blinded by external false paradigms, we have allowed ourselves to become blinded as to who we really are within. When we can no longer sense our own authenticity, it becomes impossible to discern the validity of anything outside of ourselves.

Unwrapping your true self is awakening. When you lift the veil between you and who you *really* are, you awaken. The only way to begin the process of awakening is to pay attention and bring awareness *internally* within yourself, and *externally* in the world around you. The Easter story is all about awakening. Christ emerges from the darkness of his tomb, unwraps, leaving the shroud behind, and steps into the light. Awakening is a sacred act. As each one of us begins to awaken, blossom and bloom, we bring about a new springtime in this world. It is time.

What is the Significance of 108?

The number 108 arises frequently in the yoga system: 108 sun salutations, 108 mala beads, 108 *mantras*, 108 names of God. As I began to research the meaning of the number 108, I was both overwhelmed and astonished by the number's significance throughout history, mathematics, science, geometry, astrology, spirituality and world religion. It would take pages to enumerate the many profound connections humankind has to the number 108, so I've tried to distill it all into a concise, yet meaningful, summary.

108 has been considered an auspicious number across multiple cultures and faiths since pre-historic times. Numerologically, 108 is said to be a number of completion because the sum of the digits is 9. Geometrically, the number 108 signifies "coming full circle" and being in a state of "spiritual completion" because the number 108 is a natural division of a circle. The number 108 has traditionally been connected to sacred geometry. Geometry comes from the root word "geo" which means "earth." Interestingly, the distance between the earth and sun is 108 times the sun's diameter. The diameter of the sun is 108 times the earth's diameter. The earth's diameter is 108 times the moon's diameter, and the distance between the earth and moon is 108 times the moon's diameter. The pre-historic monument Stonehenge is about 108 feet in diameter. Can this all be a coincidence?

Synchronistically, human beings have 108 *nadis* or energy channels leading to the heart. In Ayurveda, there are 108 *marmas* or pressure points in the physical body. It is said there are 108 steps to enlightenment, and there are 108 paths to God. It is also said that there are 108 veils of desire, lies and delusion, which come between man and God. "Coming full circle" is about lifting each of these veils so we can see clearly.

108 exists within us and around us. 108 is considered a "divine number," reminding us that God also is in us and around us. It seems that

the numerology in our own bodies, mathematics, geometry, spirituality and the cosmos all point to the fact that we have a divine connection.

Awakening ultimately happens when we align ourselves as human beings with our inner nature, our earthly and cosmic surroundings, as well as our Creator, Source and Spirit. Spiritual completion comes about through connection and unity. We are fully awake when we come "full circle" back to God.

Are You Awakening?

Have you been feeling different lately? Have you and your life been rapidly changing? Are you the same person you were a year ago? Five years ago? The world as we know it and life as we know it are changing at warp speed! It is all the buzz that we, as a planet, are experiencing a great shift. We are in the midst of a massive awakening, a collective advancement in human consciousness whose impact is being felt globally, even all over the universe! Our human vibration is becoming lighter, faster, and higher. It is quickening. Many people are feeling these changes physically, mentally, emotionally and spiritually. Some people are resisting the change, clinging to the old; some are oblivious; while others may be fearful or confused as to what is going on. Very sensitive people can deeply sense what is happening, and are trying to understand it, process it, and be open to the wonder of this ever increasing awareness, cognizance and consciousness. This awakening is happening to us as a collective, but is seen at varying paces among individuals, in our own timing, as we can handle and process this rapid stage of growth. This evolution of consciousness is allowing humankind to ascend to a higher state of being. We are becoming increasingly aligned with our creator, with Christ consciousness, with our life purpose, and the highest good of all of creation. Awakening is not exclusive or limited to one particular religion, faith, or creed. It is an evolutionary process simultaneously shifting us all. Humankind is moving from 3-dimensional consciousness into 5-dimensional consciousness. We are learning to see things from new angles and fresh perspectives, and we are discovering new facets of the world and ourselves. We are becoming aware of things that were always there, but never before visible. Much like the discoveries that the world is not flat or that the sun is not at the center of the universe, our world-views are rapidly changing. We are reaching new thresholds in our lifetime! How can you tell if this shift is happening to you? Here are the top 20 indications that you are awakening. See how many ring true for you.

1. Change in your interests. Losing interest in things that once inspired you. Losing interest in things that are ego-based. No longer having things in common with people you once did. No longer doing things just because they "make you look cool" or because they are "what everyone else is doing." You begin to honor what YOU really want to do.

2. Many changes happening in your life quickly. Your life is being altered, changed and rearranged: relocation, new home, career change, change in marital status, new friends, new pets, births and deaths. Once you begin to change and transform, everything else around you begins to transform.

3. Seeing signs. Increased moments of synchronicity, coincidence, happenstance and "luck." You are continuously receiving meaningful messages from unexpected sources in unexpected ways. You are having a continuous succession of "aha moments."

4. Less interest in materialism. Feeling the need to clear out clutter, downsize, simplify. No longer living to impress people. Spending money on things YOU really want, rather than on what you think other people expect you to have. No more "keeping up with the Jones's".

5. Abundance. Noticing the ability to quickly and easily manifest what you want and need. Instant manifestation. When you think something, it actually happens!

6. Authenticity. Desire to get to know yourself, to be who you really are. No longer having the need to "people please," put on "airs," play the game. Saying "yes" when you mean "yes" and "no" when you mean "no." Aligning your actions with what you know is right for you.

7. Questioning old ideas. Seeing through past conditioning and old programming. Experiencing a disconnection from old rules, outdated ideas, old ways of doing things. Seeing things as they really are as if for the first time. Seeing through false paradigms. Higher thinking. Awareness and understanding of higher truths. Outgrowing old belief systems.

8. New openness and non-judgment. A new acceptance of others despite their differences. Honoring and accepting all beings just as they are!

9. Increased creativity, insights, intuition, awareness, vision, vivid dreams, higher thinking, inner knowingness. Knowing intuitively when someone is telling the truth or not. Hearing others' thoughts. Knowing what others are thinking, clairvoyance, claircognizance, clairaudience.

10. Noticing the magical and the sacred in the ordinary. Being open and receptive to miracles.

11. Loss of fear. Feeling a strong sense of protection and confidence. Noticing an inexplicable sense of inner peace.

12. Disconnection from mass media. You have grown tired of the negativity and hidden agendas of the news media.

13. Confusion, feeling overwhelmed by the rapid changes. Feeling disconnected, disassociated, and puzzled as you assimilate these changes internally and externally.

14. Feeling a new sense of connectedness. To others, to nature, to your higher self, to God, angels, ancestors, loved ones in spirit, etc.

15. Knowing things without knowing how you know them.

16. A sense of restlessness. Anticipation of something, but you have no idea what it is. A longing to return "home," without knowing where home really is. A feeling that a change is coming, but not being able to put your finger on it.

17. Experiencing physical symptoms. Headaches, dizzy spells, ringing in the ears, chills, feeling a vibration or shaking in your body, deep fatigue, difficulty sleeping, weight gain or loss without changing exercise or eating patterns. Changes in appetites, cravings, loss of interest in meat, alcohol, and unhealthful foods.

18. Being on an emotional roller-coaster. Feeling more emotional. Awareness of more ups and downs and emotional swings. Noticing old wounds and past hurts resurface and process through you in order to be released. Spontaneously finding yourself working through the pain, and forgiving yourself and others in order to heal. The need to move on and let go.

19. Newfound compassion. Inexplicable compassion for others, for the planet, for nature, for creatures large and small. Newfound compassion for yourself, and for those who think differently than you. Forgiveness, empathy and kindheartedness for those who have wronged you. You are a peacemaker filled with kindness for all.

20. Unconditional love. Our vibration is being raised to match the vibration of unconditional love. "Christ consciousness." Newfound compassion stems from the overwhelming feeling of the vibration of pure love. You feel an overwhelming sense of positivity and can no longer be around negative thinking, negative people, negative TV shows, music, reading material, etc.

If you answered "yes" even to a few of these, you ARE awakening. You and your level of consciousness are ascending. You are moving into the NEXT dimension. If you have almost all of these, then rest assured, you are almost there!

Finding Your Tribe

Living in a small town, in a graduating class of 36, it has been difficult for my daughter to find her "clique." Music, art and creativity gush from her like a fountain. She is not into the "party scene." She is not particularly "sporty" or athletic. She would rather spend her free time out in nature with a camera, creating a collage, sitting in the grass writing poetry, or composing a new song. Just a couple of weeks ago, Hannah embarked on a European choir tour with 300 other musically inclined teens from around the state. Hannah has absolutely marveled over the fact that the other kids, like her, spontaneously break out singing Disney songs and show tunes. She has been reassured to discover that there are others who always have a song playing in their head and music filling their heart. She is astonished by how much in common she has with this group of teens, and how quickly they have clicked. With this group she feels comfortable and at ease, like she is with her own family. These are like-minds and kindred souls. She has found her tribe!

Finding your tribe feels like "coming home." When I went to my first yoga training, I too marveled at discovering that I was not alone in my uniqueness. I had never admitted to anyone that I had an unquenchable curiosity for all things mystical, supernatural and mysterious. I hadn't dared to mention that even as a child I was fascinated by nature, herbs, crystals and stones. For the first time in my life, I realized that there are others out there who are drawn to all things spiritual, metaphysical and philosophical. People who, like me, see something greater in nature than what is visible to the eye. There are other people who spend their free time stretching and rolling around on a rubber mat, meditating, praying, and saying affirmations. I found other sensitive souls who hear the whispers of God and the angels, who feel the pulse of the Earth, who sense the urgency of our times. There are factions out there who devote their lives to help, heal, and harmonize, who are here to love, teach and serve. We are healers, visionaries and peacemakers. This is our calling; this is who we are. I am no longer embarrassed to own these gifts and step into my purpose. This is my tribe.

We all have a tribe, a clan of like minds and kindred spirits, people who view the world through the same lens as we do! One tribe is not better than any other; all are necessary and essential. Finding your tribe is like liver cells knowing they belong to the liver, heart cells knowing they belong to the heart, and brain cells knowing they belong to the brain. They each have very different functions, but all are critical to the body as a whole. Finding our tribe reminds us that we are part of something greater, with a mission and purpose. We are needed and necessary. We are not alone. Just like the cells of the body, we humans are the cells of the universe. Healers are the immune system of the collective. Visionaries are the eyes seeing the way forward. Musicians are the hum of the cosmos. Artists and inventors are the architects and creators of our reality. Farmers are our sustenance. And on it goes . . . We each have our place, we all have our roles. There is no need for denial, judgment, embarrassment, or feeling like an "odd duck." We just need to find our tribe!

Are You Addicted to "Busy?"

Does it feel like you can't keep up? Are you always in a race with time? Do you break the speed limit trying to get everywhere you need to go? Do you feel like you are stuck on the hamster wheel of life? Then perhaps you are addicted to "busy!"

Neurologically it is possible to become addicted to the "high" produced by stress hormones! Stress hormones can affect the body-mind system in much the same way as stimulants. Many people have become addicted to the high of chaos and stress!

According to Albert Einstein, time is an illusion. Einstein proved mathematically that time and space are one and the same, which is explained by his theory of relativity. When you create space in your life, you create time! As a culture, we have become conditioned to believe that if we are not always busy, then we are worthless and lazy! This is slowly leading to our own demise! If we are always "doing," there is no space in our lives to experience "being." Now is the time to end the "glorification of busy!" David Allen says, "You can do anything you want, but not everything!" Inner peace is the new busy!

Instead of over-planning and over-scheduling your family and yourself, schedule space, and produce more time! Instead of adding another thing to your calendar, cross something off! Schedule in moments of inner peace. Open space leaves room for intuition, creativity and inspiration to arise. Nature quickly works to fill a vacuum. When you create space, new things spontaneously flow in.

The *Tao Te Ching* teaches, "When your cup is full, stop pouring." Let go of the need to pile on task after task, event after event, and the need to be constantly occupied. Overflowing your cup makes a mess of your life. Busy is "out," and space is "in." Browse your daily schedule or list of "to-do's." Determine what is unnecessary. Scratch off the things that you can let go. First, focus on the things you actually *want* to do, and keep those. Then focus on the things you absolutely *have* to do and keep those. What is left can be released.

Use this newly created open space to say "YES." What have you been longing to do, but haven't found time? Discern what is relevant to your life and your well-being and what is not. Consciously say "no" to the things that don't serve you, and to that which is not your work. This creates the space in your life for all of the "yeses" that have been trapped inside of you. Allow yourself time and space to honor your most treasured dreams, special talents, unique passions and deepest desires! When you step out of busy, you give yourself permission to say "yes" to being who and what you really are, and open to the sacredness of living in alignment with your "True Self." Live the life that you were meant to live, starting now.

Affirmation: Time is abundant. I have plenty of time to do everything I want and need to do. When I stop racing with time, I allow myself the space to step into who I really am.

What is Coming between YOU and JOY?

We are created by JOY, with JOY, in JOY, to experience JOY. JOY is who we are! JOY is our True Nature. So where is all of the JOY in our lives? How are we unconsciously disconnecting from the JOY that we are? How can we remove the obstacles blocking the JOY-filled life that is our birthright? The only TRUE obstacle between you and JOY, is YOU! NOW is the time to move through your unconscious, self-imposed obstacles and embrace the JOY that is already there! What is coming in the way between YOU and JOY? I invite you to take these nine steps closer toward your JOY:

1. Paying attention. Many of us become so preoccupied with our day-to-day problems, angst and woes, that we spend our lives on alert for, and focusing on, the negative. Where we place our attention, energy follows. We end up attracting exactly what we don't want . . . the problems we are fretting over. I cringed while watching *American Idol* this week when a contestant said, "I attract drama everywhere I go." Well of course she does, because this is her story, her belief. This is the message she is feeding herself and the universe. She is attracting drama by her own thoughts and words, robbing herself of JOY! Are you spending all your energy and attention on negative thoughts and beliefs? When you look for something you will find it. What if you began looking for JOY? Don't wait for JOY to find you, seek JOY. Joy exists even in the small things: a quiet moment relaxing by the fire, a cup of your favorite tea, gazing at beautiful flowers, a pleasant landscape, a walk in nature. Don't let small details distract you from the joy that is right there before you. Pay attention to the simple ways JOY shows up throughout the day. Joy is already there, RECOGNIZE it!

2. Simplification. Ever notice your joy being drained away by certain people, places, things, TV programs, activities or obligations? What is robbing you of your JOY? It is time to purge away that which steals your JOY and replace it with that which adds to it! Starting today, stop inviting in things that steal your JOY, just as you wouldn't invite an unpleasant stranger into your home. Consciously sweep out "joy-suckers."

3. Spaciousness. Is your calendar crammed with obligations and commitments every minute of every day? Are you over-committing yourself? Is there space for JOY to arise in your life spontaneously? Are you giving JOY any breathing room? That which cannot breathe cannot survive, including JOY. Make space in your life for JOY to emerge and take on a life of its own. If saying "yes" to doing certain things is causing you to feel drained, resentful or overwhelmed, it is time to say "no" to those things. The more you practice "no," the easier it gets! Volunteer to help in ways that bring you JOY because that JOY will be perceived and felt by everyone around you. Your JOY is contagious! Similarly, your lack of enthusiasm will be felt too! It is never a good idea to say "yes" due to pressure or guilt, only to bring the negative energy of anger and resentment into what you are doing! By saying "no" to things that suck the JOY from you, you actually leave room in your life for JOY to fill in those empty spaces. Make space in your life for JOY to flow in.

4. Openness. Your level of JOY is equivalent to your level of willingness to be open to it! Become keen to try new things and to come out of your comfort zone. Recently, I "turned my nose up" to the idea of a family bowling outing, recalling my embarrassing bowling snafus in high school gym class! Reluctantly I went along, and although I wasn't proud of my score, I enjoyed every moment of laughing and playing with my family! I was shocked to find JOY was there in a bowling alley! It made me wonder how much more often I would find JOY if I was open to new and different activities that I had previously shunned! Be open to the JOY hiding in unexpected places.

5. Putting yourself first. Many of us put everyone else first. When we are on the bottom of the list, we never get around to our own JOY. Even YOU are deserving of a moment of JOY! Do you feel guilty about experiencing a moment of JOY? Do you feel unworthy if you are not busily checking something off of your list? The Buddha says, "You yourself as much as anyone else in the entire universe are deserving of your love and affection." Stop putting yourself last, and observe how by bringing in more JOY to yourself, suddenly you have more JOY to share with others!

6. Creating JOY. Begin to deliberately design moments of JOY into your day. Plan JOY! Schedule JOY on the calendar. Purposefully do things that bring you JOY! Lunch with a friend, a craft project, a massage, time with a good book, a date night, cuddling with your child or pet, a good movie, a soak in an aromatherapy bath . . . Make JOY a priority. Make JOY happen. Housework, bills and taxes will always be there, but so is JOY! Put JOY on your "to-do" list!

7. Living in the present moment. We often spend so much mental energy planning, anticipating and fearing future problems and frustrations that we miss out on the JOY in the NOW! Mark Twain said, "I am an old man and have known a great many troubles, but most of them never happened." Are you stressing yourself out with problems that haven't happened and probably won't? Are you wasting the present moment ruminating over the "should's" and "could's" of the past? If you are, you are squandering the NOW! Whether you are looking back into the past with regret, guilt, or blame, or "dress rehearsing" the possibility of future troubles, you are robbing yourself of the JOY that is right here, right NOW! How much more JOY would you experience if you stayed present and enjoyed what is here in the NOW?

8. Sharing JOY. Doesn't it bring you JOY to know you brought JOY to someone else? It does for me! Neuroscience actually shows that the pleasure centers of the brain "light up" when people do something that brings JOY to other people. It is as if their JOY is our JOY! When you give away JOY, you are also giving it back to yourself! JOY is not to be hoarded, but meant to be shared! Think of simple ways you can spread JOY daily!

9. Savoring. Savoring is the anticipation of JOY. I am already savoring a tropical vacation with my husband that we have booked. It is weeks away, but just anticipating it brings me JOY. I also anticipate with pleasure my afternoon cup of tea and dark chocolate! I anticipate with JOY teaching my classes, and I always joyfully savor participating in *yoga nidra*! What do you savor? Neurologically, anticipating JOY "lights up" the pleasure centers of the brain! Just thinking about the JOY that is to come, brings about JOY!

Take these nine steps towards JOY, beginning today. If you move towards JOY, it will move towards you! If not NOW, when?

Affirmation: "I come from JOY, I embrace JOY, I live JOY, I AM JOY."

Are You Listening to Your Intuition?

Do you doubt or ignore your intuition? Personally, I will never do that again, after it recently saved my life and that of my family.

Strangely, just recently, I kept thinking about house fires throughout the day. In addition, I kept seeing posts on the Internet about house fires, and at bedtime when I settled in to read, guess what? My book was on a part describing a house fire! I was so disturbed by all of this atypical "house fire" imagery playing before my eyes and in the back of my mind, that I got out of bed and went downstairs and checked to make sure the oven and stove were off, and that there were no lit candles. Finding nothing amiss, I settled back into bed with a sense of unease. I prayed for protection and safety for my family, but was unsettled all night, waking multiple times.

The next morning my husband mentioned to me that the furnace wasn't working properly. He said that it wasn't keeping up with the thermostat setting. At first, I didn't make a connection. I planned to call the repairman sometime during the day, but went about the tasks at hand. When I finally went downstairs to check the furnace, to my horror it was almost red hot! The filter was breaking apart, and being sucked into the furnace, creating a vacuum! There were suitcases stacked up right beside the flaming-hot furnace, and the Instruction Manual for the furnace was sitting right on top, browning from the heat! It was clear that we were no more than 30 minutes from a fire or even an explosion!

Instantly, I knew this was the situation I was being warned about through my intuition! I quickly moved the luggage and the paper and anything flammable away from the furnace. In a panic, I tried to pull the filter out, but got shocked in the process! Then it occurred to me to shut the furnace down first. When it cooled down a bit, I put gloves on, and gingerly pulled the filter, a crumples up mess, out of the bowels of the furnace! I waited some time before I turned the heat back on. After doing so, I kept a close watch on the furnace the rest of the day, and all seemed to be resolved! Disaster averted . . . all thanks to the power of intuition, along with the protection of God and the angels to whom I had prayed for protection and safety the night before!

Are you listening to your intuition? If not, it is time! We all have this gift, but most people have lost touch with this subtle sense in our loud, flamboyant, fast-paced world. Some people fear that using the "sixth sense" is evil or wrong. For years I ignored and resisted my own powerful intuitive sense, out of fear and misunderstanding. I have always been afraid to share with other people how intuitive I actually am, for fear of being judged as weird or considered sinful for dabbling with my strong sixth sense! No more! In recent years, I have become open to embrace this spiritual gift that has been there for me all along. I am here to tell you that it saved my family from harm! A little reluctantly, I am coming out of my "intuitive closet" to tell you to pay attention to the subtle messages you are receiving. Your intuition could save you too!

Simplify Your Life

Is there room in your life for YOU? With the arrival of the New Year, many people have felt guided to simplify their life. In the past, simplicity has been interpreted to mean austerity or self-denial. However, simplicity is really about choosing not to draw drama, clutter, complications or chaos into your life. The "simple life" doesn't mean you need to renounce all material goods or become a hermit living in a cave. The simple life is about letting go of things which carry the baggage of stress, disorder or turmoil. By embracing a life of simplicity, you are embracing a life of ease and grace in place of struggle and strain. Simplicity brings about harmony, peace and progress. Consider the following ways to simplify the coming year!

1. Clear your space. De-clutter! Release items which have outgrown their value and usefulness and are just taking up precious space. Outward clutter mirrors internal clutter. As you begin to clear away material belongings that no longer serve you, you will find it easier to shed worn-out thoughts and ideas, burdensome emotional baggage, or spiritual obstructions. Your inner life will reflect the same renewed order and stability you've created in your visible world. Let your surroundings reflect the order, beauty and harmony you wish to cultivate within yourself and in your life. Organize your cabinets, closets and junk drawers in the same way you wish to clear away the cobwebs in your deepest, darkest, innermost corners. Notice how your life changes when you are fully clean, balanced and clear.

2. Clear your calendar. Examine your calendar, and begin to remove engagements that aren't necessary, beneficial or joyful. Let go of things that do not add to your happiness or wellbeing. I have stopped saying "yes" to the many obligatory functions, fund-raisers, business parties, and community events that do not generate enthusiasm or excitement on my part. At first it felt like the world was going to fall apart if I didn't attend! Guess what? It didn't! I now allow myself to recognize that my soul is saying "yes" when I feel excited and eager about attending. My soul says "no" when I feel pressured by obligation. If I am dreading the event, it is a "no go!" Some great advice given to me by friend and instructor Kris Wineland, is to simply respond to these invitations with the statement, "That does not work for me." Begin to look at your year and discern what doesn't work for you, and give yourself permission to utter a certain two-letter word that we often forget: "no." Month-by-month, and day-by-day, identify what can be taken OUT of your routine. No need to remove the things that you love, only the things that you dread! I'm not telling you to stop going to the dentist; this is necessary! Notice what would awaken a calmer, happier you if it was gone! Be sure to leave space for unplanned time on your calendar, and see what spontaneously arises. When you do this life becomes more light and free!

3. Clear your conscience. Practice self-compassion and self-forgiveness. Drop lower energies such as guilt, shame, regret or remorse. Wipe the slate clean, and allow these heavy energies to be absorbed by the universe and lifted from your consciousness. You did the best you could with what you knew and understood. "When you knew better, you did better." Let that be enough. These heavy energies do not serve you, they hold you back and weigh you down like heavy baggage. There is no medal, trophy or award for schlepping these old worn-out emotions along for another day! Today is the day to let them go, for if not now, when?

4. Clear your energy. Examine your life for people, places or things that drain your energy. Who or what saps you of vitality, strength and joy? Now is the time to walk away from these, and on to better things. That which dampens your energy is signaling that it is not for you. Perhaps you are in the habit of hiding who you really are from the world at large. Nothing saps your energy like keeping your "true self" under wraps. It takes no energy at all to simply rest in the truth of who you are. Who you are is peace, joy and ease. When you try to be who you think everyone else wants you to be, you become drained, because so much energy is expended trying to be who you are not, and judging and second-guessing yourself on whether you have done a good enough job at hiding who you really are! Being someone else is the job of an actor! There is a reason they make millions pretending to be someone else effectively! It is A LOT of work! Look for new ways to simplify your life so that your energy is not being drained. Examine the way you go about your day . . . your routines, chores, projects and recipes. The French and the Italians are masters at creating healthy, simple meals out of fresh, wholesome ingredients! Simplicity leaves more time to enjoy the "good life" or "*pura vida!*"

5. Clear your soul. Take a deep look at patterns, behaviors and habits that you have outgrown. Recognize the ones that are not working for your highest good: over-eating, imbibing too much alcohol, over-working, too much or too little exercise, over-scheduling yourself, indulging in too little rest or sleep. As you take inventory of these, understand which habits are working against you; these are the ones to clear away. It is not necessary to break old habits and patterns on your own. The fifth *niama* or observance in the yoga tradition is *ishwara pranidhana*, which translates as "surrender to God." We don't have to carry everything, control everything, or heal everything all by ourselves. We must learn how to surrender to the help that is already there, just waiting in the wings for us to ask. Trust that your highest good is supported by something greater than you are. Reach out and ask for assistance, and it will be as close as your next breath. Ahhhh . . . once you surrender, you will find that you can rest in the space of ease and simplicity.

Tip: You can clear your energy and space the way indigenous cultures have for millennia — with a smudging ceremony. By burning white sage around your own energy field, office or home, you clear the energy of that space . . . even if it is the space inside of yourself. This sets the intention for it to be purified and crystal clear.

Life Lessons I Wish I Could Go Back and Teach My Younger Self (and wish to share with my 17 year old)

1. Wherever you are is exactly where you are supposed to be right now.

2. The obstacle is the path. Your struggles are sacred. Meeting your struggles are moments of awakening. To learn from your own struggles to serve others is enlightenment.

3. Life is soul school, and whatever is happening right now is your curriculum. Everything that arises is a learning, that's all. All challenging, frustrating, painful situations are lessons; all blessings are lessons; all joys are lessons; all people are lessons.

4. You meet your destiny on the path to avoiding it. Resistance is futile. That which you resist stays. If you meet life's lessons head on instead of running from them and avoiding them, the struggles pass more quickly and seldom return.

5. Love what is . . . instead of forcing things to be different than they are.

6. Everything is mind. At the core of who we are is consciousness. Our thoughts create our reality. Our life is an outer reflection of our inner world. Choose your thoughts wisely.

7. Do not believe every thought you have! Many of our thoughts are simply the result of our conditioning or our imagination. Thoughts of fear and self-doubt are false; they are illusions; they are fake. Treat fear and self-doubt like doorways and walk right through them. On the other side of fear and doubt are the dreams you are seeking.

8. In order to love and accept others, you must first love and accept yourself. All of your relationships with others reflect some aspect of your relationship with yourself.

9. Whatever you dislike in someone else is really a mirror of what you haven't yet acknowledged that you dislike about yourself. Whatever you admire in others reflects the things that you appreciate about yourself.

10. Everyone you meet is your teacher; and you theirs. Whatever your relationship, that is your curriculum.

11. Don't people-please or seek approval from others for what you know is right for you. Be true to yourself. Say "no" when you mean no, and "yes" when you mean yes. When you live in alignment with what is right for you, the right things fall into place.

12. You can choose not to get sucked into other people's dramas. Let them have the center ring of their own circus!

13. You are not alone. The whole universe supports you!

14. Do what you feel inspired to do without attachment to outcome!

15. Set intentions. Life is magical, and you are the magician! You create the miracles in your own life!

16. Slow down . . . there is no need to hurry. You are the owner and creator of your personal time. You have enough time to do everything you need and want to do.

Unwrap Your Spiritual Gifts

As we make our Christmas lists, and shop for holiday gifts, let us not forget to notice our spiritual gifts and share them with others as well. We are all here to enlighten, encourage, empower and inspire others and ourselves in our own unique way. Often our spiritual gifts remain hidden or "wrapped." Perhaps it is because we feel unworthy, not good enough, brave enough, powerful enough or perfect enough to have spiritual gifts. These doubts block us from ever discovering the gifts we were endowed with by our creator. Often we don't even recognize that the gifts are there. We each have our own special spiritual gifts, and we are meant to discover them, open them and share them.

Spiritual gifts include compassion, creativity, insight, intuition, guidance, special healing gifts, wisdom, prophecy, power of prayer, teaching, counseling, leadership, energy work, empathic abilities, communicating with angels, saints and guides, manifestation, telepathy, inner seeing, hearing and knowing. You already have one or more of these gifts waiting to be opened and used! These gifts are sacred and are not to be kept on a shelf, unopened. As we excitedly prepare to give and receive holiday gifts, let us receive and share our spiritual gifts too. Here is a step-by-step guide to unwrapping your spiritual gifts.

1. Simplify your life. Our gifts get lost in the clutter of our daily lives. The busier we are, the more lost the gifts become. It is said the "devil is in the details." Perhaps this is true if we are too busy with the details of our lives to slow down enough to become aware of the gifts we have been given. It is in the space between doings, and in stepping out of the clutter of life, that your awareness of the gifts you possess will arise. Remember that you are not responsible for everyone and everything! Watch your gifts open to you as you give them time and space to be revealed and developed.

2. Raise your vibration. Humans are made of energy. Spiritual gifts are very high frequency energy vibrations. Our own natural high spiritual frequency is often weighted down by lower energies such as pride, guilt, shame, disgust, judgment, hate, fear or greed. We can consciously replace these low, heavy energies with higher ones such as gratitude, kindness, compassion, love, and peacefulness. Take charge of your thoughts instead of allowing them to be in charge of you. Choose to no longer entertain negative thoughts. Treat these thoughts like house guests who are no longer welcome. They will not stay if they are not fed, made comfortable or given space to hang out. Replace negative thoughts with positive affirmations. It is no different than changing the TV channel from an unpleasant program to a more uplifting one! When I notice low vibrational thoughts arise, I simply change the channel in my mind to one of positivity.

3. Rid your life of intoxicants. Intoxicants such as alcohol, sleeping pills, pharmaceuticals and other mind-dulling drugs lower our energetic vibration and numb us from our spiritual gifts. When we dull our senses and anesthetize our minds, we are not sensitive enough to the subtle vibrations of our spiritual gifts, and are not awake to receive them. I rarely drink alcohol, so when I do I immediately notice how much more difficult it is to access my own spiritual gifts. It is just not worth it to me to lose my own special abilities. It is my divine life purpose to put them to good use, not to throw the gifts away in exchange for being comfortably numb!

4. Rid yourself of toxins. We are inundated with toxins in our diet and environment. It would be impossible to eliminate every one of them, but we can certainly consciously avoid them. Processed foods and fast foods are full of chemical poisons that dull our connection to our higher gifts. Our water supply is full of chlorine, fluoride and traces of chemical pollutants and pharmaceutical drugs. All circuits must be connected to be able to connect to our spiritual gifts. The purer and cleaner the mind-body system, the clearer and more obvious your spiritual gifts are, and the sharper they become. For me, this alone is worth the effort of living a clean lifestyle.

5. Ground yourself. Ask any electrician, and they will tell you that energy needs grounding before it can flow properly and safely. It is no different for us humans. We need to stay grounded for the energy of these spiritual gifts to flow properly to us and through us. Humans stay grounded by going barefoot, spending time in nature, letting the soles of their feet come in contact with grass, water, sand or soil. Make sure you sit in a way that allows both sitting bones and both feet to be firmly planted or "plugged in." Drinking water and staying well-hydrated is very grounding. Also, eating root vegetables such as carrots, beets, potatoes, turnips and sweet potatoes is very grounding, as they are grown in the earth. Salt is a very grounding earth mineral, but take precaution if you have been placed on a low-sodium diet. I recommend sea salt or Himalayan salt over highly processed table salt. Reflexology foot massage or just rubbing your feet with oil is extremely grounding.

6. Pray and meditate. "Prayer is talking to God, meditation is listening." We can pray for our spiritual gifts to open for us, but it is just as important to spend time in silent stillness to actually discover the gifts that are already there. I receive so much guidance and insight through the regular practice of prayer and meditation. Many people mistakenly think sitting in silence is a waste of time, but it is actually sacred time and a powerful way to contact and connect to your inner gifts.

7. Live in the space of love. Your special spiritual gifts were designed and given to you out of God's pure love. Our creator knows exactly what you want and need, just as a parent selects special gifts for a beloved child. Once you unwrap them you will LOVE them! You will not want to return or exchange them. Just as they were given out of love, your gifts are meant to serve and to share from the spirit of love. BE love and let your gifts overflow from that love that you are.

Affirmation: "I let go of anything that is holding me back, and I open up the spiritual gifts I have yet to unwrap. I use my spiritual gifts for the highest good."

Affirmations to Heal and Harmonize the *Chakras*

The *chakras* are energy centers found in the physical body and in the energy field around our body. These energy "vortexes" help to regulate energy flow through the channels or *nadis*, the way the heart pumps blood through the blood vessels. Each *chakra* has a specific function and duty. The *chakra* system is part of our "energy anatomy," just as organs, tissues and bones are a part of our physical anatomy. Without proper energy flow, we could not move, function or live. Without proper energy flow, we come out of balance and are susceptible to illness and diseases of the mind and body. The *chakra* system is ancient. It cropped up millennia ago all over the world in various continents and cultures that had no communication with each other. The ancient Egyptians, Chinese, Tibetans, Aborigines, Mayas and Incas are all civilizations which had discovered the *chakras* and the energy body.

Affirmations are a powerful way to heal and balance the *chakras*. I invite you to discover the *chakras* and experiment with using affirmations to bring your *chakras* into harmony and balance. I will discuss eight *chakras* here, but some systems include 12 major *chakras*, and thousands of minor *chakras*.

1st Chakra: Muladhara. "The root *chakra*" is located at the coccyx and perineum and extends energy to the soles of the feet. This energy center is responsible for a sense of groundedness, stability and security. This is the most primitive *chakra* whose purpose is "survival" and the will to live. Its' color is red. Affirmation: "I am stable and secure. I feel grounded and peaceful. I am firmly rooted in who I am. I am safe."

2nd Chakra: Svadisthana. "The sacral *chakra*" is associated with the sacrum, which alludes to the "sacredness" of this *chakra*. Located in the pelvis, this is the area of the body where human life is created and sustained. If this *chakra* is not functioning properly, it is difficult to become pregnant or to maintain pregnancy. The second *chakra* is also the location of the "*hara* center" a vast "ocean of energy and strength." Yogis and martial artists learn how to tap into this "well" of energy to do the seemingly impossible. This *chakra* governs the reproductive organs. The function of the *chakra* is creativity, pleasure, abundance, procreation, enthusiasm and vitality. It is said to be the seat of "*shakti,*" the force of sacred creative feminine energy. Its' color is orange. Affirmation: "It is safe to take pleasure in life and to embrace the joy of living."

3rd Chakra: Manipura. "The city of jewels" is located in the solar plexus region of the abdomen, where our "inner jewels," the vital organs, are found. This *chakra* is responsible for self-confidence, courage, willpower, assertiveness and self-esteem. It is also responsible for regulating the energy of digestion. Its' color is yellow. I like to call it our "inner sunshine!" Affirmation: "It is safe to be powerful. I own my power and shine my light."

4th Chakra: Anahata. "The heart *chakra*" is located at the heart center and extends out through the palms and soles of the feet. This *chakra's* function is love, joy, compassion, inner peace, gratitude, self-love and appreciation. The heart *chakra* governs the heart, lungs and circulatory system. This centrally-located *chakra* is responsible for transformation of lower energies into the energy of love. Its' color is green. Affirmation: "It is safe to love and be loved. I freely give and receive love."

5th Chakra: Vishuddha. "The throat *chakra*" is located in the throat and extends into the shoulders and ears. It governs the thyroid and parathyroid glands, and the ability to hear and speak. It is responsible for communication, sound, self-expression, speaking your truth, speaking from the heart, and hearing the truth. Its' color is blue. Affirmation: "It is safe to speak and be heard. I speak from the heart. I voice the truth to make the world a better place. I am able to clearly, kindly and safely express what I think and feel."

6th Chakra: Ajna. "The third eye" is located in the center of the forehead between the eyebrows. It is responsible for inspiration, insight, creative ideas, introspection, intuition, imagination, vision, dreaming, and clairvoyance. It governs the pineal gland, which is considered our "inner eye." This gland is shaped and pigmented like the "Egyptian eye" depicted in that culture's hieroglyphics. Kissing someone's third eye helps to calm and balance this energy center. This *chakra* is the place from which prayers are sent out. Its' color is indigo. Affirmation: "I trust the vision, intuition and guidance within me. I am full of creative ideas and trustworthy insight. It is safe to use my inner vision and look within."

7th Chakra: Sahasrara. The "thousand petal lotus" or the "crown *chakra*" is located at the highest point of the crown of the head. It is centered around the fontanel, the spot where the soul enters the body in the womb and leaves the body at the time of death. This is the area where we receive the answers to our prayers and communications from God. Here we receive insight, knowledge and Truth from beyond ourselves. This *chakra's* function is Truth, higher consciousness, and bliss. It governs the pituitary gland, cerebral cortex and the central nervous system. Its; color is violet. Affirmation: "The essence of my being is light and peace. I am open to the infinite power of God. I have a unique spiritual destiny. I am divinely guided on the path that is right for me."

8th Chakra: Padaka. "The halo" and the auric field which surrounds all beings is located an arm's length above the head, and has been depicted across cultures and time as a halo, because it becomes increasingly radiant in those with deep and pure spiritual connection. Here is where spiritual awareness, ultimate truth and awakening reside. The eighth *chakra* is an energy portal where we can access divine healing energy for the highest good. It is the doorway to spiritual abilities such as healing gifts, prophecy, and doing works on behalf of humankind for the greater good. Here we disconnect from ego and become selfless. From this higher place of awareness, we are able to watch the drama of life unfold without attachment. Here we access the infinite which surrounds and envelops the window of time-space. Beyond all constructs of time, space, mind, ego, and illusion, it is our doorway to *eternity*. Its' color is white. Affirmation: "I am infinite, eternal and whole. I am beyond time, space and illusion. I am the healer and the healed. I accept and honor my spiritual gifts. I live my divine purpose."

Letting Go to Set Yourself Free

There is a Zen story about a group of monks traveling on a long journey. They carried a boat with them knowing they had a great river to cross. Once they crossed the river, they set the boat down on the riverbank and left it behind as it was no longer necessary. Without the weight of the boat, they were able to continue on their journey with greater ease, lightness and freedom. What weights are you ready to set down?

Letting go is an act of spiritual growth. The more you release, the lighter your spirit. What weights are you carrying energetically, emotionally and physically? As the monk's story illustrates, it takes a lot more energy to keep carrying things we no longer need. By letting go, you set yourself free. You become free of unnecessary weight, and free of things that stand in the way between you and your soul's highest purpose. But how do you know what to let go of? The following are ten things we ALL need to set down. If you let go of one thing you will feel a little freedom. If you let go of all ten, you will feel liberated!

1. Control. Release trying, striving, forcing, pushing, and struggling. What is meant to come to you will arise spontaneously, but only if you first get out of the way! Releasing control, and trusting God, the Universe or Source to move the right things in at the right moments is an act of faith and a powerful step towards spiritual growth.

2. Your past. So many folks allow their past to tarnish their present and their future. They hold on to resentment, regret, guilt, anger and victimhood. They cling tightly to antiquated fears, perceptions, opinions and viewpoints. Life takes place only in the now. It is time to hit the "delete" button, and free yourself from the burden of your past. Forgive yourself. Forgive those who wronged you, and do not let the past weigh you down for another day. It is gone from the reality of now. Choose to no longer allow the past to hold you under its' thumb, and you are free.

3. Fears. Fear causes contraction, confusion and avoidance. Fear is paralyzing. It keeps you stuck right where you are. It is said that everything you want is on the other side of fear. The only way to become liberated *from* fear is *through* fear. Fear is almost always a figment of your imagination. Fear is a thought, not a reality. Confront what scares you, and stare it down. What is your biggest fear? Mine is public speaking. Make it a point to do whatever it is you're afraid of. On the other side of fear is freedom.

4. Attachment to results. Much of what we do is in expectation of a specific outcome. We hope to get a "pay-off" or achieve something for our efforts. Herein, we are often disappointed and resentful. When we do not receive the praises, accomplishments, or achievements we think we deserve, we conclude that we have failed. However, when we do the right thing without expectation of anything in return, that act in itself becomes sacred. Letting go of results sets our actions free from acquiring, obtaining, or any other objective. Thus our actions become pure, and from the heart.

> "Without concern for results, perform the necessary action; surrendering all attachments, accomplish life's highest good."
>
> ~ *Bhagavad Gita*

5. Toxins. Detoxify your life of people, events, situations, television shows, news media or even a career that carries toxic energy. Detoxify yourself of negative emotions such as fear, guilt, greed, anger, hatred and jealousy. In doing so, you uncover the inner peace waiting there within you all along. Detoxify your energy field. Many of us are unaware of the energetic toxins we unintentionally pick up every day. We accumulate and carry these heavy, negative energies around with us like dead weight. It is very important to detoxify your energy field of unhealthy vibrations, which do not serve you. No different than going on a dietary cleanse to rid the bodily organs and tissues of toxins, you can also purge your *life*.

6. Judging. Let go of judging. When you judge others, you are actually judging and rejecting parts of yourself. What you dislike in others is simply a mirror of the parts of yourself that you refuse to see and accept. When you are unable to accept others, it signals that you do not accept yourself. By letting go of judgment, you are saying "yes" to acceptance. Self-acceptance is embracing the dark and the light of who you are. When you let go of judgment, not only are you giving others permission to be who they are, but you are embracing all of who you are.

7. Who you're not. What parts of you do not belong? Swami Kripalu's teacher said, "Whatever is there, throw it out, burn it out, cut it out, and that which remains is YOU." What parts of you are authentic? What parts are there to impress others? What masks do you wear to hide who you really are from yourself and from the world? What stories do you tell yourself about you? What parts of you are just sound bites from your past, replaying over and over in your mind? It is only when we learn to ignore and silence the voice of the ego that we can hear the whispers of the authentic self. Now is the time to throw out the costumes we've been concealing ourselves under and bare our souls unashamed. The bigger your insecurities, the greater your inner radiance really is. The ego works hard to muscle control over you in order to stay in charge. It does this by tearing you down with the messages "I am not good enough." and "I am not worthy." The amount of self-doubt and insecurity you have to overcome correlates directly with your true greatness. The push and pull of these forces are even. In truth we are all good enough, and we are all worthy. Letting go of who we're not is not a luxury; it's a birthright!

8. Resistance. When we reject what life brings us, we go "to war" with what is. We wrestle with denial, and struggle against what is there. Struggle and denial do not make what is there "go away," it just makes it push back harder. Imagine a game of "tug of war." Each team struggles back and forth to muscle their way to victory. If evenly matched, the struggle can go on and on. If one side simply "lets go," the other side tumbles to the ground by the sheer force of their own momentum. Game Over! When we intentionally choose to let go and lean in to what is there, whether it is pain, loneliness, illness, grief, financial struggles, etc., the game is suddenly over. Acceptance is the eternal victor. Once we learn to embrace life just as it is, the struggle is gone. Pema Chodron teaches, "What we resist, stays."

9. The "glorification of busy." Are you stuck on the hamster wheel of life? According to David Allen, "You can do anything you want, but not everything!" Inner peace is the new busy! Instead of over-planning and over-scheduling your family and yourself, schedule moments of inner peace. Let go of the need to be constantly occupied. The *Tao Te Ching* teaches, "When your cup is full; stop pouring." Let go of the need to pile on task after task, event after event, overflowing your cup and making a mess of your life. Busy is "out" and peace is "in." Browse your daily schedule or list of "to-dos." Determine what is unnecessary. Scratch off the things that you can let go. First focus on the things you actually *want* to do, and keep those. Then focus on the things you absolutely *have* to do and keep those. What is left can be released. Use this open space to schedule rest and peace.

10. Going It Alone "We're all just walking each other home." ~Ram Das. Our separation is a construct of the limited mind. Once we recognize that we are brothers and sisters on this earth, and that we share in this existence together, we realize there is no need to go it alone. Help others. Serve others. Bilaterally, don't be resistant to asking for and accepting that same help when you need it. When you ask for help, the Universe, God and all that is good sweeps in at once to assist you.

Each of us is attached in some way to ancient, outdated conditioning. This obsolete patterning works against us in becoming the best version of ourselves. It is time for a new paradigm. We can choose our own world, our own life, our own story, and our own way. We must sift through all of who we are and discern what is conditioning and what is Truth. By letting go of things that do not serve our highest good, we change our own experience. "Letting go" invites joy, freedom and fulfillment. Let go of all ten above, and become weightless! By giving up what no longer works, you move out of the way of the flow of grace. You open yourself up to unknown blessings. Letting go sparks the fire of the miraculous.

Am I on the Right Path?

We are all walking the journey of life, each one's path unique. We each have a purpose and a calling. Do you know yours? Ultimately, our own special path is meant to take us each to the same destination: oneness, unity and wholeness- back to God. Like wild geese, we are all headed home. How do we know if we are on the right path, or even on the path at all? Being on the right path is being in alignment with your soul's highest purpose — the reason you were incarnated. Of course, as humans it is our nature to second-guess our path and our purpose. The following are some hints to guide you along.

You feel momentum. When you are on the right path, there is an inexplicable momentum behind you, like tailwinds behind a plane. Your journey seems almost effortless. Things fall into place without manipulating, maneuvering or interfering on your part. You are empowered by energy beyond yourself . . . the flow of grace. You don't have to know how to reach your destination, have a plan, or even know where you're headed. You will intuitively sense the next step forward. As you take that step, the next step naturally arises. It is like having your own internal GPS, leading you one turn at a time. However, it is important to know that you don't set the pace, that you must honor and surrender to the impeccable timing and rhythm of grace. Where you are on the path is called NOW. Here and now is the only part of the journey that matters in this moment.

In contrast, when your path is wrong, you encounter one roadblock and difficulty after another. You meet with obstacles large and small. You know you are headed in the wrong direction when grace is not there to guide, assist and support you along the way. If there is a great deal of "friction" and frustration, you are headed in the wrong direction! The benevolent forces of the Universe — God himself — is trying to get your attention. Until you pay attention, the messages will become louder and louder and increasingly uncomfortable! I suggest listening the first time you feel guided a different way.

You love it! When you are on the right path, it feels right! You know it; you feel it. It is unmistakable. You have a renewed zest for life! You are filled with excitement and passion, and wake up each day excited for it to unfold. You are full of gratitude. The right path is the one that brings you joy! You have a skip in your step and a song in your heart! Alternately, if you lack enthusiasm and inspiration, this is a message from your soul, that you are headed in the wrong direction. If you feel like you are just trudging along, bored, disengaged, weighted and weary, you are off course!

You are safe. When you are on the right path, God, the universe, and all that is good, is there behind you, backing you up, supporting you, surrounding you and protecting you. You will notice that harm does not come to you. We are safe when we keep to our paths. You might even notice fear and anxiety diminish as you intuitively sense this protective shield surrounding you. However, when you are not on the right path, it is like being lost in the woods — you can't tell where you are or where you're headed. You feel bewildered, confused and afraid. You are no longer in the safety zone. You may notice that you attract chaos, drama and problems into your life. You may observe that the wrong people show up — people not out for your highest good. You may attract illness and disease. You may be met with danger, obstacles, hindrances, and suffering. The walk is not easy on the wrong path; things get increasingly messy and uncomfortable, urging us to change direction.

You encounter synchronicity. People, events, songs, quotes, emails, phone calls, letters all come your way at exactly the right moment in time. You immediately see their relevance, connection, and know their purpose. Coincidence becomes commonplace when you are on your path! Life seems to converge and align at just the right moment. You magically receive what you need when you need it. Obstacles fall away as you walk towards your unique destiny. Moments of synchronicity are "road signs" or affirmations that you are headed in the right direction!

Are you on the right path? This is article is your message. Here is your sign!

Seven Things Thriving People Do Differently

There is something different about thriving people, a certain *Je ne sais quoi*. They stand out and seem to exude radiance and joy. You know immediately when they walk into a room that there is something special about them. Most of us just think they are "lucky" or were handed a good lot in life. However, thriving is a choice, one that can be made by every one of us either consciously or unconsciously. Here's what thriving people do differently. Beginning today, I invite you to make the choice to THRIVE!

1. They beat to their own drum. Thriving people pave their own way, walk their own path, and stand in the light of their own truth. They are not dependent upon approval from the "crowd." They know who they are, and are comfortable in their own skin. They stand secure in their own uniqueness. The *Tao Te Ching* teaches, "When you are content to be simply yourself and don't compare or compete, everyone will respect you.'" Thriving people are authentic people! They are who they say they are, and what they say and what they do align. They keep their word and stand in their truth, whether it is popular opinion or not. Thriving people refuse to go along with anyone or anything they instinctively know is not right for them.

> "To remember who you are, you need to forget who they told you to be."
>
> ~ Anonymous

2. They hold hands with fate. Whether you resonate with the word God, Great Spirit, Higher Power or the Universe, thriving people walk with the creator, trusting in the benevolent love, help and support already there in their midst. Thriving people don't try to MAKE things happen, they allow things to unfold in their own way and according to natural timing. Thriving people trust in "the flow." They allow their lives to unfold according to the natural course of things. Nothing is forced. For me writing is all about tapping into "the flow" and letting thoughts and ideas move through me. Once they arise, it is essential to seize the moment and put these thoughts to words and words to paper! When I ignore this flow, I lose some great nuggets. The writing process has helped me so much as I learn to tap into the greater flow, knowing there is a plan better than my own. It is taking that leap of faith and trusting that things will unfold perfectly if you just relax and get out of the way!

> "Do not struggle. Go with the flow of things, and you will find yourself at one with the universe."
>
> ~ Chuang Tzu

3. They appreciate what they have. Thriving people focus on what they do have instead of coveting what they don't have. They don't focus on their aches and pains, but on the parts of themselves that feel vibrant and healthy. For them, being thankful is a way of being. Their attitude is positivity and gratitude. Through this outlook, they are actively participating in the "law of attraction," often without even knowing it!

> "Better to lose count while naming your blessings than to lose your blessings to count your troubles."
>
> ~ Malthie D. Babcock

4. They practice kindness. Thriving people are first kind to themselves. They don't berate or criticize themselves. They practice self-compassion. They keep their own tank filled through self-care, not driving themselves too hard, listening to their body, and honoring the needs of their soul. By practicing kindness with themselves, they simply exude that same kindness towards others. When you fill yourself with kindness and compassion, it simply radiates from you!

> "If compassion doesn't include yourself, it is incomplete."
>
> ~ Buddha

5. They do what they love and do it with purpose. (. . . and they don't worry about doing it *perfectly*.) When you are doing what you love, you are filled with love, and love is the highest energy form there is!

When people do something they love, they sparkle and shine. Love is expansional energy, where perfectionism, in contrast, is a contractive energy. These two opposing forces don't thrive side by side. Thriving people let their purpose be serving others, rather than striving for perfection to serve their ego or for personal gain. Because their intention is to serve, rather than to appear perfect, what they do comes with ease. Do what you love, with the intention to serve and enjoy doing it imperfectly! Go and do the things that light you up, and you will shine from the inside out and you will help others shine too!

6. They believe in themselves. Thriving people don't become distracted by naysayers, self-doubt or fears. They don't allow anyone to rain on the joy of sharing what they love. They believe so steadfastly in who they are and in what they do, that lower energies roll off of them like rain on a duck.

> "To accomplish great things, we must not only act, but also dream, not only plan, but also believe."
>
> ~ Anatole France

7. They don't get distracted from their purpose. Although they may take a break to rest and enjoy life, thriving people stay focused on what they are here to do. They don't get caught up in too many distractions, or let themselves get stretched too thin. They intuitively know when to say "yes" and when to say "no." Thriving people watch very little TV, and avoid getting saturated by the negativity of the media. They avoid gossip, drama and negative people. They consciously choose how they fill their life, instead of getting caught up in disorder. They eliminate chaos and clutter so they can stay balanced, focused and grounded. They realize when they have too much on their plate and when they need to scale down, step back and reboot! They continually reevaluate what needs to stay and where they need to let go.

A Prescription for Self-Care

As an Ayurveda practitioner, if I could write a universal prescription that would prevent every known disease of the body and the mind, then I would write a prescription for "self-care." All disease, mental or physical, arises from an imbalance in the mind-body system. The ancient healing science of Ayurveda teaches that it is impossible to catch any "bug" or pathogen if your mind-body system is in a state of balance. It is only when we have a "chink in the armor" of our immune system that pathogens can slip in and illness is able to arise. Why are so many people sick today? Because we wait until we are sick to begin to administer care for ourselves. Illness is our soul's way of directing us towards the vital business of loving and caring for ourselves! The truth is if we got enough sleep, ate right, rested, set adequate boundaries for ourselves and lived a harmonious existence, health would prevail. Often, overeating is a misguided attempt at self-care. It has a quick "band-aid effect, "covering-up" the areas when we are lacking in care for ourselves. Here are ten powerful ways we can love and nourish ourselves into well-being.

1. Fresh air and sunlight. People rarely get sick in the summer when they spend more time outdoors in fresh air and sunshine. It turns out that spending time in nature has a profound effect on the immune system, so much so that nature has been nicknamed "vitamin N." The sun, the wind and the air around us are profoundly healing to the mind-body system! Get outdoors!

2. Moderate exercise. The key word here is "moderate." Often our culture thinks that if a little is good, then more must be better! This is not the case with exercise. Moderate exercise lifts the mood, increases metabolism, and helps fire up the immune system. Movement increases blood flow to the body tissues and the brain. Moderate movement such as yoga, walking, *tai chi*, *qui gong*, biking and swimming increases energy and enlivens the mind-body system. Strenuous or excessive exercise is not an act of self-care, but self-flagellation. It has a negative impact on the mind-body system, depleting vital reserves and activating the stress response. Strenuous movement is aging to the body and depleting to the immune system. Ayurveda recommends regular moderate exercise as opposed to vigorous activity for optimal health and harmony.

3. Adequate sleep and rest. Recently, I accidentally overslept by 30 minutes. I was astonished at how relaxed and refreshed I felt the rest of the day! In contrast, my son stayed up till 2 am at a sleep-over, and was up early the next morning. He became sick with a cold by the next evening. Sleep and rest are pillars of self-care in Ayurvedic medicine. If you shortchange yourself here, it is impossible to look, think or feel your best! Suggestion: take a daily rest time in *Savasana* or a similar restorative yoga pose for 10-20 minutes to recharge. It has made a huge difference for me!

4. Honoring our needs. There are two areas of critical needs: physical needs and soul needs. Honor natural physical urges such as hunger, sleep, elimination, urination, coughing, sneezing, passing gas, etc. A Zen saying is, "What is enlightenment? When you're tired, rest; when you are hungry, eat; when you are sleepy, sleep. That is enlightenment." Equally important are the needs of your soul. Soul urges include prayer, silence, creativity, imagination, intuition, and dreams, visions and passions. Do not apologize for answering the innate needs of your mind, body or soul. To denounce these leads to disharmony and suffering.

5. Nourishing foods. The foods you eat are the building blocks of who you are. Nourishing foods support health, energy and longevity. Eating the foods you were created to eat help you embody the most vibrant, and vital you. The most nourishing foods are whole foods including fresh organic fruits and vegetables, seeds, nuts, whole grains, and organic dairy products. Eating the way your body was designed to eat is a practice of self-care.

6. Boundaries. Setting boundaries means giving yourself permission to walk away from negative situations, conversations, arguments and controversy. Give yourself permission to avoid disharmonious people, events, or places. Setting boundaries means saying "no" to things that are not your "work." For example, I know that it is not my work to bake cupcakes for a bake sale, my work is to share wellness and healing. When you identify and clarify your purpose, it becomes clear what is and what is not your work. To say "yes" to things that are not your purpose is in effect saying "no" to who you are. Stop people pleasing, and start pleasing you.

> "If you spend your life trying to make people happy, you spend your life."
>
> ~ Cheryl Richardson

7. Playtime. Joy and pleasure aren't luxuries, they are necessities. Play rejuvenates the soul! Don't underestimate the power of fun to reinvigorate you! Psychologist Dr. Brene Brown says, "The opposite of play is not work — the opposite of play is depression." Know that it is as essential to adults as it is for children to incorporate playtime into each and every day. The games might just be a little different!

8. Positivity. Engage in only positive self-talk. Shut down negative thoughts as soon as you become aware of them. Negative self-talk never accomplishes positive self-change, it only batters the soul. Purge negativity out of your thoughts and conversation. Louise Hay recommends looking at yourself in the mirror first thing in the morning, gazing into your eyes, and saying "I love you, (name)." Start the day with positivity.

9. Natural cycles. Just like the moon, the seasons, the tides, and all elements of nature, human beings go through cycles. We go through hormonal cycles, energetic and emotional cycles. Women transition through menstrual cycles, and cycle through puberty, peri-menopause and menopause. Instead of resisting these cycles or trying to ignore or push them away, embrace these natural cycles as part of who you are. Honor how you feel. Accept and allow the shifts in energy and mood instead of fighting against them. Let them be exactly as they are. If you have a low-energy day, simply move slower. If you feel fatigued, rest, knowing energy and mood can ebb and flow like the tides.

10. Help and support. How often is help offered to you and you turn it down, knowing you really should have accepted it? We often look at receiving help as a sign of weakness. Refusing help is letting the ego overshadow the soul. Begin to say "yes" to help when it is offered, and *ask* for help when you need it. Most people neglect asking the benevolent forces of the universe for help. God, the angels, your passed over loved-ones and ancestors are there waiting for you to ask for help. They don't want to interfere, so they wait for you to ask! You will be amazed by the help that arrives when you call upon these higher energies!

The following process, recommended by author Esther Hicks, has made a profound difference for me! Try making a list with two columns. In the first column, list what you will do this week. In the second column, write what you would like God or the Universe to do this week. When the list is complete, see how many of the things on your "to do" list you can shift over to the second column and let the Universe accomplish. How much you soften and lean into the support that is already there is directly proportional to how much you will be supported. Move the ego out of the way, and be supportive of yourself, asking for and receiving the assistance your body, mind and soul are begging for!

Think of self-care not only as self-healing but also as a practice of health maintenance. Today I am not only giving you permission to do these things, but a prescription to practice these ten ways for the mind, body and soul to thrive.

Step into Your Light and Shine

Like many others, I believe we are entering into a special time on Earth. It is time for each of us to step into the light — our own light. I firmly believe we are all created to shine. We are all "light workers!" Everyone is born worthy and equipped with everything they need to shine their light in a unique way in this world. What stands in the way of you shining your light? Only you! When you recognize you were created to shine, you deserve to shine, God wants you to shine, you are beautiful enough, smart enough, wise enough, and powerful enough . . . you already ARE enough, you step into the light of your soul. You cannot help but radiate your own inner light. It is each of our calling to shine lighter and brighter, and shed anything that stands in the way of doing just that!

Here are ten necessary steps towards shining your special inner light:

1. Accept yourself. Embrace yourself, love yourself, befriend yourself. Celebrate your uniqueness and love it. Your individuality is your strength, not your weakness! You are rare, exceptional and exclusive. You were put here to do something no other being is here to do, and to do it in a way that is distinct to you. Trying to be like everyone else means standing in the shadows. You were born to stand out, not to fit in! Be courageous enough to show the world who you are, stepping out of the shadows and into the true light of your soul.

2. Release your past. You are not your past. Who you are only exists in the present moment. You are now. Dismiss your mistakes, your guilt, your shame and your doubt as lessons learned. Leave your shadows behind, knowing you only exist in the now. Don't let the past rob you of the present, or steal away your light. The past is irrelevant. As long as you continue to beat yourself up with your past, you are only expressing your shadows, not living in your light. Light shines only in the present moment.

3. Seize your birthright. We all are created to do great things, not just a select few. You were made to be powerful. Your body may be temporary, but your soul is infinite. Step into infinity, and remember who you are, who you came here to be, and what you came here to do. Not to do so is an affront to your soul. Greatness is your birthright just as much as it is anyone else's.

4. Trust in yourself. Take a leap of faith in YOU. Be your own *guru*, listen to your inner voice, your intuition, the voice of your highest self. To ignore these is to disregard your soul. Insight, intuition, instinct and inner calling is the expression of your soul. Believe in what is in your heart and honor it. The heart is the seat of the soul. Trust yourself, and trust your own divine path.

5. Embrace your passion. Explore it! Follow the voice of inspiration. What does your soul long to do most? What fires you up? Here is your clue to your life's work, your soul's purpose. What step can you take today to honor what you are passionate about in life? Do this without apology or regret. To squelch your passion is to put out the sparks of your own inner fire, to shut off your own inner light! That which ignites you is your purpose, it is how you will shine!

6. Serve and share. Whatever you passion is, allow it to be shared in a way that serves this world. Large or small doesn't matter in the world of spirit. Just go forward and serve humankind with your own personal vision. Share the light that shines within you, and light the way for others.

7. Stand in your truth — be authentic. It is safe to speak your truth. It is what you were put here to do. Now is the time to separate yourself from the trap of "what other people will think." You will never step into your light this way, by getting everyone's "permission." If you are trying to say what you think others want to hear, you aren't being true to you. People really don't want to hear what you think they want to hear. They want to hear the truth. Be your truth, speak your truth, and live your truth, and you will shine.

8. Be supported. It is said that "God's work does itself." Shining your light instead of crouching in the shadows is God's work. When you're on the right path, living your purpose, standing in your light, you are doing God's work, and you'll be amazed at how easily things flow. God's work is easy, man's work is hard. God removes all the friction. Pay attention to the subtle hints, guidance and clues he puts in place on your path. You always have help at your side as you do God's work, in the form of angels, saints, passed over loved-ones and beings of light. The more you soften and relax into the support that is already there, the more support you allow yourself to receive.

9. Open — step into possibility. Don't allow what you think you know to get in the way of what is really there waiting for you. Don't let knowing get in the way of being. Don't get attached to specific outcomes or certain ways of doing things. Be open to the unexpected. Step into your light and enjoy the ride! Control and perfection only dim your light. How much you open is directly related to how far and wide your light will shine!

10. Practice self-care. You can't expect to shine if you aren't nourishing and caring for yourself. If your body and mind are tired, depleted, and decayed, you fade instead of flourish. Your spirit withers. If I forget to water my flowers, and don't give them sunlight, their blooms fade away, and they begin to wilt. How much more is this the case with human beings? It is up to you to tend your own garden. It is in your hands how much fruit you will bear. Self-care involves nourishing diet, adequate rest, being compassionate with yourself, speaking only kind words to yourself, guarding yourself from negativity, and saying "no" to projects that drain away your energy and time.

Now is the time to Step into Your Light and Shine!

Don't Do Yoga, BE Yoga

I experienced a huge personal awakening last week during an unpleasant encounter with someone who made it quite a challenge to be the loving person that I strive to be. How do you love someone who is very difficult to love? It came to me: I don't have to strive to love them, I just have to **BE LOVE**, and then the loving happens all by itself. In my yoga practice, I noticed, I don't have to "do" the pose, if I just embody the pose. When I am in tree pose, I become that tree. When I am in hero pose, I am a hero. When I am in warrior pose, I become the worrier. When I am in child pose, I am a child.

In order to really "do" yoga, you have to **BE YOGA**. The word "yoga" actually means wholeness and unity. Yoga means to yoke together the mind, body, spirit and breath. Breath is life-force energy or *prana* and is understood in yoga practice as the "spirit of God," which animates us and gives us life. Yoga is **oneness**. It is complete integration. Ultimately the purpose of yoga is to bring about oneness with God, but in order to become one with God, you first must become one with yourself.

Biblically is said that "the kingdom of God is within," and that "We are created in the image and likeness of God." That is our journey, wholeness and oneness. Jesus was a powerful example of that oneness when he said, "I am in the father and he is in me; I and the father are one." This oneness is available to all of us.

Today, I don't have to act peaceful, if **I am** peace. I don't have to take it easy, when **I become** ease. I don't have "do" healthy, if I embody health and wellbeing. I don't have to strive to be loving, when **I AM** love. When **I AM** love, the creator and I are one. I would like to thank that difficult person last week for *teaching* me who **I AM**.

Li Po's poem "Zazen on Ching-t'ing Mountain" brings this point home:

> The birds have vanished down the sky.
> Now the last cloud drains away.
> We sit together, the mountain and me,
> until only the mountain remains.

What is Your Personal Mission Statement?

Businesses often have mission statements describing their vision and purpose. For Shining Lotus Yoga and Wellness, our mission statement is "To inspire, encourage, empower, enliven and enlighten." This is what we are all about, and this is what I strive to do in every class. If businesses should have mission statements, how much more so should individuals in order to clarify their life's purpose! What is your personal mission statement? If you don't have one yet, now is a great time to develop your own.

A personal mission statement clearly defines your individual vision and purpose, distinctly and succinctly. It identifies who you are and where you're heading. In order to write a mission statement, it is important to know yourself and where you see yourself going. Use the following four questions to create your own mission statement.

1. Who am I? Begin to differentiate self from non-self.

> What is me and what is not me? (You are not your job, your status, your achievements, your religion, race, culture or gender.)
>
> Who are you really, without your ego?
>
> What are your strengths?
>
> What is unique and special about you?
>
> What is your fundamental personal philosophy?
>
> What is true for you?
>
> What are your core values?
>
> What are your beliefs?
>
> Think of one word that best describes your overall essence. This word will be a key word in your mission statement.

2. What is my purpose? Our purpose is what we are compelled to do in order to serve in this world. We are never too old to have a purpose or to serve. Our purpose will develop, change, shift, grow, and evolve as we age.

> What are your priorities?
>
> What are you good at?
>
> What inspires you?
>
> What do you enjoy?
>
> What are you passionate about?
>
> What enkindles your enthusiasm and "lights your fire?"
>
> State your purpose:

3. Where am I heading?

> In what direction do you see yourself going?
>
> Where do you see yourself in 5 years? 10 years? 20 years?
>
> What would you like to accomplish in this lifetime?
>
> What would it take to make your life feel complete?
>
> Define your personal vision as you see it.
>
> I see myself . . .

4. What is my mission? Combine the most essential elements from the three steps above into one clear succinct statement. Your personal mission statement should start with the word "I."

My personal mission statement is: "I share wellness, mind, body, and spirit." I'd be delighted for you to share yours with me too!

Trying vs. Being

When I first began to practice yoga, balancing poses seemed unobtainable! I held myself frozen in "tree pose," gripping the floor with my toes, and contracting every muscle. I had, even the muscles in my face! This much effort made it impossible to hold the pose. Once I stopped trying so hard the pose was surprisingly attainable. It was the same with headstands. When I got into the pose, I noticed that if there was too much determination, too much stiffness and tightening, I'd fall. It was in softening into the poses, relaxing my effort that I was able to stay, even if I started swaying! There is a Zen proverb which teaches "If you aim for It, you are turning away from it." When trying too hard, we get in our own way! Our true nature is *being* not *trying*. As long as we are trying and straining, we are moving away from the ease and peace that is our birthright. But how do you accomplish anything without trying?

This lesson can be learned from my two precious furry children, a dog and a cat. The two couldn't be more different, but both teach me and inspire me! Bodhi, the dog, begs for attention, yipping, whining, jumping and pouncing until he is gratified. Country, the cat, on the other hand, shows little interest in attention, preferring to sleep in a sunny spot. Ironically, despite the vast difference in effort, the result is the same; both animals receive abundant love and attention. The lesson we can learn from this irony is that we can often get the same results with less trying. My Enlightened Eating students are often shocked that when they move away from excessively strenuous and vigorous exercise to a more moderate workout, that then they lose weight! My foray into yoga balances teaches that many times we can get even *better* results with less trying! Who knew? When I hold a bar of soap too tightly, it slips out of my hands! When I hold it with ease, I get clean!

Where in your life are you trying too hard? Where could you relax into just being and get the same or even better results? When everything in life is about trying, the joy and ease that is patiently waiting for us is shrouded. Tireless trying creates a pattern of stress and strain in the mind-body system. Stress and strain produce imbalance and dis-ease, which eventually presents as disease.

In our culture, we are conditioned to believe that "becoming" is of more value than "being." What if we try being, and let the becoming happen all on its' own? Being is becoming! The laws of gravity keep the earth orbiting the sun effortlessly! Flowers open and bloom in their own time without struggle, just by being flowers. Trees change colors without even trying, because it is their nature. There is no effort necessary. As a part of nature, why would humans be any different? Instead of trying, relax into being . . . "Let go and let God."

Tao Te Ching #48 reads:

Less and less do you need to force things,
until finally you arrive at non-action.
When nothing is done,
nothing is left undone.

True mastery can be gained
by letting things go their own way.
It can't be gained by interfering.

What Can Dogs Teach Us about Stress?

The garbage truck, the UPS man, the mailman, a random bicyclist and the doorbell all have one thing in common at my house. They completely throw my dog into a tizzy of fright and panic! Even the doorbell ringing on TV triggers a frantic barking fit! The family cat really loves to push the dog's stress buttons, and then revel in it! The interesting thing is, that out of all of the things that unnerve him, none is actually a real threat. It is all his imagination! All of his stresses are illusions of his own mind, complete misperceptions. The garbage truck, the mailman and the doorbell mean him no harm whatsoever!

Perhaps it is the same with humans. We all react to situations the way the dog reacts to the doorbell. Most of our reactions are actually false alarms. We lose sleep, send our heart rates and blood pressure soaring. We create headaches and heartaches over many things that we perceive to be threats. We snip and growl out of habitual reaction and conditioning, rather than because the dangers are real.

The only way to shift our minds out of these patterns of false reaction is to begin to witness our own behavior, just as I witness the irrational behavior of my dog with the garbage truck and the mailman. Only when we become aware of our own illogical ways of relating to perceived stress can we consciously choose a more peaceful, relaxed and calm response.

Mark Twain put it best, "I've had a lot of worries in my life, most of which never happened." In other words, most of our worries and fears are manufactured by the mind, simply figments of the imagination. What if we began to just watch worries arise, then before reacting, stop and see if they actually prove true? So often we get caught up by the stories our minds create around our fears. Not unlike the dog, we end up in our own frenzy of emotion due to our imaginings. How many false alarms do you allow to steal away your peace? You can be like the dog, all worked up over the same neighborhood kid ringing the doorbell day after day, or you can choose ease. As humans, we can be watchful observers of our own behavior, and then choose our reactions with awareness. Yoga philosophy calls this "Witness consciousness." We are the only species with the ability to witness ourselves and then consciously select a better response.

As for the dog . . . he needs a 'dog whisperer' . . . Ding-dong!

> "Be patient and loving with every fearful thought. Practice observing your fears as a witness, and you'll see them dissolve."
> ~ Dr. Wayne Dyer

Flowing Water Never Decays

The verse "Flowing water never decays" from the *Tao Te Ching* has never meant more to me than now. It has been quite difficult as my family has watched my beloved grandmother decline physically. Aging is of course inevitable, but grandmother is a very genteel, delicate little southern lady, and, quite honestly, she rarely lifted a finger in her life. The "baby" of the family, her mother doted on her, and did just about everything for her. She never learned to do for herself. Eventually she met my grandfather, a man who absolutely adored her, and who quickly took over where my great-grandmother left off. My grandmother was well taken care of, to put it mildly. Although she is one of the most beautiful souls I have ever had the privilege to know, she lived a life of ease. She never did her own cleaning, laundry, ironing or cooking; granddaddy did it or paid someone to. In her day, exercise and movement were simply unheard of. She never owned a treadmill or a gym membership. Without any exercise, or even any form of physical work, her already fragile and delicate frame grew increasingly delicate and weak, as she lost muscle mass and bone density.

Grandmother ended up with severe osteoporosis, and has been living with it for decades. Her posture is challenged by a "dowager hump," making it difficult for her to stand upright. Over the years, her bones have broken by just walking down stairs. At one point or another, almost every bone in her body has been broken. She is as fragile as an eggshell. A few weeks ago, my grandfather was helping her out of bed and three vertebra in her back completely crumbled into "dust." This has caused a great deal of pain, and now she cannot move at all. This lack of movement has caused edema in her limbs, and fluid to congest around the heart and lungs. If "Flowing water never decays," then stagnant water certainly grows stale. Grandmother's health has never been more perilous than now.

Witnessing the decline of my precious grandmother has increased my passion and desire for sharing the practice of yoga more than ever.

Yogis are purported to live astonishingly long and healthy lives. There are even reports of yogis in the Himalayas who are said to have lived hundreds of years. "Flowing water never decays . . ."

Since our bodies are 70% water, yoga is certainly a way to keep the waters within us flowing. Yoga works its magic by moving the fluids in the body every time we come into posture practice. Yoga poses help move lymph through the lymphatic system, and increase blood flow to the organs and tissues. Yoga postures help lubricate the joints, move fluids from the glands, and stimulate the kidneys and bladder to move out waste and toxins through the urine. Yoga stimulates the digestive system, and helps keep digestion and elimination regular. Yoga promotes sweat, flushing out fluid toxins through the skin. Yoga also helps regulate the flow of energy through the energy channels, moving blockages and stagnation. It increases the flow of breath, along with release of toxins through the lungs during exhalation. It is no wonder that yoga is purportedly the practice of longevity!

I cannot promise that you will live for hundreds of years if you take up yoga practice, but I can promise that you will certainly prevent some of the setbacks that don't have to be a "normal" part of aging after all. "Flowing water never decays . . ."

The Seven Doors that Stand between
You and Your Soul's Highest Purpose

An ancient Zen proverb says "The obstacle is the path." Without facing the obstacles before us, we will never reach our ultimate destination, which is to serve the world in our own special way. I like to think of obstacles as doorways. Once we are able to walk through obstacles, there is no longer anything between us and our soul's highest purpose. Obstacles are merely illusions; they are not really standing in our way. It is only when we believe in these obstacles, and give them energy, that they stand in our way like a locked door. For every door we encounter, we ourselves hold the key. If the obstacle is really the path, then whatever stands in our way is the door! Awareness of the illusions standing in the way between you and your life's purpose, or *dharma*, un-shrouds the way forward.

When you recognize these six doors, they become gateways that open to your life's greatest work.

1. Self-doubt. "I am not worthy." "I do not deserve this." "Why me?" "I can't!" "I don't have the right education." "I am not the cool kid." "I am not from a privileged family." Do these sound familiar? The real question is "Why *not* you?" We are all created to be great! We hold on to these deceptive beliefs out of fear . . . fear of failure. When we believe these misperceptions, we never try. The people that are able to be with self-doubt and shine anyway are the ones who go on to do great things. As long as we believe we are inadequate, we will never walk through that first door. To walk through the door of self-doubt we truly must believe each one of us is created to make a difference and to do great things. No, there is nothing special about you, because we are ALL special. The illusion is that there is any one of us who is not extraordinary.

2. Fear. "Fear = false expectations appearing real." Fear is an illusion. As long as we live in fear, we stand frozen and never move forward through the doorway of courage! The only way to conquer fear is to be with your fears. Practice approaching what you are afraid of, going straight towards that which makes you anxious, uncomfortable or fearful. When you embrace your fears, they evaporate like the mirages they are. Don't let the delusion of fear stand between you and your life's work.

"You get in life what you have the courage to ask for."

~ Oprah Winfrey

3. Time. "I am too busy, there's not enough time." "I am too old." "It is too late." Many of us have cultivated an adversarial relationship with time, as if it is us against time. What if we shifted the belief to "Time is really on our side." We reaffirm our perceived barrier of time each time we say "I don't have enough time to . . ." My personal affirmation and *mantra* to overcome the illusion of time is "I have enough time to do everything I want and need to do." Stop fighting with time and make friends. Walk through the doorway of time. Einstein himself rejected the concept of time through his study of physics, stating that time is only an illusion.

4. Scarcity. "I cannot afford . . ." "I do not have the means." "I am broke." "When I get enough money, I will . . ." "I don't have enough." "There are already too many people doing this!" These are the illusions of scarcity that stand in the way of reaching your goals and achieving your dreams. The truth is that there *is* enough, there is always enough. God and the universe are entirely in support of equipping you to live your destiny. We are born equipped with everything we need in order to achieve our soul's highest purpose. God has already provided each of us with the special talents, gifts and strengths needed to do what we were created to do. We may have to be resourceful and use our creativity in order to make things work out. We are duped into thinking we can only do what we were put here to do once we get everything we need. We waste time spinning our wheels trying to get rather and just doing. Everything we need is already within.

5. Ego. "I can't ask for help, I am in this alone." "I won't look cool, what will everyone think?" "What if I fail or goof up?" "What if I look like a fool?" "What if I fall on my face?" Ego works to preserve the status quo, but the ego isn't who we really are. The ego is the "small-self," but the soul is the highest self. Don't let the "small-self" tell the "big-self" what to do! The small-self will keep you small, the big-self is here to do big things. Don't be afraid to ask for the help of family, friends, angels or God himself to do the work you were meant to do. By grasping tightly to your current reputation, you can never achieve your highest potential.

"I let go of who I am to become who I might be."

~ Lao Tzu

6. Negative thoughts. You do not attract what you want, you attract what you think. You ARE what you think! In order to change your life, the first thing you must change is your thinking. For us to live our soul's highest purpose, our thoughts must vibrate at the highest frequencies. Thoughts of worry, guilt, shame, lack, and greed have low vibrations. Negative thoughts will never move you towards your highest purpose. We automatically believe our thoughts as if they themselves hold some great truth. The fact is most of our thoughts are just thoughts, and most thoughts are illusions, nothing more than conjecture and imagination. Next time you have a negative thought, give it this litmus test, and ask yourself the following questions created by author and motivational speaker Byron Katie: "Is this true? Do I absolutely know it is true? How do I feel when I think this thought? Who would I be without this thought?" Remember that negative thoughts will never lead you in a positive direction.

Are you on the right path? If you're not, this is article is your message — your wakeup call! Here is your sign!

Packing Guide for the
Journey of Life

In the 9th grade I decided to join an Explorer Scout troop at the urging of my friends. I attended the meetings regularly, as we planned for a long hike and camp out in the North Carolina mountains. At long last, the day came. My buddies talked me into carrying all the junk-food and soda we'd need for the weekend, along with my sleeping bag and other camping necessities. As we began our ascent up Glassy Mountain, it didn't take long to realize I was overloaded for the journey. I was miserable! My pack was so heavy that my back, legs and shoulders ached. As we scaled the mountain at the steep points, my pack threatened to pull me backwards off the mountain, partnering with gravity to send me crashing onto the rocks far below. Thankfully, my tenacity and desire for survival were strong enough to keep me aloft. A typical teenager, I whined all the way to the top where we camped. When we arrived, I was so exhausted, I couldn't move. I was too exhausted to enjoy the glorious scenery and the magnificent view. I was too tired to eat, so I immediate rolled out my bag and slept while my buddies enjoyed the treats I so precariously lugged up the cliffs of Glassy Mountain.

I learned one thing from Explorer Scouts: If you carry too much, you'll weight yourself down and have a miserable journey, unable to enjoy even the destination. This lesson can be applied to life. You can't and shouldn't pack everything you own to hike through life. You must be very discerning. Below is a "Packing Guide for the Journey of Life" — the things to take and the things to leave behind.

Things to take:

1. God, spiritual mentors, prayers, angels, guides, and passed over loved ones. Unseen, they are protecting you and supporting you, every step of the way.

2. Those dear to you. Family and friends, this is your *sangha*, your clan, your tribe.

3. Your values, morals and integrity. These are your armor; shield yourself with them daily.

4. Your dreams, passions, and heart's desire. These are the key to your life's highest purpose.

5. Love, kindness, gratitude and compassion. Adorn yourself with these daily. They are the only beauty products, accessories and baubles you'll ever need.

6. Your individuality and authenticity. Bring along only who you really are, and leave the heavy masks and false personas behind.

7. Creativity. This is something psychologists say we all have, but few actually use. Creativity is a resource and treasure trove of unique ideas to help you explore and plunder life. It will get you out of even the toughest predicament, and will show you a way to manifest anything you need along the way.

8. Courage. So often courage is the only thing standing in the way between who we are and who we wish to become. Go to places that scare you. Walk towards what terrifies you. The obstacle is the path.

9. Faith. Believe in yourself and in the journey. Trust that life unfolds exactly as it is supposed to, in perfect timing.

10. Openness. Be open to the people, places and experiences you encounter on your journey, without judgment. These are your teachers.

Things to leave behind:

1. Perfection. Perfection is impossible and non-existent. Unless you are a surgeon, precision and exactitude will bog you down like my over-weighted backpack. Free yourself up to be "good enough." In doing so, you move with lightness and ease.

2. What others think. My dad always said "What others think of you is none of your business." We spend more time thinking about what others think of us than others actually think of us! We are none of their business, and they are none of ours. Caring what others think about us is an obstacle and a hindrance. Real or imagined, leave their judgment and opinions behind for them to carry, not you, and keep moving forward.

3. The past and the future. Each step in life exists only in the here and now. Journey through life taking one step at a time. The present is all that matters, because now is the only reality; the past and the future exist only in your mind. I remember once walking a long distance through heat and sand, carrying a heavy load. If I looked back to see how far I'd come, or looked forward to see how much further I had to go, I felt exasperated. So I looked down and just watched as my feet took one step after the other, arriving to my destination without the angst I would have had if I kept looking back or forward.

4. People-pleasing. There is no pleasing everyone, so strive to please yourself. Some people spend their whole lives being the person (sister, father, mother, son, wife, daughter) they perceive others want them to be, and they never fully experience what it is like to just be themselves. Other say "Yes" when inside it is really a "No!" Try on your own shoes, and walk in them a while. I assure you they are much more comfortable than hiking through life in someone else's!

5. Guilt. It is said that guilt is one of the heaviest energies. It drags us down. Let go of what you did when you were naive, immature, inebriated or just operating from a lower level of awareness or consciousness. We are not our pasts. The past does not define us. Who we are exists only in the present. We can choose the person we are to be and leave those unwanted parts behind.

6. Fears. This is the lowest and heaviest energy of all. Fear is like wading through quicksand, or walking through life wrapped in heavy chains. Fear is an illusion, a mirage on the journey. Once we walk through it, we realize that 99% of what we fear only exists in our own imaginations.

7. Worn-out beliefs. Set aside old, unproductive or outdated viewpoints about yourself, life and the world. If we didn't do this on a regular basis we'd still be trapped in the belief that the world is flat, and the sun is at the center of the universe. Don't stay shackled to attitudes, beliefs, or dogmas that no longer speak to your heart. Grasping on to stale beliefs is like carrying the weight of old decaying food in your pack.

8. Striving. Here's where we "let go and let God." Striving is like swimming against the current, or taking the whole journey walking uphill. Switch out striving for allowing. Life doesn't have to be a struggle. That which is meant to come to you will come to you effortlessly, in its own way and in its own time.

9. Wanting. We are so often side-tracked and confused by all the wanting. Marketers are experts at getting us to want! When we are enticed to "want" we are forced to "strive." We get caught up in the hamster wheel of wanting-striving-wanting-striving. Wanting is an illusion, because when we finally get what we want, we move on to a new want, and the hamster wheel of wanting and striving starts turning all over again.

You must pack as efficiently for life as you would for a long hike up a mountain! For life is a long journey, uphill most of the time. Along the way I have begun to set aside that which hinders, blocks or weighs me down. Thankfully, I've learned a lot since the 9th grade!

Paradise

There exists a warm, breezy, lush, dwelling,

A tropical Island, fertile, peaceful, serene.

A place I have sought after in my travels,

My lifelong quest for that one special, magical place that feels like home,

A place that appears often in my dreams,

A place I almost grasp just before it disappears or evaporates.

At last I located my Island paradise, where I least expected.

It is not on a map, but is buried deep within my heart.

It has been waiting with great anticipation,

Longing to be discovered, visited and inhabited . . .

Ancient, timeless, and precious, like sunken treasure or the lost Atlantis.

I found my lost paradise by simply walking through the door of my heart,

and into the realization

I can visit my own private island retreat anytime I choose.

Experiments in Love

If we had to choose one thing that is at the essence, the core, the very meaning of life, most people would say it is LOVE. Swami Kripalu says, "Love is the highest practice . . . the only breath . . . the treasure of life. First we must build the foundation, and that foundation is love." The reason I practice and teach Kripalu yoga is because it is based on the foundation of love. The love is more important than the postures or any other element of the practice.

At the Kripalu Center, in the "Transformational Teaching" module, we created our own "experiments in love." Inspired by this, in the yoga classes I taught this week, we intentionally brought love into our yoga practice, and set the intention to bring more love into our lives. At the beginning of class, students designed three "experiments in love," and I would like to invite you to do the same.

1. An experiment in love for yourself. Without loving yourself first, you do not have the capacity to love others. In fact, Laura Williams says, "You can only love others as much as you love yourself." For the next seven days, think of ways you can be more loving towards yourself. This might be allowing yourself to sleep 15 minutes longer, or getting up and savoring your cup of coffee or tea without rushing into your day, or spending quite time relaxing on your porch or deck, or whatever makes you feel loved by you. For myself, I chose to practice self-reiki daily for a week.

2. An experiment in love for your family. Mother Teresa said, "Love begins at home." Think of ways you can be more loving to members of your family. An extra kiss and hug. Being more attentive. Being a better listener and more present when they are speaking. Choosing to do their favorite thing or make their favorite meal. They don't have to know what you are doing, just make this your little experiment, and notice what happens over the next 7 days as you choose to intentionally bring more love into your home.

3. An experiment in love for others. Jesus taught his followers "You shall love your neighbor as yourself." This is why it is so important to love yourself first. Make an "experiment in love" with people outside of your family. It could be smiling at the cashiers when you are in the store. It could be making an effort to offer compliments to everyone you encounter. It could be to reach out and call someone who has been on your mind, or send a card or letter. Think of some way you can spread love beyond your family and out into the world.

Notice what happens over the next seven days as you practice your experiments in love. It is with love alone that we can transform our lives and the world.

> "Plant seeds of happiness, hope, success, and love; it will all come back to you in abundance. This is the law of nature."
>
> ~ Steve Maraboli

Life is a Playground

As a culture, according to author and researcher Dr. Brene Brown, "We wear exhaustion like a badge of honor . . ." We try to out-do one another with our lists of accomplishments. We brag about how many things we ticked off our "to-do" lists. We boast about how many hours we worked, and about how few hours of sleep we got away with. Americans get a lot done, but as a whole, we are over-stressed, under-rested and overwhelmed. Where is playtime? Are we happy?

Dr. Brown goes on to say that "The opposite of play is not work; the opposite of play is depression." "We're a nation hungry for more joy." And play is the best medicine! For the mental health of our country, we as adults need more play, without guilt and without apology. But most of us don't remember how to play or even what it is. How do we even begin to define play as grown-ups?

Dr. Stewart Brown lists seven properties of play:

1. It is **purposeless**. There is nothing to accomplish, no "carrot" for doing it other than enjoying the very act. Play is something we do just for its own sake, without needing or expecting a result.

2. It is **attractive** in its own right in alleviating tension or boredom.

3. It is **voluntary**. Play is something that doesn't require any convincing or coercion. No reward or pay is necessary for you to engage in this activity.

4. You **lose track of time**. In play, time seems to fly by, standstill, or both! Time seems to be warped when you engage in your form of play.

5. The **ego fades**. Play is an activity in which you lose yourself.

6. It is **improvisational**. Play is creative. There is spaciousness and openness. One "goes with the flow."

7. There is a **desire to continue**. This is an activity you are not looking forward to finishing. It is an activity you want to return to again and again.

How many activities in your life meet these seven criteria? How often are you engaging in these activities? How could you be involved in them more?

The sage Erasmus said "The highest form of bliss is living with a certain degree of folly." Jesus said "Unless you become like little children, you'll never enter the kingdom of heaven." He also said, "The kingdom of God is within." Heaven is described as full of wonder, awe, peace and joy, and apparently it is already there within us. Perhaps when we become more like children and treat life as a playground, it is then that we will have a piece of heaven on Earth.

Taking Your Vacation Back with You into Your Life

As many of us are returning from vacation, I am reminded of a quote I recently read:

> "Instead of wondering when your next vacation is, maybe you should set up a life you don't need to escape from."
>
> ~ Seth Godin

This quote got me thinking about how we can bring our vacations back with us into our lives, allowing us to continue to savor that same joy, ease and relaxation back in the "real world!" Setting up a balanced life is the best way to create optimal mental and physical health. Here are a few ways we can live lives we don't need to escape from!

1. Conscious relaxation. Our bodies have certain places where they hold tension and stress. By taking a few moments to consciously relax these points, we can create a sense of ease in the body and mind. Try the following exercise: Consciously relax the walls of the abdomen; the root of the tongue; the muscles of the face; the area between the eyebrows; the scalp; the area between the shoulder blades; the back of the neck; and the hinge of the jaw. Now take a few moments to notice what it feels like in this more relaxed body. Repeat this practice any time you like, at your desk at work, in traffic, or after a stressful encounter, phone call or email.

2. Conscious breathing. Our breath informs our entire mind-body system. Slow deep breaths communicate a sense of calm and relaxation. By consciously slowing and deepening the breath, we shift ourselves out of "stress response" and stimulate the "relaxation response." Try taking three deep breaths, deliberately slowing down the exhale, while intentionally softening and relaxing the body on the out breath. This exercise takes less than a minute, and you will FEEL the difference!

3. Time outs. Give yourself a "time-out." I remember giving my kids "time-outs" when they were whiney, cranky or just plain naughty. It was really ME who needed a moment of peace! A vacation is really a "time-out" from the stress, pressure and hectic pace of life. Why not create a mini-vacation by putting yourself in time-out? Every week, block your calendar with several hours, or even a whole day, of free, unscheduled time. You deserve time for YOU in your own life. Time to do nothing or time to do anything you really want to do. This is NOT time to catch up on bills, phone calls, emails, workouts, grocery shopping, etc.; this is "free time" just for you! Let this time be your gift to you!

4. Let go. Take one thing off of your calendar every week — I am not talking about crossing off something on your "to-do" list! You're already doing plenty of that! I actually mean to look for things that you can choose to not do without a huge repercussion. One of the main problems with our everyday lives is that we are over-scheduled and under-rested. What activity can go, so you can open yourself up to more freedom and space in your daily life? What can you remove so you don't need to escape the hectic pace of life, but live a balanced daily life instead?

5. Pampering. Pamper yourself. Indulge in "vitamin P" — *pleasure!* Here's a chance to add something you love to your calendar in place of that something you just removed. On vacation, people read a good book, get a massage, play a round of golf, tennis, or their favorite game. Pamper yourself on a regular basis even when you are not on vacation. Schedule a "date" with your favorite luxury. Use this time for something that makes you feel special and happy . . . even if it is just a bite of chocolate, a cup of tea, time in nature, listening to soft music or a good podcast.

6. Just say "no." "Honor your top priorities. If it is not a definite 'yes,' then it is a 'no.'" ~ Cheryl Richardson. "No" is an empowering word which allows us to set boundaries and safeguard our time and energy. Often we feel saying "no" is unkind, but saying "yes" to something you are not moved or inspired to do is being unkind to yourself. Don't do things you are half-hearted about. Saying "no" to these opens up time and space in life to say "yes" to you! Saying "no" more often allows time for your real passion and purpose.

> "All the mistakes I ever made in life were when I wanted to say 'no' and said 'yes'."
> ~ Moss Hart

Are You Being Kind Enough to Yourself?

In her book *The Top 5 Regrets of the Dying*, nurse Bronnie Ware says that after spending 8 years treating the dying, "My biggest lesson was to be more gentle with myself . . ." Apparently the biggest regret of the dying was that they hadn't been kinder . . . to themselves! Why are we so tough on ourselves? I am pretty sure as human beings most of us are hard-wired that way. But isn't life hard enough without us beating ourselves down more? What would the world look like if we were all kinder to ourselves? Here are six ways to be kinder and gentler with yourself, beginning today.

1. Self-care. There is a Zen saying: "The path to enlightenment is simple: When you're tired, rest; when you're hungry, eat; when you're sleepy, sleep." Being kind to yourself is listening to the signals your body is sending. As long as you're fighting against the body instead of honoring it, you are not being kind. Don't even wait for the body to have to tell you it needs something, because this is a signal something is already out of balance. Treat your body as you would a luxury automobile. You wouldn't forget to have the tires rotated or the oil changed! Our bodies are the vehicles in which our souls travel through life. What if we really took care of our body's needs as if it were a precious child? What if we started working with the body instead of against it? Can you imagine how great you'd feel, how much energy you'd have, and how much you would accomplish? Honor what your body needs when it needs to feel enlightened and enlivened!

2. Time to "be." Neale Donald Walsch said, "We are human beings, not human doings." In this culture, we base our self-worth almost entirely on what we have done or accomplished. What if we began to base it on who we are, more than what we do? If all we ever do is "do," it can be difficult to discern who we really are. Meditation practice is a great way to get to know yourself. Meditation can be as simple as sitting quietly outside in nature, or sitting, breathing, relaxing, feeling, watching and allowing. There is another Zen saying, "Everyone should meditate 20 minutes a day unless you are really busy, then meditate for an hour." As the Beatles sang: *Let it be . . .*

3. Nourish yourself. Take time to eat foods that really nurture you. Eat wholesome, nourishing foods that leave you feeling light and energized, not heavy and sluggish. Take time to enjoy your meals and snacks! Don't rush around and eat while standing at the kitchen counter, sitting at the desk, or driving in the car. Take time to prepare your food with love rather than eating food made on a conveyer belt or assembly line. Allow yourself to relax, taste, and enjoy your meal! You are worth it!

4. Goof off. Our culture programs us to set goals and work tirelessly until they are accomplished. We consider ourselves "lazy" if we aren't always ticking something off of our "to-do" lists. We think we are accomplishing more this way, but we are actually accomplishing less! By giving ourselves time to decompress, lighten up, and refill our tanks, we return to the tasks at hand more joyfully, and with renewed energy and enthusiasm. This perceived "unproductive" time is actually the fuel that helps propel us forward towards meeting our goals. We all need a healthy balance between rest and play! I am my own worst "boss," but I have resolved to become more like the ant, doing things bit by bit rather than trying to move mountains all at once! In this attitude I have found great joy, and I still accomplish what is needed!

5. Maitri. *Maitri* (Sanskrit), or *metta* (Pali), is defined as loving-kindness or unconditional friendship, including with one's self. Loving-kindness and compassion cannot be cultivated towards anyone else until first given generously to oneself. To love others more, we must first love ourselves wholly. *Maitri* emphasizes relaxing the inner critic and cultivating self-acceptance. I cringe when I hear people beat themselves up with negative comments like, "I'm so stupid." or "I'm so fat." We judge ourselves so cruelly and harshly. Are you friends with yourself? Would you treat a friend the way you treat you? Would someone want to be friends with you if you treated them the way you treat yourself? Being friends with yourself is about loving yourself just the way you are, without having to change anything. *Maitri* includes a practice of self-compassion and self-love. Promise to never again utter a harsh word to yourself, either in thought or in word. *Maitri* is about cultivating ways to be more gentle, loving and kind to yourself. I recommend making a commitment to doing one kind thing for yourself every day for 21 days as a practice of *maitri*. Perhaps it is taking time to walk in nature, having a relaxing cup of tea, taking a cat-nap, practicing yoga, massaging your feet, or taking an aromatherapy bath. Do whatever speaks to you as an act of kindness and friendship to yourself. This can be any simple activity that always brings you joy. This alone will refresh your soul, and kindle an intimate friendship with you. I also invite you, for the next 21 days, to offer a daily prayer of loving-kindness to yourself. The following is a simple loving-kindness prayer: "May I be happy and free. May I be protected and safe. May I be healthy and strong. May my life unfold smoothly with ease." Repeating this prayer daily in your own fashion or form, nurtures the seeds of compassion within us, and as it grows for ourselves, it begins to expand out towards all beings.

6. Self-affirmation. Affirmation is a practice of avowing that you and your life are worthy and good. Affirmations are positive statements made in the present tense as though they have already happened. Using affirmations in your daily life has a powerful uplifting effect on your mood and spirit, promotes increased self-esteem, and can help you achieve your goals. You can write your own affirmation and place it somewhere you will see it and read it every day; I suggest the bathroom mirror or the dashboard of your car. You can also practice affirmation meditation by repeating the affirmation silently to yourself for several minutes. Both of these are effective ways of introducing the powerful effects of affirmation into your life. Here are some examples of effective affirmations: "I love and accept myself exactly as I am." "I accept all of the abundance that is flowing to me now." "I am happy and successful." "I am calm and peaceful." Feel free to come up with your own affirmation that expresses what it is you would like to genuinely feel. Then repeat the affirmation daily until you feel it is true in every cell of your being.

Practicing kindness towards our selves is the first step forward towards creating a kinder, gentler world in which to live and raise our children and grandchildren. Don't wait until your deathbed to recognize that you should have and could have been kinder to yourself all along . . .

Let the Real You Come Out to Play

Have you ever felt "different"? Have you ever had the awkward feeling that you're just not like everyone else, or that you don't fit in? That is because you are different! We are all different! What if every cell in the body acted exactly the same? How could we function? What if everyone was a glamorous Hollywood actor? Who would fix our broken bones or repair our broken cars? We are all here to serve a purpose, and each one is special and unique. It isn't weird to be different; it is weird to be "normal!"

There are some people who spend so much time and energy trying to be like "everyone else" that they lose touch with who they really are. They have to have the same jeans, sunglasses, sneakers, and haircuts. They have to like the same things, think the same things, and do the same things as everyone else. They spend tremendous time and energy convincing everyone they fit in! They say the "right" words, they post images of themselves doing all the "right" stuff, and they would never be caught dead being themselves.

These folks haven't discovered **self-acceptance**. Many spend their whole lives rejecting who they really are in exchange for an alternative that "appears" on the surface to be kosher. In reality they are rejecting their true identity. When you reject who you are, you are rejecting your creator who designed you for a special and unique purpose. Who you *really* are is not a mistake. You are not a freak of nature. You are exactly who you were meant to be.

I had a powerful experience walking down the streets of Paris on my way to teach my first yoga class. I literally saw and felt myself "step into who I am." In that moment, saying "yes" to teaching yoga was saying "yes" to being me. Be warned, being yourself is *not* always the easy path! I can attest first hand that being a yoga instructor and healthy eating coach (with a southern accent) is a huge challenge in a conservative Midwestern community in which burgers, brats and beer rule! It often leaves me feeling awkward like the **odd-one-out.** It takes a lot of **courage** to be authentic to yourself, amidst the tremendous pressure to conform.

No one else can tell you how to be YOU! Not your teacher, boss, spouse, parents, friends or the popular group — no one. No one knows how to be you but you! By spending a life-time rejecting the **true-self** over and over, many people have forgotten who they really are! People are waking up middle-aged completely alienated from themselves! Our life-long efforts have been spent training ourselves to be like everyone else, not cultivating self-acceptance, individuality and connecting to our inner truth. We have lost ourselves along the way!

Give yourself permission to be who you really are. Start today! Practice being you. Be authentic! Be who you are, say what you feel, do what you love. Relish your own uniqueness without apologizing to anyone. Nothing feels better than living in your own skin and dancing in your own shoes! Stop rejecting who God fashioned you to be. Bow to your creator and embrace the beauty of who you truly are. Let the real you come out to play! You were put in this world, at this moment in time, for a reason! This world can't be great without YOU being YOU!

YOU are your own *GURU*!

The biggest questions in life are:

Who am I?

Why am I here?

What is my life's purpose?

What should I do now?

Where do I go next?

How do I find love?

How do I serve?

What is the meaning of my life?

We've all wrestled with these questions and searched for the answers. The answers are not "out there." They are "in here." You already have the answers to all these questions; they are just buried deep inside. In fact, no one else can answer these questions for you! The only one who really knows your answers is you! How do you uncover these truths hidden inside? How do you become your own *guru*?

How to find your inner guru:

Slow down. Your inner voice gets lost in the day to day chaos that hijacks thoughts, energy and time. Each moment is packed. Our calendars are full! We are unable to hear the soft whisper of truth murmuring in our hearts because we don't give ourselves the time or space to actually listen to the wisdom of our souls. What can you cross off of your calendar? What commitments can you let go? What on your schedule is standing in the way of you and your higher purpose? The time to remove it is now!

Say NO. When we say "yes" to things which don't inspire or move us, we are saying" no" to things which give our life meaning. When we clutter our limited time with things we are half-hearted about, they stand in the way of our whole-heartedness! It has been said, "Don't get good at what you don't want to be doing." Once you start moving things out which don't stir your soul, your divine purpose has space to emerge. I recently read an article which asserted that the "devil" really *is* in the details! The "devil" foils our divine plan by keeping us too busy with monotony!

Say YES. To your passion! The things which we feel excited and enthusiastic about are our life's purpose! We were given the desire to do these things because we are intended to do them, not set them aside or ignore them! Your life's purpose isn't anything you don't feel drawn to; it is that which you are energized excited about the most! If we deny ourselves these passions, we are saying "No" to our life's purpose! Let your passion become your purpose!

Follow. God sprinkles little "bread crumbs" of insight to show us the way. Life is like a scavenger hunt, with little hints, tips, and clues, guiding us along, one step at a time. We aren't always led at the pace we desire, but we are always led and always at the right pace to the right place! Look for the clues, notice them, and follow them. BIG warning: If you get off your own path, the clues get less subtle and increasingly unpleasant! Notice the gentle, soft cues; don't wait for the hammer to fall! God will do what he needs to do in order to get your attention!

Spend time in quiet. The answers are in the silence. They are not on the radio, the TV, Facebook, or the phone! Give yourself enough silence to listen to you! Your soul is trying to get through to you but its whisper is drowned out by constant noise. Meditation is the fastest doorway to the voice of your soul. Spend 15 to 20 minutes in silent meditation daily. The answers to your life's questions begin to surface quietly and subtly in the spaces between your thoughts.

Rest. Our society as a whole is exhausted and stressed out. Our thoughts are racing just as fast as we are! Exhaustion clouds the mind and wearies the soul. Clarity and insight are disrupted by fatigue! It is when we feel vibrant and alive that we are illuminated! In a recent training I attended, it was suggested that everyone take a 20 minute *savasana* every day and a 1 hour *savasana* once a week. (*Savasana* is a relaxing yoga pose, resting on the back in a lying position.) I have begun to practice this myself, and the results are profound! Give yourself permission to rest. Busyness is not a substitute for substance, meaning, or purpose! Real meaning lies beneath all of the busyness.

Spend time in nature. Nature is wisdom in physical form. Nature is inherently intelligent, and we ourselves are part of nature. When we lose touch with nature, we lose touch with ourselves. Returning to nature, we are immersed in the beauty and intelligence that is our birthright! The answers we are searching for take living form in the natural world. In nature, the answers are right before our eyes, waiting to be discovered. When we're holed up in cubicles, wired to electronic devices, we're separated from the wisdom of our own nature.

Trust. Trust that the answers you are seeking are also seeking you. Trust that you will keep meeting your destiny over and over again until you finally recognize it and welcome it. What keeps showing up in your life? What is it trying to say to you? What is it trying to teach you? Know that your life's purpose is attracted to you and you to it, like a huge magnet. Your destiny continues to be revealed to you in many different forms until it gets your attention. Who you are and why you're here is hard-wired into your DNA. Every cell in your body knows the answers to your life's questions. Trust what your inner guidance is telling you, and be guided by the answers that are knocking on the door of your heart.

Ask. Ask for support. Ask for help. None of us are meant to go it alone. When we work together, miracles unfold. Once you discover your life's purpose and what you're meant to do on this earth, ask your loved ones, friends, acquaintances, even strangers for their help and support as you step into your destiny. But do not stop there. Ask for the support of God, the angels, saints, guides, passed over loved ones, ancestors, and Jesus, Buddha, or whoever is your spiritual teacher. It is not weakness to ask for help. Help is empowering, and with powerful help, it is impossible to fail!

We are all meant to be *gurus*, wise teachers who affect this world for the better. However, we are currently conditioned to let our desk jobs, the rigorous schedules we impose on ourselves, and our own insecurity hold hostage the wise one within. The whispering voice of our highest self has been drowned out by the noise of modern life. What if we begin to watch and listen now? If you've never met a *guru*, it is time to look within.

Weekend Review

Life spins and swirls at an incredible pace! Most of us can hardly keep up, much less make sense of it all! One thing I know for sure is that life keeps teaching us the same lessons in different ways, until we finally learn them. Often we are too busy to even become aware of these teachings, much less learn them! We are frequently unavailable to the wisdom, insights and truths right underneath our noses. We wouldn't want to keep repeating the first grade over and over again because we failed to pay attention, but we unwittingly do this in life, over and over! Life lessons can become quite noticeable, aggressive and attention-grabbing if we fail to take notice of the subtle messages! One can never underestimate the importance of taking time and space to ab-sorb, reflect, digest, process and assimilate what life is here to teach us!

For a few moments, try becoming a spectator, a passive observer of your week. What was this week here to teach you? What new truths did you uncover? What new lessons did you learn? At the week's end, re-flect back, and answer the following questions. (I suggest writing your answers in a journal.) With this increased awareness of your week, notice the insights, wisdom and understandings which would have otherwise gone unnoticed.

- What new events came into my life?

- What new experiences did I have?

- What new people did I meet?

- What new purchases did I make?

- What shows, movies and books have I taken in?

- What were these events and people here to teach me?

- How was my overall energy and mood?

- What made me uneasy or uncomfortable?

- What did I avoid?

- What brought me joy?

- What inspired me?

- What new things did I start?

- What did I complete?

- What came to a close?

- What did I leave undone?

- How did I disregard or neglect this week?

- What difficult choices did I make?

- How did I serve?

- How did I give love?

- How did I receive love?

- What did I do special, just for myself?

- Where did I spend the majority of my time, and with whom?

- Where am I doing too much?

- Where am I doing too little?

- What lessons did I learn?

- In just one sentence, what was the overall theme or purpose of my week?

I suggest making this process of reflection a practice at the end of each week. If you do so, you'll find by year's end that you will have avoided many of life's strong-arm, attention-grabbing tactics, and you will have definitely passed from first grade!

Creating Space for Grace

"Space" is valuable "real estate" in our busy lives. The cost of the space in your life is equivalent to what you must give up to keep it. Perhaps you're giving up time, breathing room, your health, freedom or peace of mind. Often we keep our days, calendars, and lives utterly and completely filled. How often do we take time to quiet the mind and listen, reflect, digest and assimilate the truths and teachings that life presents us?

Space is openness. Space is emptiness. Space is silence. Space is a vacuum. If we deliberately fill every nook and cranny of space in our lives, there is no room for grace to flow in. Is there something unnecessary and inconsequential taking up "prime real estate" in your life? Is something robbing you of the space for grace? If so, imagine what might be crowded out of your life: time with family, down-time, self-care, health and healing, creativity, living your dreams, eating well, spiritual growth?

Grace is defined as unmerited divine assistance, given to humans for their regeneration or sanctification. Deepak Chopra says that "To live in grace is to experience that state of consciousness where things flow effortlessly and our desires are easily fulfilled. Grace is magical, synchronistic, coincidental, and joyful. But to live in grace we have to allow nature's intelligence to flow through us without interfering." What is interfering with the flow of grace in to your life? What can you release to allow room for something healthier, better and more satisfying to come in?

How do you learn to release those things which consume the space for grace? My own litmus test is to ask myself three questions:

1. Is it a definite "yes"? If not, then it's a "no."

2. Am I doing this because I really want to, or just because I want to win others' approval?

3. Do I **love** this? Or am I **inspired** by this? If not, it's a "no."

These questions can help clear the clutter in a drawer or in a room, but also in your life. After all, space is space, and grace is grace. Are the right things taking up **prime space** in your life?

List, in order, your top five priorities.

1.

2.

3.

4.

5.

List, in order, the five things which demand the most time/space in your life.

1.

2.

3.

4.

5.

Now list five things in your life that you don't **love**, which aren't a **definite** yes, or which do not **inspire** you. These are the things you need to clear away to make room for grace to flow in.

1.

2.

3.

4.

5.

Elise Cantrell

Do you recognize any discrepancies? Is what you need to release clear? Begin to create space for grace today, and allow new possibility, enchantment and joy to flow to you effortlessly.

Sacred Geometry:
The Power of the Triangle

A friend of mine recently recounted to me how as a child she devised her own science experiment. She created a cardboard pyramid, and placed it over a freshly picked flower. She placed a second freshly picked flower, from the same plant, beside the pyramid. In a few days the flower sitting beside the pyramid had withered, dried and crumbled. After 30 days, she removed the flower from beneath the cardboard pyramid, and it still appeared fresh and intact. However, after removing it from the pyramid, in a few days it too withered and crumbled. I told her we should all live in pyramids!

The four sides of a pyramid are composed of triangles, the geometrical shape of power and strength. In new relativity theory, called causal dynamical triangulation (CDT), all of space-time is said to be composed of tiny triangles "glued" together. CDT asserts that the walls of time and the different dimensions are triangulated. This accounts for the law of cause and effect and the geometrical shape of reality.

When contemplating the power of the triangle, I can't help but envision the pyramids of Giza which have stood for millennia in the Egyptian dessert. The space shuttle is made of thousands of tiny triangle-shaped tiles. A carpenter uses a triangle to strengthen the architectural structure of whatever he builds: roof tops, the framework of a house, wooden fencing. The Holy Trinity in Christianity is a sacred triangle.

At the center of our physical body, right at the bottom frame of the ribs, you can feel the rib cage form a triangle that houses the solar plexus and many vital organs. This area is the very center of the human physiology. The very core of the human frame itself is a triangle. In the yoga system this area is considered our "power center." It is said to be the storehouse of vital energy, will-power, inner strength, courage, determination and purpose.

Elise Cantrell

I often practice yoga with a mirror for alignment. I can't help but observe the beautiful geometry present in the human body during yoga practice. Yoga itself is sacred geometry brought to the human form. If geometry can have such a powerful effect on something as fragile as a flower, or as grand as a skyscraper, what effect can this sacred geometry have on our own being? The Sanskrit word yoga means to yoke or unite. As we practice yoga, perhaps we yoke the same power inherent in sacred geometry and draw it into our being . . .

How to Do What You Love, Succeed and Thrive!

Most people never get to enjoy a career doing what they love. Work is one thing, and fun is another. There is a mind-set that these two can't go together. I think this is exactly what keeps people from achieving greatness in what they do. It is because their time and energy is completely consumed doing something they *have* to do instead of what they *want* to do. This alone sets us up for mediocrity. There are all kinds of excuses: "I'll never be able to support myself doing that." "It just seems too good to be true that I could do what I love all day, and not only survive, but thrive!" "There is too much competition in that field." Or "I'm afraid." And the list goes on. Just as a great recipe leads to a delicious dish, there is a recipe to absolutely thrive at doing what you love. Here are the ingredients!

1. Do what you love! If you could do anything in life what would it be? What is your passion? Harnessing the fire of your passion and desire will carry you far. You will have inexplicable drive and energy behind you, carrying you forward like a sailboat that has caught a strong wind. Your efforts will seem effortless. You will have boundless energy available to you if there is passion behind it. You will move full-steam-ahead without the friction of halfheartedness, boredom or monotony.

2. Do it with love. Throw yourself into your work wholeheartedly! Love is the most important ingredient behind anything we do. Love is the formula for success. Do what you love, love what you do, and let love be the origin from which all you do emerges! Love is an inexhaustible, infinite, and potent field from which to live, work and act. When you come from love, you are serving this world directly from the source, and that endless well-spring contains everything you need. Love is success.

3. Serve. Let your passion serve others, help others, heal others, and inspire others. Does what you do come from a place of giving back? Are you generous or just taking? When it is your deepest desire to serve in whatever way you are called to, doors open. When you are willing to serve, everything you need to do so will be provided.

4. Leave doubt behind. Don't second-guess or question how things will work out or how things will unfold! Let things unfold naturally! Trust your intuition at all times. Trust in divine timing. Trust in the wisdom of your soul. Doubt is an illusion. Walk right through the doorway of doubt without fear, and enter the field of dreams. Close the door of doubt behind you and live in the realm of infinite possibility.

5. Be authentic. Be yourself, and don't be afraid to do what you love, and do it YOUR way. Be unique. Don't do it a certain way just because everyone else does. Don't seek approval. Let who you are really shine through in what you do. Be unapologetically you! Trust in who you are, and don't dilute it! Stand in the radiance of your own light!

6. Do it with integrity. Be honest with yourself and others at all times. Never compromise your integrity. Remain upright and honorable in all you do. Do what you say, and say what you do. Integrity is the leavening that allows you to rise higher and higher. Without integrity, we are heavy and sinking.

7. Trust. Trust that you will have an abundance of time, energy and resources to do what God put you here to do. When you are doing what you love, with passion and integrity, "the force is with you." Never doubt it!

8. Believe! Believe in yourself. Believe in your purpose. Believe in what you do. Believe in your calling. Believe in what you were created to do. Believe that dreams do come true. Believe in the flow of grace. Believe in the power of love. Toss out logic and reason, and follow the wisdom of your soul. Know that wisdom is a divine gift! Dive into your dreams fully, and don't look back!

9. Find balance. The fire that fuels your passion is the same fire that can burn you out! When you are passionate about something, it is tempting not to stop and rest, but this is critical to keeping your momentum going. Stay in balance by taking care of you! It is vital to fertilize success with a balanced formula of work, rest and play.

I didn't create this recipe, this formula found me. I had no formula in mind as I set out to do what I absolutely love, but in retrospect I am aware that these are the ingredients that allowed me to do what I absolutely love, and thrive. If I can do it, so can you!

Elise Cantrell

Free Yourself

There is a popular story in meditation circles about a man who walks down the sidewalk and falls into a deep, dark hole. He is stuck in the hole for a long time, frightened and scared, until he finally manages to free himself from the hole. The next time he is walking down the sidewalk, he falls right back in the same hole again. It still takes him hours to get out. When he walks down the same sidewalk again, he is on the look-out for the hole in hopes of avoiding it, but not seeing it, he again falls into the same hole, and is stuck there until he is able to climb his way out. The next time he walks down the side walk he spots the hole, and tries to walk around it, but winds up falling back in again. After climbing out of the dark hole this time, he decides to start taking a different sidewalk. Once he starts taking a different sidewalk, he never falls into the hole again.

How often do we continue to fall into the same holes in life? How many times have you climbed out resolving never to see the inside of that hole again, only to fall in again? If we keep walking the same path, we'll keep encountering the same hole! It is once we resolve to take a new way that we can avoid the old pitfalls. Clearly, from this story, change must be conscious, but it also must be skillful. In order to free ourselves, we must not only try to avoid pitfalls, but deliberately choose a different path.

No so long ago, I began to notice that when I take my dog on a walk, I take the same route, day after day. There are many different avenues, paths and trails around Kohler, WI. Why am I staying on the same one? Sometimes we get stuck in the same groove, like repeating the same track over and over again on a CD. In yogic philosophy, this is called *samscara*. A *samscara* is a deeply rooted pattern of existence, which is very hard to change. As I became aware of my habitual walking pattern, I also began to become aware of other patterns in my life that I seemed to be repeating unquestioningly. As they came to light, I noticed many of these ways of doing things actually didn't really serve me, but stayed in place more as a result of habit than anything else. With the awareness, I set out with intension to break up some of these patterns. My first act to undo my own *samscaras* was quite simple. I began to think of new walking routes on which to walk the dog every day. Years ago I was able to break a bad habit of keeping the TV on while I was doing things around the house, the habit of background noise. With all of this external noise, I couldn't hear my own thoughts; perhaps on a subconscious level I didn't really want to. One year, for Lent, I gave up TV. This 40 days broke my old pattern, and opened up a whole new world of being at home with silence, with my thoughts, and with myself.

Once I became comfortable with taking a variety of walking routes, I began to expand my inquiry into intentional change into other areas. What are some other things I can do differently? Where else can I free myself up? Trying new make-up, experimenting with dry shampoo, tossing new experimental ingredients into my recipes. I began investigating new meditation techniques, investigating new ways of coming in and out of yoga poses, coming up with new sequences in my own yoga practices. I even drummed in a drum circle and LOVED it! A whole new world was opening up for me. For once I was living outside of my own box, an imaginary box I had slowly over time created for myself, and which held me prisoner to preconceived ways of doing things, when in many cases there was a better way. How freeing it is to jump out of the groove! Looking at things in fresh new ways, and even turning my thinking "upside down" has led to my greatest moments of insight, creativity, and genius! What would happen if you came out of your comfort zone?

Ask yourself these questions:

1. Why am I doing things this way? Am I on "autopilot"? Am I doing this out of pattern or habit, or by conscious choice?

2. Is this the most skillful way I could choose to do this?

3. Am I getting the results I want to get?

4. What would happen if I consciously chose to go about this in a different way?

Your life is a result of the daily choices you make and the patterns which you continue to reinforce. If you aren't happy with your life, then change your patterns. Leap out of your *samscaras*. Look at things in new ways! What are you keeping yourself from discovering and enjoying because of being stuck in limited patterns and ideas? What happens when you remove outdated labels, tags, habits, expectations, and restrictions? What happens is that a whole new world opens up! Out there is a world of things to try, and explore, and enjoy!

Living with Paradox

Paradoxical observations of my life:

1. The more I hurry, the longer things take. When I slow down, I get things done.

2. When I try too hard, I fail; when I stop trying, that's when I succeed.

3. The harder I work, the less I accomplish. When I relax, things seem to complete themselves.

4. The less I want, the more I have.

5. The more I like myself, the more others like me.

6. The bigger my expectations, the greater my disappointment. When I don't expect, I am always amazed.

7. The more I try to change things, the more they remain the same.

8. When I don't interfere, things change by themselves.

9. The more I try to help, the less helpful I am. By being present and supportive, help is no longer necessary.

10. The more I give, the more I receive; and the more I receive, the more I have to give.

11. When I agonize over perfection, everything seems flawed.

12. When I let things be as they are, I realize they are as they should be.

13. When I chase after something, it eludes me. When I remain still, it comes right to me.

14. When I run from my fears, they chase me round and round. When I confront them, they flee from me.

15. When I am too hard and firm, I inevitably break; but when I am soft and flexible, nothing can break me.

16. When I resist, life pushes back harder. When I allow, life flows effortlessly.

17. When I take time to play, I get more work done.

18. I am controlled by my own need to control. When I release control, I liberate myself.

19. The real price of things is the amount of peace I have to give up for them.

20. Perfection is imperfection, and imperfection is perfection.

Paradoxical observations of others:

1. The more money people have, the more it has them.

2. When people follow the crowd, they leave themselves behind.

3. When people eat to live, they remain healthy; when people live to eat, they cause disease.

4. When people drink alcohol to feel better, they always wake up feeling much worse.

5. The more people brag, the less their self-confidence.

6. The harder people try to be liked, the less likable they are.

7. The more "superior" people try to be, the more common they are.

8. A "know-it-all" really knows nothing. It is only in a place of not knowing where one can learn.

Staying Balanced and Grounded
During Times of Transition

Fall is nature's most profound reminder that life is full of transitions
and changes. Change is obvious all around us, as leaves change colors
and fall to the ground, leaving trees bare and the earth blanketed. We
observe animals, insects and birds scurrying about, anxiously attempting to secure safe passage into winter. In the fall, the winds pick up,
swirling around as if to remind us of the winds of change. This time
of year the natural world vividly demonstrates that nothing is perma-
nent. Some changes are gradual and subtle, and other changes, like
fall, are dramatic and dynamic. Even positive changes can cause us
to feel ungrounded, unstable and imbalanced. When we experience a
change in career, relationship status, finances, health, geographic location, surgery, home renovations, a milestone birthday, a new addition
to the family, or a newly empty nest, it is common to be confronted
by a sense of unsettledness. At these times, mind-body imbalances can
easily arise. The more sudden and profound the change we encounter,
the more abrupt and severe the disturbance is to the mind-body system.

**Assess whether you are experiencing any of the following mind-
body side-effects of change:**

1. Have you been more absentminded, forgetful, or spaced out?

2. Have you noticed a change in appetite?

3. Has your digestion been more delicate, weak or irregular?

4. Do you notice increased intestinal gas or constipation?

5. Have you noticed stiffer muscles and joints?

6. Have you observed cracking and popping noises in your joints?

7. Have you had more difficulty focusing and concentrating?

8. Have you felt more fretful, anxious, or worried than usual?

9. Have you had difficulty sleeping, more restless sleep, or waking between the hours of 2 and 6 am?

10. Have you noticed a sense of restlessness, or moving from task to task without really accomplishing anything?

11. Does your mind seem to be racing from one thought to the next?

12. Have you experienced moodiness or mood swings?

If you have noticed three or more of these, you are experiencing the physical and mental imbalances that often accompany change or transition.

When experiencing these effects, it is a signal that we need to regroup, reconnect and rebalance. Ayurveda, the ancient 5,000 year-old healing "science of life" has its own special prescriptions for dealing with the symptoms of change and transition. The aim of Ayurveda is to always keep the mind, body, and spirit in a state of wholeness, harmony and balance. We often can't control the way things shift around in life, but what we can do is care for ourselves in a way that enhances our ability to adapt to the changes we face. We must consciously readjust our life-style to meet change in a balancing way. Following are Ayurvedic natural recommendations to help safeguard the mind-body system from the uncomfortable side-effects of change.

Ayurvedic diet recommendations for transitions:

1. Add more root vegetables, which are extremely nourishing and grounding.

2. Eat warm, moist, *cooked* foods and beverages such as soups, broths, stews, herbal teas and stir-fry.

3. Increase fluids, which are instantly grounding due to their heavy, liquid nature.

4. Increase organic dairy products. Dairy products are highly nourishing and soothing, and promote a sense of comfort. Think of how babies are instantly calmed and gratified by a bottle of milk.

5. Increase nuts, seeds, healthy oils and whole grains. These too are soothing, healing, and nourishing, and rejuvenate the mind-body system, helping to prevent us from becoming depleted.

6. Reduce caffeine and alcohol. These substances are agitating to the mind-body system, and throw it further into imbalance.

7. Avoid red meat, which increases inflammation, anxiety, and is difficult to digest.

8. Avoid eating cold or raw foods.

9. Avoid fast food, junk food, or processed food.

10. Include sweet juicy fruits, which promote a sense of "sweetness" in the mind-body system.

Ayurvedic lifestyle recommendations to help acclimate to transitions and change:

1. Avoid excessive movement, travel, trips and errands.

2. Avoid loud noises and over-stimulation of any kind, such as TV, radio, bright lights, nail-biting movies or novels, loud parties, heated conversations, or crowds.

3. Take warm soothing baths with aromatherapy oils such as rose or lavender.

4. Get adequate rest and ample sleep. (Note that these are two separate things.)

5. Engage in self-massage and other self-care.

6. Spend time in nature.

7. Practice grounding yoga poses such as hindi squat, lotus, mountain, child's pose, and goddess.

8. Practice restorative yoga or *yoga nidra*.

9. Take leisurely walks.

10. Curl up by the fire with a good book.

11. Listen to soft, soothing music.

12. Practice meditation regularly.

13. Walk barefoot on the earth. Lie on the bare ground.

14. Avoid overly strenuous activities.

15. Stay warm, and keep out of wind.

16. Stick to a set daily routine for meals, bedtime, and awakening.

Sticking to a nurturing, soothing and supportive diet and lifestyle routine can make all the difference as the winds of change blow our lives around, taking us in new directions.

Life Lessons I Learned from Writing a Book

It has been several years since I began the adventure of writing *40 Days to Enlightened Eating*. Had I known in advance how much work was involved in writing, editing and publishing a book, I can honestly say I would have run in the other direction as fast as I could without looking back! Fortunately, "ignorance is bliss" . . . at least until it was too late, and the book was written! I was too far in to go back!

What a learning experience this has been! In fact, the lessons learned in the book writing and publishing process can be applied to life in general! Here are the hard-won life lessons I learned over the past few years!

Think of everything you begin as a rough draft! Just get started with whatever it is that you want to accomplish! Don't think it has to be flawless the first go-round. In fact, just plan on revising anything you take on in life! You can edit is as many times as you need to, until you get it just right! I cannot begin to explain how many revisions, changes, corrections and edits were made in order to create something I can be proud of. Things have been added and subtracted, shifted and moved. In life too we are free to edit and revise things until we get things just right and can be proud. Let it be OK not to get everything right on the first, second, even third try! Keep editing away at life, day by day, and eventually you'll have a masterpiece!

Perseverance is the path. You can ask my parents, I was a strong-willed child. (I am a Taurus.) My stubborn, dig-in-your-heels approach to life, made me a challenge to parent! I was a source of many frustrations — theirs and my own! My parents often marveled at how I wouldn't let something go until I made it happen. My grit and determination often wore them down, and got me my way. I don't give up! In book writing and publishing, this quality has been an asset. If I gave way to difficulty and challenge, there would be no book! It was sheer perseverance and persistence that allowed me to give birth to my book.

Perfection is an exercise in futility! No matter how many times you edit, there is no perfection. There are still flaws in the book: a missing comma, an extra space, a typo. Perfection does not exist. But something doesn't have to be perfect for it to be great! And this comes from a self-admitted "recovering" perfectionist. Allow things to be great without agonizing over the perfection of every tiny detail. Only God is perfect! Be accepting of your own imperfections!

Divine timing is real. Nothing comes to fruition until the universe is ready! As hard as I tried to reach a September deadline, the book was delayed until November. At first I was devastated by this glitch in my time schedule. That is until it dawned on me that it would be released right in peak holiday shopping season and on the cusp of the New Year's dieting craze. Only God could have planned the timing this well! In our limited views we often mistakenly think things just aren't working out for us, but instead divine wisdom comes along and works things out even better! Allow things to flow on their own. Trust that God's timing and unfolding of things is far more intelligent than we are. The order in which things happen and come together don't always make sense until we see the big picture.

Often we can't see the forest for the trees! Interestingly, after pouring over the manuscript countless times, uncovering the tiniest inconsistencies, punctuation errors, and typos, my editor and I could no longer see a much larger error, a discrepancy in the appendix and table of contents. Thankfully the publisher caught it! Sometimes it takes another set of eyes to point out the forest that is right there among the trees! As a former art teacher, I should have known how important it is to step back and look at the full picture! This same thing can be said about life. Sometimes we get so caught up in the day-to-day details that we fail to recognize what is right before our eyes. It is important, from time to time, to take a look at your life from a different perspective. Look at it as a whole, instead of just the minute parts. Here is where we have the greatest revelations and insights!

Leave space! Books contain blank pages, margins, space between words, sentences and paragraphs, and space between the end of one chapter and the start of the next! The concept of space is powerful in writing books and in life. As I worked out spacing margins, chapters, and leaving space for journaling in the book, I became aware of how important it is to plan in empty space in my life. We need blank pages, margins, and spaces in life to give ourselves room for the unexpected. We also need space to process and integrate what life teaches us, or else it just blurs together! Can you imagine what a book would look like if everything was crowded together without spacing? Just as space is deliberately left between chapters, margins and the beginning and end, how much more so can our own lives benefit from inserting space intentionally! This was a revelation for me, and I have begun to insert space in my schedule for pauses, for reflections, and for the unexpected.

Feel free to rearrange! Create your own life in a way that makes more sense and flows more easily! I wrote the book as I taught "Enlightened Eating" classes. Then, by trial and error, chapters were moved, changed and adjusted, to make things flow just right. Rearranging the chapters was almost like rearranging a room in order to have better *feng shui*! Nothing is set in stone. If the flow of your life is not working for you, feel free to rearrange things to make it work optimally!

Alchemy exists! If you believe in yourself, and believe in your work, strive to serve others, and are passionate about what you do, that is alchemy! Yes, these are the magical ingredients to achieving anything! There are endless amounts of energy, ideas, time and creativity, if you do what you love, love what you do, and do it with love!

Some people will resent you for shining your light. Shine it anyway! Along this path I was surprised and hurt by the reactions of a very small number of acquaintances. Not everyone has been happy, kind or supportive. There have been a few individuals who have seen this journey of mine as a threat or competition. They have made comments which have been hurtful, or have acted rude and resentful. At first I was baffled by this behavior. Then I realized that their resentment is really about themselves, and not about me! Instead of shining their own light brighter, some people will try to darken the light of others.

This behavior arises from a place of fear, insecurity, or "contracted consciousness." Know that people like this are doing the very best they can at the level of consciousness at which they are operating. Be compassionate, forgiving, and wish them well. But don't be deterred by those who don't rejoice in your efforts, just keep moving forward, and let your light shine!

Some things take on a life of their own. Many days it seemed like the book just wrote itself. It was merely my hands at the keyboard, but the insights, ideas, and flow of words came from somewhere beyond me! If I said I did this all on my own, I'd be lying! Something bigger than me was also at work! I think life works the same way. There is a powerful, loving and creative force beyond us, full of wisdom and intelligence, guiding and leading us, writing the story of our lives. It is just up to us to let that magnificent force flow through us! Some call it the universe, I call it God. When we allow God to work through us however he wants, great things become possible.

> "All that is good comes from God because God is ALL that is good. When we define God; we limit God. When we place limitations on goodness, we crush it. When we believe there is only right way to reach souls, many souls go unreached. When we allow God to work through us however he wants, great things become possible."
>
> ~ Elise Cantrell

A Walk Among the Dead

The first time I ever heard about "death meditation" was in my 200 hour yoga teacher training with Ganga White. He described how in India it is customary for the dead to be wrapped in a burial cloth, placed on a wooden raft, set aflame, and then floated down the Ganges River into the darkness of the night. At the urging of his *guru*, Ganga went to the riverbanks of the Ganges to practice "death meditation." From dusk until dawn, Ganga sat on the riverbank in a state of watchful awareness as each flaming raft that was a former life passed by. He was deeply touched and experienced a profound shift from this experience.

Upon hearing this story I admit I had quite an aversion to the thought of a death meditation. Since that time I have read and listened to numerous accounts of death meditation, with a mix of repulsion and curiosity. Early this summer, however, the death meditation smacked me over the head when the husband of a friend was struck and killed by a car while riding his bike. Feeling her pain and anguish over this tragic loss became a death meditation in and of itself. You cannot have a friend lose her husband without considering the prospect of losing your own. Upon even considering such a thing, you look mourning, sadness, loss and impermanence right in the face. You hold space for your own worst fears. The feelings of compassion that emerged for this friend were a reflection of the feelings which arose in me at the thought of a similar demise.

Although I spent the summer experimenting with various meditation techniques, I consciously avoided engaging in a formal death meditation. Finally, I gained the courage to actually look death in the face. Unlike Ganga White, I didn't go to the banks of the Ganges River. After all, death has no particular preference for India. Instead, I stayed close to home. For my meditation, I chose a walk among the dead. Near my home is a cemetery with a walking trail, that up until then I had avoided like the plague. For my death meditation experience, I chose to enter the gates, and take a meditative walk along a path lined with graves.

As I first entered, I immediately realized that I was the only human being around that was actually alive. I did not feel fearful because of this, it was just an observation, and I walked further down the path. I recalled how my father taught me to drive stick shift in a local cemetery, and how he said jokingly that I couldn't kill anyone there because they were already dead. As I walked on, I noticed one side of the path was lined with graves, but there were just trees and grass on the other side. I felt as if I were walking the line between life and death. In this moment, I was between two realms. Then I noticed that there were plots available for the not-yet-dead, waiting patiently for expected new occupants. Here I sensed that death is ongoing and unending. It always has been, and always will be. Ironically, there is no death for death. I found that I didn't really have any emotion for the lifeless bodies lying below the neatly piled earth, but I wept for the ones who had lovingly and painstakingly placed flowers or American flags by the headstones in loving remembrance. It was the survivors who unearthed my compassion. Then I came upon the grave of a child. This one halted me in my tracks, and almost brought me to my knees. As a mom, this is my deepest, darkest fear, and here I was looking it right in the face. It wasn't pretty. I felt my gut wrench as I imagined the parents who had to lay their child to rest much too soon. Death isn't fair. Death isn't predictable. Death doesn't show favoritism. Death isn't kind.

As I walked further, I came to a point where headstones populated the landscape heavily. On either side of me, as far as my eye could see, I was surrounded by a sea of tombs. There were many colors, sizes, and shapes. Each bore a different name and a unique message, but their meaning was all the same. These markers were all that was left of a life . . . a stone with a name and a date. This seemed rather unremarkable considering some of the things I imagined these people once accomplished, and the lives they once touched. This was yet another reminder of the impermanence of all our passions, our efforts, our goals, our deeds, our accomplishments and even our love. Next, I noticed the silence . . . the stillness . . . There was something beautiful there in that vast expanse of silent stillness. I sensed rest, peace, contentment and an arrival to a place where there was no need to try, no need to do, and no need to impress. It was complete. There were no goals, no deadlines, no cell phones, no emails. There was just rest. As I exited the cemetery, I breathed a sigh of relief that I had now left death behind me . . . But had I really?

Unplugged!

I awoke this Monday morning to find to my horror that the internet was "kaput." I had so much work to do online! I fidgeted with wires, rebooted, went through the internet repair program several times, pressed random buttons, etc., to no avail. I waited on the phone for what seemed like an eternity to speak to technical support, which brought me no closer to a solution. I would have to wait for a technician who would promptly arrive between 12 and 4 p.m. I am not a TV watcher, so quite honestly for the first hour or so I was at a loss! As I paced around restlessly, I felt totally disconnected from the outside world!

Then I decided to bake some healthy scones, which were delicious! And I love to cook! After that I took the dog for a leisurely walk. Noon came and went. No knock at the door. No repair men. I did some writing, made gazpacho for lunch. I practiced yoga and meditated, all the while expecting to be interrupted by the doorbell. No such luck. The kids arrived home from school. Four p.m. came and went. I read a health magazine as I awaited the technician's knock. The knock finally came at 5 p.m. and by 6 p.m., I was reconnected!

What I began to realize by 6 pm, however, was how relaxed I felt. I was renewed! I became aware of how over-stimulating always being connected through a fiber-optic wire actually is! I was awed at how much I accomplished during the day! I felt peaceful, calm and relaxed, yet I had caught up on so many things! This was a powerful, perhaps life-changing mishap! A blessing in disguise! Lemons became lemonade! From here on out, it's media-free Monday for me!

The Law of Expansion and Contraction

Have you ever noticed a pattern in life where things seem to be at their darkest, smallest, saddest and scariest right before there is a profound shift, growth and awakening? Right before our lives expand, we inevitably experience the natural contraction which heralds the next expansion.

Life is a playful interchange between the forces of expansion and contraction. The law of expansion and contraction is the same law that governs the most primary component of life, the *breath*. Breathing in and out is probably the most fundamental and obvious relationship between the two forces. One depends upon the other, and each precedes the other. There has to be an even exchange. The exhale must happen first before the lungs can expand once again with breath or life-force. The lungs must expand and contract in order for life to take place.

In all of life there is a necessary balance and flow between these two forces: giving and receiving, doing and not doing, having and doing without, action and inaction, work and rest. Every force in the universe breathes and has a life of its own. There is a necessary give and take. One must precipitate the other in order for expansion and contraction to comfortably function in our bodies and in our lives. We must work so we can enjoy the fruits of our labor. We must give in order to receive. We must receive in order to be able to give! If we overdo just one, the other cannot take place. We must become smaller to become bigger! Notice the deepest of exhalations happen right before the most invigorating inhalations.

Contraction is the tightening, narrowing and decreasing stage which allows space for expansion to occur. Expansion is boundless and liberating. If we stay stuck in contraction, our lives remain underdeveloped and stagnated. It is like having the exhalation without taking in another breath! Fortunately breathing happens all on its own without thought, practice or intention. We don't have to try to breathe.

We may notice the law of expansion and contraction at work in our mood, appetite and energy. Jobs, finances and even the economy and politics go through states of expansion and contraction. When we notice these things come and go, instead of getting too attached to one state of being or the other, rest in the comfort that the two elements are partners in the dance of life. One cannot exist without the other!

Where do you wish to expand in your life? Where do you need to contract in order to allow this to happen? Be aware that even without your intervention, life does this for you all on its own. We often just need to relax and let it happen.

Begin by just taking a deep exhalation. In the space after the exhale know that you are resting in a state of "pure potentiality." Know that expansion is on its way. Then draw an expansive breath in, allowing your whole being to expand and open. You are expansion. You are evolution. As the breath fills and expands the lungs, your awareness, intelligence, wisdom, and life-force take on the form of expansion. Be that expansion!

Enough

I have a friend who used to exercise 4 hours a day, striving to be skinny enough, desperate to be a smaller size. Although she already looked great to me, she squandered away time with her family and friends, her talents, passion, energy and creativity in exchange for the treadmill — all in the name of reaching that perfect number on the scale. Despite the excessive exercise, the perfect number never arrived because it was never skinny enough.

Another friend recounted to me how when he first became a store owner he was ecstatic. He loved his job. The store was very successful. He opened a second store. With the second store, he was more stressed and less happy. However, both stores were great successes, so he opened a third store. At this point, he became overwhelmed and miserable. He eventually sold all three stores, because it became too much. He was at his happiest with just that one store. His mistake, he admits, was in wanting more. He said his lesson from this is to stop when you are already happy. Learn to be satisfied with "enough." Ancient Chinese sage Lao Tzu famously advised, "When your cup is full, stop pouring."

Westerners have long come to believe that if a little is good, more must be better! With this in mind, we end up overdoing everything! If vitamins are good for us, then we need a whole handful! If exercise is good, more must be better. If success is good, more must be better! If one slice of cake is good, more is even better! The sickness of our times is in never recognizing the sense of enough. Instead, we have created a culture of super-sized everything, all-you-can-eat buffets, houses people cannot afford, mountains of credit-card bills, along with mountains of debt, all in search of enough. People are in a pattern of over-exercising because they are over-eating. People are over-spending because they are over-wanting. People are over-working because they are over-spending. We live in the illusion of never having enough. We are not satisfied with what is. We are never good enough, skinny enough, strong enough, rich enough, smart enough, talented enough, happy enough, and perfect enough. We never seem to have enough time, enough energy or enough money.

In the current economy, many minds are entrapped by the illusion that there is not enough to go around. They feel that for them to succeed someone else must fail. Businesses try to cut employees, and bamboozle competitors. Coworkers throw each other under the bus, desperate to get further and stay ahead. People are afraid to be happy for others' good fortune, as if there is not enough good fortune to go around. This limited thinking is false. We have become like hamsters stuck running around the wheel of life, seeking something which is ever elusive: **enough**. As long as we keep chasing more, we will never stop running long enough to see **enough** is already here. When we are waiting for enough, we don't give ourselves permission to enjoy what we already have. We are never satisfied with what is, as long as we're stuck in the deception that more is better. What if we recognize that enough is enough? We already *have* enough, we already *are* enough. The paradox is the fact that we only **reach** enough by realizing that what we have at any given moment is enough. Like my friend on the treadmill, stop chasing. Stop and appreciate what is already there. This is the only way you will finally attain **enough**.

Enough
by David Whyte, *Where Many Rivers Meet*

Enough. These few words are enough.
If not these words, this breath.
If not this breath, this sitting here.
This opening to the life
we have refused
again and again
until now.
Until now.

Non-Striving: Life is Like a Cat

My first love arrived into my life when I was five. Her name was Wiskers. She was black and furry, and loved me as much as I loved her . . . but only when she wanted to! I remember fits of tears when I tried to hold and cuddle Wiskers and she wanted no part of it, leaving me behind with bites and scratches! But when I was less available to her, doing homework, playing, or otherwise engaged, Wiskers was right there demanding my attention, impatiently and relentlessly! From this experience alone, I learned volumes.

Have you ever observed that when you seek out a cat, it wants nothing to do with you? It insists on having its own way with things. It is only when you stop trying that the cat comes to you on its own, begging for *your* attention. It's as if the invisible force of our "efforts" has a repelling effect, and "not trying" is almost magnetic. Perhaps cats are here to teach us something about the flow of life.

Often times, replacing striving or grasping with just *being* allows life to come to us when *it* is ready. Life-force is said to have its own innate intelligence and wisdom. In trying too hard, our efforts just get in the way. Have you ever noticed that what is forced almost never works out? When we tamper with the natural flow of things, we ourselves become the obstacle. Herein lies the yogic principle of "non-striving." When we strive and effort, we begin to go against the natural flow. Non-striving is about trusting things to unfold just as they should on their own. It is about having faith in the inherent wisdom of God, nature and the universe. It is about understanding that nature itself has its own intelligence. Nothing has to be forced in the natural world, the sun comes up every day on its own. Plants and trees bear fruit without any intervention. The grass grows; seasons change. There is no striving in nature. Things have their own natural rhythms and timing. We as human beings are part of nature. Perhaps we should let things unfold "naturally," without allowing our limited intellect and imperfect reasoning to intervene.

When I strain to be creative, new ideas are elusive. When I *must* write, come up with a new recipe, or create a yoga class, it is impossible. When I allow it come to me when it is ready, the ideas flow like rain. And when it decides to rain, sometimes it pours, and I cannot even contain all the thoughts and ideas that come flowing in.

When we spend our life striving and efforting in order to force things to fit into our fixed notions and rigid time constraints, we strain the body and mind. We end up creating patterns of strain in the mind-body system. Overall unease develops as the mind and body war with each other and work against the natural, intelligent flow of life. Straining is not only unnecessary, but it is unhelpful. People who stay entrapped in patterns of strain often end up with strained looks on their faces. They live strained lives. Nothing flows, because strain tightens, restricts and holds. Strain creates and builds tension in the mind-body system and in the flow of life. If we can't relax the body, we can't relax the mind. If we can't relax the mind, then we can't have peace. Softening this tension removes the barriers to the natural flow of wisdom and grace.

The *Tao Te Ching*, an ancient Chinese text often considered to be one of the wisest books ever written, teaches this same concept. Chapter 24 reads: "He who rushes ahead doesn't go far. He who tries to shine, dims his own light. He who defines himself can't know who he really is. He who has power over others can't empower himself. He who clings to his work will create nothing that endures. If you want to accord with the Tao, just do your job, then let go."

Force only creates resistance. Where you strain and strive, you meet with opposition. When you accept, allow and wait, the natural flow of things unfolds in perfect timing and in just the right way. The magic is in trusting in the innate intelligence of the natural way of things. It is the greatest paradox of life that the more we strive, the less we achieve. When we step back and just allow things to flow, life comes to us soft and cuddly, rubbing against our leg, purring, giving us exactly what we wanted all along . . . but only when it is ready.

Elise Cantrell

"Don't try to force anything. Let life be a deep letting go. See God opening millions of flowers every day without forcing the buds."

~ Rumi

"Do not struggle. Go with the flow of things, and you will find yourself at one with the mysterious unity of the Universe."

~ Chuang Tzu

Turning Your Thinking
Upside Down and Inverting Your Perspective

There is a Seinfeld episode in which George Costanza decides to see what happens if he starts doing everything in the opposite way from the way he is conditioned. He consciously treats people, money, experiences, and things in an entirely reverse way than he has before. Miracles begin to happen! Everything begins to work in his favor. He comes into lots of money, becomes "popular," gets offered his dream job, etc. It is said that "If we always do what we've always done, then we'll always get what we've always gotten." If you want to see transformation in your life then you yourself must first shift your thinking. Try inverting your perspective.

In yoga theory, the head is the home of the rational mind, ego, logic and intellect. The heart is the home of the soul, eternal wisdom and expanded consciousness. In yoga's physical practice, an inversion happens when you deliberately get the heart above the head, and this requires turning upside-down. Inverting your thinking also requires deliberately shifting your thinking upside down, and allowing the heart to override the rational mind. Thinking with an awakened heart-mind, or *bodhicitta*, is thinking in unity with the limitless compassion, wisdom and insight of the heart. It is there where a higher awareness exists, beyond logic or the ego. From the heart we delve into the timeless wisdom of our eternal soul. In order to powerfully transform our lives, we must invert our thinking in a way that puts the heart before the intellect. Leaving reason and logic, and making choices and taking action led by the illuminated wisdom of the heart, gets radically different results. Our choices, actions and words become more awakened and enlightened. The intelligence of *bodhicitta* far surpasses that of human logic. It is a place of eternal truth, deep understanding, unbounded creativity, universal perception, luminosity, clarity, insight, kindness, compassion, love and peace, flowing from the mind of the heart.

Perhaps we lost touch with this center of thinking when man went from crawling about on all fours to standing, when suddenly the head was physically placed above the heart. This transition may have shifted the direction of humanity. Perhaps now is the time to shift our consciousness back to this wiser, more enlightened, center of thinking and being. Perhaps it is time to shift our thinking from our minds to our souls. Perhaps George Costanza's theory of inverting our thinking is actually genius. Perhaps inverting our perspective is the key to changing our lives and changing our world. Perhaps this is what enlightenment really is, a moving out of our head and into our heart.

Uncloaking Joy

Ever since I was a child I have dreamed of living in an island home. This probably stemmed from childhood summer vacations to Fripp Island, SC, where we rented a home right on the ocean. These were good times! As an adult, from time to time, I still have a strong desire for island life: quiet, carefree and warm, abounding in fruit trees, ocean breezes and lush vegetation. I have even caught myself drooling over episodes of House Hunters International's "Island Homes."

On a particularly miserable day, I found myself wanting more than anything to escape to my island dream home! This was a deep craving for something "better" than my life as I perceived it. As I was meditating, the thought came to me: "Your island home is right here, right now." I felt as if I'd been struck by lightning! I melted into tears, recognizing that I had been giving up the beauty and joy of what I already had in imagining some "castle in the sky." For most of the world, my home is a fantasy. For the homeless, any home would bring joy. I wasn't seeing or appreciating what was right before my eyes. I was giving away my own joy! This was a "light bulb" moment. Hence forward I began to abide in the joy that already is, instead of frittering it away on an alternate reality! In the words of Guillaume Apollinaire, "Now and then it's good to pause in our pursuit of happiness and just be happy."

I wonder how many opportunities for joy completely escape us only to be eclipsed by our fantasies, disappointments or illusions? How sad it would be to have lived a life full of joy, but never having even recognized that it was there! How many ways do we miss out on our own joy? What if we embrace whatever joy is already present, without feeling shortchanged, and without longing or craving for anything more?

Focus on joy. If we dwell on misery, then misery seems drawn to us, and misery is our destiny. Where we focus our mind, energy follows. If we focus on joy and positivity, then we draw ourselves toward it like a magnet. Eastern cultures, in general, place more emphasis and reflection on joyful moments such as accomplishments, victories, and good deeds. For the most part, Westerners spend a disproportionate amount of energy dwelling on shortcomings, failures and sins. It seems we overlook our own moments of joy in lieu of our disappointments. It is as if joy is cloaked for us. Rita Schiano says, "Talking about our problems is our greatest addiction. Break the habit. Talk about your joys." By glazing over the positive aspects of our existence, we squander away opportunities for joy. Stop looking for problems. Stop focusing on the imperfections, which are few, and focus on the joys, which are many. By practicing this alone, it will seem as if a veil of darkness has lifted and a light has begun to shine!

Give yourself permission to feel joy. Don't feel guilty for having joy, be grateful. I believe our culture has conditioned us to overlook and dismiss our own joy out of guilt for the suffering that exists in the world at large. Suffering has always existed and always will. Each of us, at some point in our lives, has suffered. Suffering is inevitable. But to dwell on suffering is to be ungrateful for the joy that is there at the same time. Savor the joy that is present, knowing that all circumstances and situations are ever-changing. There is no reason you should not feel joy because another is suffering. Refusing to feel joy does not remove the suffering of anyone. In fact, it adds to the suffering. To allow yourself to feel more joy is to bring more joy into existence. Many of us feel that we have no business feeling joy as long as there are others out there who are lacking it. Sacrificing our own joy in no way increases the joy of anyone else. In the words of Jack Gilbert, "To make injustice the only measure of our attention is to praise the devil." To appreciate joy is to amplify joy. To dismiss it in deference to the ongoing hardships and afflictions that exist is to only magnify agony. Joy is there, it is up to us to uncover it and abide in it. Be aware of how you interpret your world. It becomes exactly what you perceive it to be. In what ways do you give up your own joy? In what ways do you fail to recognize the joy that is already there?

Experience childlike joy. Children are always available to joy. They are masters at uncovering joy in the simplest things and in unexpected ways. I have marveled at how much joy my children find in an empty cardboard box, a stick, a balloon, or blowing bubbles. Something as simple as a ball can bring about hours of smiles. Perhaps somewhere along the way we have over-complicated the path to joy. Just being in the presence of children reminds us that joy is a simple thing which rarely involves trying or striving. It is about discovering the wonder and amazement present in simple things.

Notice what brings you joy. Recognize the joys you have. Look joy in the face, be there with it, and embrace it. See if you can discover joy in unexpected places. See if you can become comfortable being with joy. I invite you to create your own list of things in your life that bring you joy. It may include your morning cup of coffee, curling up by the fire, snuggling up with a pet, a walk in the woods . . . whatever it is, write it down. Allow yourself time to reflect upon and to behold your own joy.

Now be grateful. Gratitude is a profound doorway to joy. It instantly brings you into the present moment, and focuses your awareness on the joys which are already present. What are you grateful for? When we focus on the things we are grateful for, we immediately recognize that there is nothing lacking.

> "Joy is the highest energy of all. It's the magical sense that everything is possible. Joy springs from appreciating the gifts within each moment. Joy allows you to attract and create your present and future moments at their highest possible levels."
>
> ~ Doreen Virtue

Balancing Life

As difficult as it is to balance on the yoga mat, I find it much more complicated to stay balanced in life. Just when I think I've got it all worked out, something swoops in and throws me a curve ball, sending me way off balance. Although we can't predict the curve balls that come our way, living a balanced life can be a conscious choice. As you will find in any balancing pose on the yoga mat, the more stable and balanced you are in the pose, the more at ease and at peace you feel!

An easy way to detect an imbalance in your life is to begin to see where your life may be lopsided. Look at your life as if it were placed on an old fashioned set of scales. Would those scales be balanced, or are they tipping to one side or another?

What kind of balance do you have between work, rest, play and relationships? Is there a balance in your life between giving and receiving? Does care for yourself equate to the care you provide to others? Is your eating balanced during the day, or are you saving all the calories for the evening? Do you allow yourself to be stressed out all day, only to numb out in the evening with too many drinks or zoning out with the TV? Where is the balance?

More importantly, is there a balance between your mind, body and spirit? Is your mind beating up your body, willfully pushing you into a "punishing" exercise regime? Or conversely, is your body having its way with the mind, lazing around on the couch without mental stimulation, physical activity, or motivation. Are you letting the physical body fall into disrepair, or are you actively participating in your own wellness? Do you put all of your time and energy into intellectual pursuits, or achieving the ideal physique, while neglecting your spiritual path? Are you living a life of balance?

What is it in your life that tips the scales at the expense of something else? Is it worth it? In the yogic healing science of Ayurveda, when the mind, body and spirit are balanced, there is no possibility of illness. It is only when one or more of these come out of balance that we are confronted with a sense of dis-ease which eventually manifests as disease. Staying in balance is work, but it is a lot less work than bringing balance back once you have lost it!

Eight Ways to Refill Your Tank

If you have recently been feeling exhausted, I just read an article online that asserts solar flares could be to blame! Apparently a sense of "jet-lag" is a side-effect of solar flares! Feeling exhausted, worn-out, depleted or fatigued is also a sign that your "tank is running low." After a particularly hot and extraordinarily busy summer, it is entirely possible that any fatigue is a result of more than just solar flares. Summer "vacation" was once a time to laze in the sun, but in the age of electronics it has become busier than ever, leaving many of us worn out and fatigued. In Ayurveda, yoga's healing sister science, fatigue is considered a sign of an imbalance. When we find ourselves imbalanced, if we keep doing what it is that is causing the imbalance, things can escalate and eventually result in disease. Regaining balance is really as simple as "refilling your tank." Cars can't run on empty, and neither can we! We do not have anything to give when we have neglected filling our tank.

There is a parable told by the Buddha in which two acrobats are discussing how best to remain safe when performing together. If either of the acrobats is in harm's way, then chances are that the other acrobat is also unsafe. The first acrobat suggests that they each focus on keeping the other safe, and then they will both be safe. The second acrobat suggests that they both concentrate on keeping themselves safe, and then they will both be safe. Finally, they conclude that the only way to ensure their well-being is if they both concentrate on keeping themselves as well as the other one safe. It is only then that they can be assured of being free from harm. When we forget to focus on ourselves, and only focus on others, we are forgoing a "safety net" for our own wellbeing as well as for those who depend on us. In order to take care of others, we must also practice tasking care of ourselves.

Here are eight suggestions on how to "refill your tank":

1. Rest / sleep / deep relaxation. Get at least 8 hours of sleep a night to replenish the mind and body. If you are tired during the day, do not hesitate to rest a little while. When I am feeling particularly worn-out, I will take a restorative yoga pose, like legs up the wall or reclining bound angle on a bolster, for 10 to 15 minutes. Other times I will practice a self-induced *yoga nidra* (a yogic deep relaxation technique). It is amazing how rejuvenated I feel when I rise! Meditation is another way to rest the body while also giving the mind a respite, while in a state of quiet stillness. It is said that 15 minutes of meditation is equivalent to 1 hour of sleep! I find my daily meditation practice vital to my energy and well-being. After meditation, I find I am deeply refreshed and renewed in a way unparalleled by anything else.

2. Nourishing foods. The only way I have the energy to teach multiple yoga classes, write, and care for my active family is by eating foods full of vitality and life force: fruits, veggies, nuts, whole grains, and legumes. I also try to work in "super-foods," brimming with nutrients and life-force: berries, avocado, walnuts, almonds and salmon to name a few. When I deviate from this, I notice my energy level correspondingly plummets! Junk food and fast food actually rob us of our energy, depleting the mind-body system. Not only are these foods lacking in vitality, but they require undue energy from the body to digest, process and then detoxify!

3. Time in nature. Nature itself is profoundly healing and replenishing. In nature we are surrounded by soft therapeutic sounds, colors and textures. We breathe fresh clean air and are bathed in warm sunshine. There is an inherent, calming, medicinal-like quality present in the natural world. Sometimes referred to as "vitamin N," nature replenishes, renews and invigorates us, simply by being in its presence. Taking a gentle walk down a quiet wooded path, or simply sitting in the grass, or by a stream, lake or pond, can quite dramatically vitalize the mind, body and spirit. The Japanese actually call the practice of spending time in nature "forest bathing!"

4. Space. Give yourself space. Schedule in "down-time." I find that when things get too hectic, I begin to actually "crave" a sense of space. This is your soul's way of nudging you back into balance. I find if I don't actually schedule "space" for myself, life takes over!

5. Self-care. When you are feeling depleted, and exhaustion ensues, it is time to practice "radical self-care," nurturing yourself without a drop of guilt. Take a nap, indulge in a massage, or practice self-massage. Listen to relaxing music. Spend time alone. Journal. Eat chocolate. Indulge fully in whatever it is that your body, mind and spirit are asking for. Give yourself what you need when you need it. Self-care is not a luxury, it is a necessity. When fatigue sets in, and you feel drained, take a "mental health day" and spend the day caring for you as you would care for a small child. When you give back to yourself, your tank refills, and you have the energy and strength to give back to your work and to others.

6. Conscious breathing.

"Life is in the breath. He who only half breathes, half lives."

~ Yogic Proverb

Breath is integral to yoga. Breath is "life-force" or *prana*. The quality and depth of our breath directly corresponds to the quality and vitality of our own life-force. Sometimes all we need is to pause a moment, and focus on breathing deeply. The involuntarily act of yawning is the body's way of accessing *prana*, but we can also access it deliberately with *conscious breathing*. One safe and effective breathing technique I like to use is to simply take a deep breath in, hold the inhalation for a count of three, then consciously extend the exhale by breathing out slowly and relaxing into the out-breath. Repeat this technique three to five times and it can have a potent effect on energy level! Just as we take in food to gain energy, the breath is another way we access renewed vitality.

"*Prana* can relax, heal, and transform."

~ Swami Srinivasananda

7. Play time. Sometimes I forget to play! In fact a lot of times I forget! As a "recovering type A," I often catch myself being overly driven, too serious, and absorbed in my "to-do" lists! I notice how rejuvenated I feel when I take time just to "play" and do the things I love. Whatever you love to do, take time to do it! Notice how your tank is instantly filled just by giving yourself permission to play!

8. Time with loved ones. There is something magical about spending time around those you love and who love you unconditionally. Being in the space of love is powerfully healing and rejuvenating to the soul. Unconditional love is who we really are and the source of our strength and light. We are reminded of this when we are enveloped in the space of love. When the soul is weary, seek out those you love. Spend time encircled in this mutual love, whether it is with a beloved pet, a child or grandchild, family or friends. To refill your spiritual tank, simply bask in love.

A Zen master was asked by one of his students, "What is the secret to enlightenment?" His answer was simple, "When you are hungry, eat; when you are tired, sleep. This is the secret to enlightenment." It is my hope that you are now enlightened.

The Art of Balancing Effort with Surrender

I recently heard a story about a meditation student who went to his Zen master and asked, "If I practice all of the teachings just as you have instructed, how long will it take me to achieve enlightenment?" The Zen master answered, "It will take 10 years." Then the student asked, "But if I work twice as hard, and practice extra hours every day, then how long will it take me to find enlightenment?" The teacher answered, "In that case it will take you 20 years."

Is it possible to try too hard? Achieving anything in life is truly a balance of effort and surrender. So often it is in over-efforting that we are slowed down. Over-efforting is often a hindrance because it is depleting, and steals time and energy away from other important aspects of living. This morning my son brought me one of his soccer cleats. The shoe strings were in a horrendous knot. He had been struggling and pulling at the knot with all of his might, only making things worse. Once I was able to loosen things up a little, the knot came out almost effortlessly. How many times do we get "tied up in knots" over things, only to keep tugging tighter and tighter, making matters worse? Sometimes it takes loosening up for progress to be made.

One of the best-kept secrets out there is in balancing effort with surrender. I have found that, for me, the difference exercising 1 hour a day versus 2 hours a day is about 3 pounds on the scales. My time is precious, so the extra hour a day is simply not worth the effort. If I expend my energy and effort on that 3 pounds, then I must sacrifice something else, perhaps something which is much more important. Therefore, I surrender to weighing 3 pounds more.

I am always in need of finding a way to balance effort and surrender, trying and allowing. The following are seven ways to balance effort and surrender in your life.

1. Ask for help. Acknowledging that you need help is the ultimate act of surrender. Admitting you cannot possibly do it all and do it all well is quite humbling. For me this is particularly hard to do. However, I have no family close by and my husband often travels for work. Asking for help is admitting I am human, not a robot. I ask my children to help out with chores around the house, my husband helps with grocery shopping and cooking. Occasionally, I need the help of a friend. What a relief it is to finally ask and receive the help you need.

2. Harness momentum. I have found that when I am not in the mood to work on something, it takes two or three times the effort. I find that when I am up for the task, I knock it out in no time. I have learned to ride this wave, and use it to my advantage. When I feel in the mood to iron clothes it seems like nothing. At other times the task seems daunting. This applies to almost anything, from errands to chores. Try working at times when there is willingness, instead going against the grain. When I am moved to write, I write, and the words flow effortlessly. When I am moved to practice yoga, I practice, and the postures magically unfold. If I were to force either one, I would lose the joy and triple the effort.

3. Do what you love. Although I work hard writing, planning classes and teaching, I love it! If I were writing and teaching calculus, the effort involved would be insurmountable. I'd feel like a small dog trying to pull a large bolder. But I love yoga, I love sharing it, and I love learning more about it myself. Because I am able to do what I love, things flow with much less effort. Love of what I do, and loving the people I do it for, helps me to balance effort and surrender. Interestingly, we are all different. My husband actually loves yard work. He finds it relaxing and therapeutic. For me, it is taxing. On the other hand, he hates paying the bills, and making phone calls. In our home we divide up the tasks according to our preferences. When done this way, household tasks require less effort.

4. Wait. I have found that plowing forward is not always the best course of action. Sometimes things actually work themselves out with no effort at all. I can think of numerous times when I paused and waited a bit, and problems have simply resolved themselves; then I am grateful I haven't wasted extra time, energy, and effort. Ask yourself "Is this something I could wait a bit to work on? Is it possible that this problem will work out on its own?" Often it is our own impatience which creates needless effort.

5. Enjoy down time. I find it imperative to give myself moments of down time. If I am on the go constantly, I burn out even if I am doing what I love. Surrendering to my own mental and physical fatigue is powerful. I find that if I give myself breaks, whether that be a cup of tea on the porch, taking time to meditate, taking a peaceful walk, or simply sitting in nature, I am able to refill my tank. With a full tank, moving through the twists and turns of life require less effort.

6. Practice self-care. Self-care is taking care of you. The airlines are always reminding us that we need to place the oxygen mask on ourselves first, before we help others. This is because those who are depending upon us need us to be available to help them. When we are depleted, we are useless. In this state, any amount of effort is too much. When we care for ourselves, we have energy to expend and give back. Self-care is to surrender to your own limitations, and recognize your own humanity. Self-care includes adequate rest, play, exercise, and eating foods which impart energy and vitality. It is about giving yourself what you need when you need it.

7. Have compassion. Sometimes we drive ourselves more than we would ever drive anyone else. We expect more of ourselves than we expect of others. We are harder on ourselves than anyone. Having compassion for yourself is a form of surrender. Don't ask yourself to do anything you wouldn't ask or expect of anyone else. We do not demand too much from others because we have compassion for them. Return that same compassion to yourself.

Are you taking care of you? Where are you straining? Where are you needlessly expending your effort? Where can you surrender and effort less? In order to find balance between effort and surrender, ask yourself the following three questions:

- What is it that I want most in my life?
- Where am I putting my effort?
- Where do I need to surrender?

Surrender takes courage. Effort must be skillfully applied and balanced with surrender in order to get what you want most in life, otherwise you end up running in circles. A reflection on where you need effort, and where you are actually putting it, will lead to a powerful awakening of when it is necessary to try, versus when it is necessary to let go. Just how long will it take you to find enlightenment?

Life is Like a Yellow Brick Road

When I was a child, our family had a vacation home in Beech Mountain, N.C. Some of my best childhood memories are of going to the "Land of Oz" theme park there on the mountain top. As kids, we were mesmerized walking down the park's yellow brick road, experiencing Dorothy's journey for ourselves! The theme park is now closed, but I hear that you can still see the remains of the Land of Oz from the chair lifts at Beech Mountain ski resort.

As an adult, it occurs to me that the venerated film *The Wizard of Oz* fits perfectly with the themes of yoga and life. After all, we are each walking down our own twisting, turning, winding path. Along our journeys we encounter friends, foes and fears. We experience the effects of good and evil. I believe the film has so much intrigue because it mirrors life itself. Let's look at the significance of what is encountered along the yellow brick road.

Munchkins remind us that we are never too old to play, laugh and have fun. The child-like giggles of the Munchkins, the Lolly Pop Guild and the Lullaby League remind us to nourish our own inner child. What are you doing today to connect to the child within?

Glenda, the Good Witch of the North, shows that goodness exists, and always wins out. Grace and goodness always have your back. Surround yourself with love, light and positive energy, and your own life will be magical!

Toto represents our animal guide or "totem." If we pay attention, animals have so much to teach us. According to Native American tradition, they each represent a different "medicine" and come in and out of our lives to guide us along the way. Over the past couple of years I have begun to tune in to the animals which appear around me. I often go online and look up their symbolism. I am always struck by how this information rings true for me at the time. As a dog owner, I notice how powerful animal companionship is. Toto is a reminder that we are never walking alone.

The Scarecrow shows us that we must listen to our own inner wisdom. It is the walk down the path of life that cultivates this wisdom. The sciences of yoga and Ayurveda both teach learning by "direct perception." This is the philosophy that true learning and wisdom come only through your own real experiences. Interestingly, the Buddha instructed his followers to not believe the things they are taught until they find out for themselves.

> "Can't you give me brains?" asked the Scarecrow. "You don't need them. You are learning something every day. A baby has brains, but it doesn't know much. Experience is the only thing that brings knowledge, and the longer you are on earth the more experience you are sure to get."
>
> ~ L. Frank Baum,
> *The Wonderful Wizard of Oz*

The Tin Woodsman reminds us that if we don't take care of our bodies, we become rusty and stiff. If our body isn't functioning well, we fail to move forward on our journey, and we get "stuck" right where we are. It takes flexibility to adapt to the twists and turns of life. We must listen to our hearts. It is the heart which guides our destiny. In yoga theory, the heart is not only the seat of the soul, but the seat of the illuminated mind as well.

The Cowardly Lion reminds us that courage isn't about not having fears, it is about facing them and proceeding anyway. It is by facing our fears, even as we are afraid, that we cultivate courage.

> "You have plenty of courage, I am sure," answered Oz. "All you need is confidence in yourself. There is no living thing that is not afraid when it faces danger. The true courage is in facing danger when you are afraid, and that kind of courage you have in plenty."
>
> ~ L. Frank Baum,
> *The Wonderful Wizard of Oz*

The haunted forest, full of lions and tigers and bears, represents our own demons. We have to walk through our fears and face them head-on to get to where we are going in life. Our path is sometimes scary, but it is crucial to keep moving forward anyway. In Zen it is said that "the obstacle is the path."

Flying monkeys represent those people who mindlessly follow the bidding of others. They are easily led astray. They have no discernment of what is right and wrong. Even as they pulled the stuffing out of the scarecrow, the monkeys were the ones without the brains. Don't be a "flying monkey." Think for yourself!

The poppy field reminds us that sometimes we are asleep to the beauty that is already there. Being asleep to the amazement of the present moment is one of the greatest obstacles to moving forward on our own yellow brick road. Awaken to the splendor of here and now.

The Wizard represents the tempting impostor. Don't pretend to be someone you're not. This only creates a false sense of power. Sooner or later you'll be found out. Don't let ego grow bigger than who you are. Just be yourself. Is the real you "hiding behind a curtain?" Sometimes we use the curtain of material things, name brand cars, or clothing to create an image of something we're not. Be aware that other people are not always what they seem to be on the surface. Sometimes as you get to know people better, they are not really who they say they are. Make sure you pay attention to who is really standing behind the curtain.

The Emerald City represents illusion. Things are not as they seem. Initially the city appears beautiful and magical. But we find out this is all a hoax. *The Wizard of Oz* is nothing more than a man who has no better answers to life's problems than anyone else. Yoga is about uncovering and removing illusions. Interestingly, the Buddhist name for the "devil" is "mara," or illusion. Perhaps it is illusion which is our greatest enemy. The Emerald City reminds us that there is no magical fix for our difficulties and problems. The solutions and the way forward is within us, not somewhere out "there." Instead of seeking answers somewhere else, find them in yourself.

The Wicked Witch of the West teaches us: Don't cower to your fears. Your fears are not invincible. Do not hide from them, they will find you! Do not let them hold you prisoner. It is only when you face what you are afraid of that you conquer fears once and for all. When you confront your fears, they simply melt away.

Dorothy represents that part of us which is searching for something more to make us happy and whole. It is only when we realize that our true search is more internal than external that we find our way home. That place **"somewhere over the rainbow"** is within. That "somewhere" exists right here, right now. The true journey is in finding how to be at home with yourself. The real wisdom is that you never have to go searching for your heart's desire. The real wisdom is in discovering that everything you ever searched for exists in this moment, inside of you.

Truly we all walk down the **yellow brick road** of life, searching for what we already have. We are confronted by obstacles, fear and illusions as we go through life. Without flexible and healthy bodies, positive energy, open hearts, inner wisdom and courage to move forward we'd never return home. Herein lies the yoga. Yoga is a practice which encompasses all of these things. Healthy and whole, you can walk down the path of life with a spring to your step and your head held high, knowing you are already home.

Hidden Treasure

The other day my son and I were in a shop, and we came upon a collection of "geodes." We were both taken by the wonder of these stones, probably for different reasons. Geodes are stones which look like normal rocks on the outside, but when they are sawed in two, the inside is exposed as something really special. Inside there is a spectacular formation of crystal clusters. Plain on the outside, they are quite exquisite once you look within.

It occurs to me that people are much like these geodes. The real beauty, and the actual treasure, lies hidden inside of us. We are often tricked by the outer shell. Perhaps we find out a big burly guy with tattoos is really a gentle teddy bear. The elderly lady with the tan leathery skin is filled with inner wisdom, knowledge, kindness and understanding. The quirky artist with blue hair is really a sensitive soul. Many times I have made judgments about people based on the external "shell" only to find an exquisite radiance and beauty waiting to be discovered beneath the outer covering.

What brilliance am I missing out on if I fail to take the time to look inside? I have vowed to be as open as possible to outward appearances, and take the time to look deeper before I determine anything more. The geode is a great reminder to look beneath the surface. This stone itself is a physical manifestation of what inner beauty is all about.

Have you ever looked to see what is hidden within *you*? Have you taken the time to examine your own interior? Our culture is so obsessed with external appearance that we often forget that the inside is where the true jewels lie! What if we spent as much time looking on the inside as we do focusing on our outward image? In the end, what stays is what we carry on the inside of the shell . . . As I age, I may look just like any ordinary stone, but when opened up, I hope to be as dazzling and spectacular as a geode!

"This shell is not me. I came as the royal pearl within."   ~ Rumi

Conversation: Speaking Skillfully

"When words are both kind and true, they can change our world."

~ Buddha

I remember when I was younger how often I put my foot in my mouth! This was because I was speaking faster than I was thinking! Or perhaps in some cases, I wasn't thinking at all. Thankfully, the practices of yoga and meditation have helped me to cultivate a bit more awareness in my conversations, and I would like to share these with you! Pause and ask yourself the following questions before the damage is done!

1. Is what you have to say an improvement upon silence? Often we talk just to fill up space, or make ourselves feel better during moments of awkward silence. When we say things just to fill the void, this is when we have our biggest regrets! Consider the following wise quotes on silence:

"Never say anything that doesn't improve on silence."

~ Richard Yates

"Be silent or let the words be worth more than silence."

~ Pythagoras

"Silence makes idiots seem wise even for a minute."

~ Carlos Ruiz Zafon

"He who does not understand your silence will probably not understand your words."

~ Elbert Hubbard

"Silence is the source of great strength."

~ Lao Tzu

"Speech is silver, silence is golden."

~ German proverb

"When you have nothing to say, say nothing."

~ Charles Caleb Colton

"Wise men, when in doubt whether to speak or to keep quiet, give themselves the benefit of the doubt, and remain silent."

~ Napoleon Hill

2. Is what you are saying true? Across all religions, faiths and philosophies, truthfulness is considered sacred. Truth is revered. In yoga, *satya*, Sanskrit for truthfulness, is one of the Five *Yamas*, or restraints. In *The Four Agreements*, Don Miguel Ruiz teaches us to "Be impeccable with your word. Speak with integrity, say what you mean. Express what you really want." Lying actually creates a stress response in the body. Polygraph tests don't really detect lies, they perceive the stress response. If you are tempted to lie, begin to examine what is at the core of this need to lie. We only lie for three reasons: ego, fear, or compassion. We most often lie because we are embarrassed to admit the truth. "I meant to do that." Embarrassment is really an encounter with ego. People often lie to inflate their egos. This creates a false perception of who they are. When people lie to inflate their egos, they are telling us in a subtle way that they are not comfortable with who they are. They feel inferior. Be comfortable with who you are and what you have accomplished, whether you just learned to ride your bike or whether you rode with the Tour de France! It makes people much more comfortable to know you aren't the world's greatest expert at everything! People just want you to be human like they are! People lie for fear of getting caught.

3. Are you speaking your truth? I cringe when I look back at the many times I should have spoken up and didn't! Speaking your truth is finding your voice, and this takes courage. With age and maturity, I have found that courage to speak up and speak out has increased, but there is always further to go. Not speaking your truth is agreeing to something you don't believe in. If you don't speak your truth, what are you teaching? Perhaps this is how kids learn to passively go along with peer pressure or bullying. Speaking your truth is powerful and empowering. Lives could be saved, wars prevented, souls could be saved by the simple and courageous act of speaking your truth.

4. Are you using flattery? There is a difference between compliments and praise and downright flattery. Flattery is excessive and insincere praise that is intended to further one's own interests. Flattery is all about motive. What are your intentions behind the compliment? Are they about kindness and sincerity, or about getting something you want from someone? Flattery is phony and false. When it is all boiled down, flattery is just a pretty little lie.

5. Is what you are saying kind or compassionate? I understand that the Buddhist tradition has a practice in which you are not to speak about anyone who is not present. This rule is designed to prevent needless gossip. I have found that it is so easy to get sucked into gossip without even meaning to, and then regretting it later. If you find yourself speaking about someone, ask yourself if what you are saying is kind and compassionate. And it is just as important to talk with kindness and compassion to yourself. The other day I couldn't figure out how to use an unfamiliar gas pump at a gas station that I don't usually frequent. I ended up needing the help of the attendant. I heard myself saying, "I guess I am too dumb to pump gas." What??? It pierces my heart when I hear someone put themselves down, or berate themselves, and here I was doing it to myself! We should be our own number one fan, admirer, and supporter. Be compassionate with yourself, and speak to yourself and of yourself with kindness. Don't forget to show yourself the same compassion that you endeavor to show to others. I would have never told anyone else they were too dumb to pump gas! Never be the one to put yourself down.

6. Do you keep your word? My son has a way of looking at me with his soft brown puppy dog eyes, and he can get almost anything he wants. I have found myself saying "yes" when the answer really needed to be "no." When this happens, I end up going back on my word. What am I teaching my son? Having integrity means your word is impeccable. Say what you mean. Do what you say.

7. Do you honor confidentiality? Do you create a safe environment for others in support and intimacy? Do you share what you are asked not to share? Do you share private information or gossip with others?

Refraining from sharing personal information of others is an act of conscious and skillful speech. It is an act of trust. When something is said to you in confidence, hold that confidence sacred.

8. Is what you are saying well-timed and appropriate? As kids, my brother and I got very good at assessing whether it was a good time to ask Mom or Dad for something we wanted. It was with this awareness that we were able to get what it was we wanted more often than not! We knew never to ask Dad for something the moment he walked in the door from work. Things didn't work out so well when we did that! There are certain times when our words are appropriate and other times the same words may be inappropriate. Timing is everything! There are certain things you may say at a party that would be poorly timed at a funeral. Anyone who uses Facebook can recount some of the inappropriate posts they've seen. Facebook is the latest way to put a foot in your mouth!

9. Can you avoid rudeness and sarcasm? Rudeness and sarcasm are biting! We've all been witness to moments when we observed a customer being rude to a waitress. In all honesty, it takes everything I have not to be rude to telemarketers interrupting my life to try to sell me something I don't want! I was raised as a gracious Southerner, and am married to a New Yorker. It is a miracle we made it through our first year of dating! His sarcastic remarks, meant in humor, were hurting my feelings! It took him a while to realize that sarcasm wasn't something I was accustomed to in the Southern culture, and he needed to tone it down for us to get along. Thankfully he did. He became more conscious of the way his remarks landed. Sarcasm can be hurtful even if it is meant as a joke. If the other person isn't laughing, then the joke has failed! Be conscious of how your remarks are received.

Christmas in July?

When I was in college, I worked as a leasing agent at an apartment complex. One of the residents was a warm and friendly older gentleman named Chuck. Chuck was very popular among the residents. Everyone loved Chuck so much so that they fondly called him the "mayor" of the apartment complex. One day, as I was showing apartments, I noticed Chuck's Christmas tree lit up through the sliding glass doors of his balcony. The only reason this was strange was because it was July! I thought to myself that Chuck, a single guy, still hadn't bothered to take down his tree.

The next time I saw Chuck I asked him "Isn't it about time you took down your Christmas tree?" His answer astonished me. He said, "I leave my Christmas tree up 365 days a year, because I believe that every day is Christmas. Every day is a gift." Immediately I saw so much wisdom in this kind older man. No wonder he was so well-loved! What a positive outlook, to live every day as if it was a gift. He truly shared that gift with everyone he met, always cheerful, warm and friendly.

We often get caught in the daily grind, running around harried, just trying to make it through the day. When we let ourselves get "wrapped up" in chores, to-do's, frustration and stress, we fail to see the gifts right there before us. The underlying joy and peace available to us all goes unrecognized, and we come away feeling depleted. What if we lived every day as if it was Christmas? The gift is already there waiting to be discovered, as if it has been sitting there under the tree all along. I would like to resolve to live every day as a gift. I'd like to give that gift back to my family, to my students, to my friends, and to the world at large. It is a gift that Chuck gave me 25 years ago, and one too valuable not to share. My personal affirmation for July is that "I will see every day as a gift, and with care I will unwrap each moment with joy and ease."

I don't know if Chuck is still living. What I do know is that Chuck really lived. He viewed each day as a gift. At age 19, I had not yet begun to practice yoga, but little did I know, I had already met a yogi. *Namaste*, Chuck!

Cultivating Courage

"Life shrinks or expands in proportion to one's courage."

~ Anais Nin

I admit, I am not the most courageous person. In fact, in many cases, I am a big "chicken!" I am afraid of heights, terrified of public speaking, and when I first started teaching yoga, being up in front of a large group of peers was extremely intimidating!

Recently, my family and I watched a movie called *I Bought a Zoo*. The movie is based on the true story of a widower, Benjamin Mee, and his children, who in a flash of courage bought a dilapidated zoo against the advice of everyone he knew. This turned out to be a powerful and life-changing experience, as he stepped into his destiny. His words have stayed with me:

"All it takes is 20 seconds of insane courage, and great things will happen."

~ Benjamin Mee

For my birthday back in April my dear friend gave me a necklace with the word "courage" inscribed on it. Knowing me well, she knew this was the right word coming at the right time. This necklace has become a powerful intention in my life, inspiring me to cultivate more courage.

Since being given this necklace, I have begun to reflect deeply on courage. I have only but begun to live my life with more courage in recent years. For example, not knowing what to expect, we moved our family to France for almost 2 years! Also, it was a huge act of courage for me to deviate from the expected "norm" for a Kohler, WI, housewife, and become a certified yoga instructor. I've had a few people look down their noses at me just because of this. It takes courage to teach yoga, healthy eating, and meditation in the conservative Midwest. These practices are NOT always readily accepted! I have been criticized, judged, and condemned for teaching eastern practices here in the heartland! This has saddened me.

For me, it is an act of courage to send out my newsletters each week. I hold nothing back, and bare my soul in hopes that my words may touch someone in the right way at the right time, even if it is just one person. There are always butterflies in my stomach before I press "send!" However, I deeply am moved to share yoga, wholeness, health and harmony. These are practices which have greatly enhanced my own life. How could I keep this to myself?

I am discovering that living with courage is not about being unafraid, but about becoming comfortable with having fear. Getting comfortable with fear requires actually "being" with your fears instead of running away, zoning out, checking out, ignoring them, or pushing them away. The Native American Indians have a practice of naming their fears. Once you begin to name them, they begin to lose their mystique. Our fears are no longer strangers. Meditation instructor Jonathan Foust humorously suggests "having tea with your fears." Eleanor Roosevelt said, "You gain strength, courage and confidence from every experience in which you stop to really look fear in the face."

On the first night of meditation teacher training at the Kripalu Center, we were asked to come up with a word which would express our intention for the workshop. My word, inspired by my necklace, was "courage." Out of 55 instructors, I was the only one who made "courage" my mission that week. As I spent time in silence, in meditation, and in some of the deeper practices of yoga, I found that courage was not only helpful, but crucial. You do not engage in these practices without all your "stuff" coming up . . . and up it came. Instead of checking out, I stayed with it. I let fear be there. In doing so, I noticed that I became less and less afraid of fear! I began to become curious about my fears instead. I let myself see them, and we met face to face. What I found is that when you don't run from fear, it has no hold over you! Standing your ground with fear and looking it in the face is a powerful practice. When you are no longer afraid of fear, fear simply dissipates. Courage is not about no longer experiencing fear. "Cultivating courage" is simply the practice of "making tea" with your fears. That being said, I am still not planning on sky-diving, bungee jumping or zip-lining anytime soon!

> "You have plenty of courage, I am sure," answered Oz. "All you need is confidence in yourself. There is no living thing that is not afraid when it faces danger. The true courage is in facing danger when you are afraid, and that kind of courage you have in plenty."
> ~ L. Frank Baum,
> *The Wonderful Wizard of Oz*

What Stands between You and Feeling Free?

I can't help but laugh out loud when I remember our cat "Country" as a kitten. She was enticed into endless episodes of chasing her tail. Occasionally, she caught her tail and held it tightly in her teeth. She would get a look of great satisfaction as she captured the furry critter which had been following her around. Then a perplexed look would appear across her face. Eventually, it would dawn on her that it was she who had caught herself, and it was she holding herself prisoner! Finally, she would reluctantly release the tail, letting herself go, looking a little sheepish.

How often do we humans entrap ourselves too without even being aware of who it is holding us back? What is it that you are holding on to, which stands in the way between you and feeling free?

I have an uncle who has so deeply ensnared himself with rigid ideas and fixed notions about the world, his religion, other people, and life in general, that he has virtually imprisoned himself and his family on a 30 acre compound in Mississippi. He home-schools the kids, and home-churches them, fearing that they might be misled by anyone other than himself. He fears that they may come into contact with germs and get sick. He also believes the apocalypse is on its way, any time now. In his attempts to protect himself and his family, he has created a prison for them instead. Although this prison has no bars, other family members fear that once grown, the children may never be able to leave from an emotional standpoint, as they are socially awkward and have little contact with other people, let alone kids their ages. This life is all they know.

I know this case is a bit extreme, but now consider yourself. Are you also in a prison of your own making . . . one without bars? Recently, I came to the realization that I have ensnared myself too. I became aware that I have a very adversarial relationship with time. Yes, time. We are not friends. It's almost as if I am at war with time! I always feel as if I am battling against time to do the things I want and need to get done. When I allow this to happen, I feel pressured, and I end up stressing myself out unnecessarily. While meditating, I realized that time wasn't holding me prisoner, my *perception* of time, and my relationship with it, was what was holding me prisoner. In other words, I have been chasing my own tail, and holding on to it for dear life, wondering why I felt trapped! My own false perception that there was never enough time to get things done held me prisoner. It caused my body to tighten and tense, almost tying myself up as if bound in the ropes created by the tension of my own muscles! I believe my concept of time is a result of cultural conditioning rather than reality. The French seem to always find plenty of time to enjoy life *"sans souci,"* without worries! As an expat living in Paris, I witnessed this myself.

What if I open up to time, and make friends with it? What if I embrace time rather than let it hold me hostage? My new daily affirmation is: "Today there will be enough time to do everything I want and need to do." This has already had a profound effect in my life. There has been a huge shift for me. Just by changing my own preconceptions and prejudices about time, I feel freed and much more relaxed! I finally, finally let go of my own tail! I can't express to you how good this feels!

Letting go of what stands between you and feeling free opens the door wide to new possibilities, to exploring life joyfully, and fully. Letting go is about softening and relaxing into what is. Letting go is about not clinging to expectations or making assumptions as to how life should be. As we ease the tension and gripping in our minds, the whole body relaxes as if the chains are falling away. New space opens up in our joints, muscles and bones, and also in our lives and in ourselves. I fell in love with the following quote from Dr. Wayne Dyer: "As I un-clutter my life, I free myself to answer the callings of my soul." What is it that you hold on to? Now is the time to release your own tail . . .

The Sound of Silence

I have only shared with a few people that during my most recent yoga teacher training at the Kripalu Center for Yoga and Health, I spent 3 days in silence. Unannounced to the group until the first night, we were to spend 3 days in silence! Now I know that those of you who know me well are rolling in laughter at the thought of that! At first there was a little bit of anxiety about keeping silent for so long! But actually, it wasn't that difficult, or even that bad! In fact it was quite enlightening!

Let me share with you my journey into silence! Here is what I observed . . . We often talk just to fill space.

In silence, things become clearer, and I became aware of more subtle thoughts, inspirations, and insights.

Constant chatter is often a way we attempt to distract our minds from reality, or from being in the present moment. We use it as an escape.

I had more energy available for other things when I wasn't expending it on talking for talking's sake.

I noticed how much better food tasted, and I could taste more subtle flavors when not distracted by talking during a meal. I was really present when I ate.

I could hear my body actually speaking to me intelligently. Honestly, it said, "Go pee, stop holding it." And another time, "You make me carry too much." And, "You give me too much responsibility."

Sharing time together in silence with other people actually enhances the intimacy of the moment. There is an energetic connection just being in the presence of one another.

Instead of talking, I became aware that I could consciously give off positive thoughts or positive energy to others without words.

I also noticed that I could almost instinctively sense the thoughts that other people sent out. It was as if words just make it easier to understand what people think and feel, but without words we can still perceive it on an energetic level.

It dawned on me that this must have been how it was before language developed.

I became aware of not saying things which *should* have been left unsaid, such as criticisms, judgments or complaints. And I hoped I could still leave these things unsaid once I resumed talking.

I became aware that we use talking just to fill awkward silence or awkward moments instead of just being with the awkwardness that is there.

Instead of using talking to distract myself from aversions or moments of awkwardness, I began to be with these moments as they were, with courage. I named the feelings which were arising and I looked them in the face. As I did this, those feelings simply began to dissipate.
The most difficult part for me was not extending politeness, like saying "thank you" and "please," or "good morning." I felt rude, and noticed I began to judge myself when I had to withhold these strongly conditioned responses.

Meditation came with much more ease during the days of silence, and I was able to go deeper than ever before. I now see why Jesus and the Buddha went out in the wilderness for contemplation, and why yogis retreated into caves for periods of deep meditation. It is amazing how much deeper one can go without a chance of the phone or doorbell ringing, or a child or pet interrupting. There is such peace knowing you will be undisturbed! That peace allows you to reach the next level! In the end I learned a great deal from the time I spent with silence. I actually can't wait to do it again . . . this time for 5 days! I realized that you can learn much more from the "sound of silence" than you can

Elise Cantrell

from the sound of your own voice! I enjoyed my silence so much that I brought home my "In Loving Silence" badge, just in case mom needs some time in silence around here!

Be Kinder . . . to You

At the end of each yoga class, as my students rest in *savasana*, the pose of final relaxation, I pray for them. I ask God to give them what they need when they need it, and ask that they each are blessed in whatever way they need to be blessed. During my most recent 10 days at Kripalu Center for Yoga and Health, upon deep reflection and meditation, I came to the realization that I forget to ask this very thing for myself. I also came to the realization that *I* often don't give myself what *I* need when *I* need it. How ironic!

After a recent demanding week, it came time to plan next week's classes. I noticed that I was atypically resistant to going upstairs into my private yoga space to practice and to plan. I already had a good idea what I wanted to base my class upon and what I wanted to do. As I began to warm up, something entirely different came about. My resistance to planning and practice was strong. Instead of "cranking it out," I practiced self-compassion and self-acceptance. I surrendered into what was there . . . low energy, a tired body and a stiff mind. What came was the unexpected. I felt a shift. As I accepted what was there instead of forcing what was not, I felt the resistance soften. I "let up" on myself. I found myself in a beautiful *yin* practice, with soft compassionate poses allowing long, tender holds, ending in deep releases.

In this practice, I realized that it is my own determination which sometimes holds me back. Driving myself relentlessly actually creates "friction," often *slowing* my momentum. It is only when I "lighten up" on myself that resistance melts away, and I am able to move forward or even move at all.

When the human body meets a hard surface like a hard floor, the body must soften or the excess pressure will cause pain, and even create bruising or injury. If the skin, joints, bones and muscles soften their resistance, in that non-efforting, pain and injury are averted. What can we soften in our lives to avoid injury to our mind and spirit? What can be "let up" on to reduce the "friction" in our lives so we can move forward with ease?

Can you sense what is pulling you down and holding you back? Where do you need to surrender? Where can you be kinder to you? Kindness is your strength, not your weakness. Where can you give yourself permission to soften and relax? Where can you soothe away the friction in your life?

The source of the friction in your life is YOU! You are the cause, and you are the cure. You are the obstacle, and you are freedom from that obstacle. The choice is up to you. Kindness dissolves resistance. It eases friction; it is the cure to what ails us. Do you give yourself what you need when you need it? Are you being kind . . . to you?

Transformation

Just this past weekend, I spent hours on Saturday and Sunday working on the bibliography of my book. I had only three more sources to cite, when the computer locked up. I had to reboot, and when I did this I lost everything. I was working through a bibliography website, and, unbeknownst to me, my daughter had registered on the website too, using the same family email address. No matter what I tried, I could only pull up her account. It was as if my account never existed! When I became certain I had lost an entire weekend of work, I admit, I lost my yoga cool, especially because I was working towards a deadline! I broke down into tears, and I uttered a few choice words I normally would never use. I felt my heart race, I could feel my blood pressure rise, and it felt as if my head would pop off! I felt every muscle in my body tighten up! For at least an hour I was a mess! I couldn't even wrap my mind around starting over again!

I thought about opening a bottle of wine to calm my nerves, but without a clear head, I certainly couldn't get the work done. Instead, I went upstairs and hit my yoga mat. Here I lost track of time, I let go of the book, the deadline, the bibliography. I stretched, breathed, sweated and turned upside down for a good hour and a half. In this time I transformed!

After I was done, I took a hot bath! It was in relaxing into the hot water that I realized that nothing external had changed. The bibliography was still lost, and the deadline was still around the corner. However, I felt completely different. I was relaxed, I could think, and I had the newfound resolve to start over. The only thing that had changed was my mind. In this moment I was transformed. I have heard the Zen saying that everything is "mind." But in this moment of transformation, I actually understood exactly what this saying meant. When I fell apart, my mind was a mess. I couldn't think! I looked at the whole situation through the mental lens of stress and anxiety. The whole situation seemed overwhelming.

On my yoga mat, my heart stopped racing, my blood pressure lowered, physical tension melted away, and I began to breathe again. As my body relaxed, my mind followed its lead. I emerged from the mat a new person, with a new mind. It was through the lens of a calm, clear mind that I could see that this wasn't the end of the world, and that the process would go much faster the second time around. More importantly, I was transformed in a more profound way. I saw how powerfully our frame of mind defines the fabric of our lives. I saw that, truly, when you change the mind, everything else is transformed. Transformation often happens when we are put through the fire, and this situation became an opportunity for me to know how powerfully the mind frames each and every life experience. Viewed through aggravation, panic and frustration, life looks so much different than when viewed through quiet, calm and composure. Next time you "freak out" over something, breathe, meditate, and or practice yoga to simply remind your mind that everything is mind.

Flowing in the
Current of Grace

There is a famous story about Swami Kripalu. He was a strong swimmer. However, during the rainy season in India, the Narmada River flooded over its banks quite suddenly. Swami Kripalu was nearby, and got swept into the raging river. The rush of the water and the power of the current immediately washed him away, and he found himself deeply submerged. He swam vigorously and struggled to reach the surface of the water to get a breath of air, but no matter how hard he swam, he was unable to make his way to the top. Finally he began to drown. As he was drowning, he heard a voice he believed to be the voice of God. It simply said, "Stop swimming!" So he relaxed his limbs, and let go into the flow. It was then that the water itself brought him to the surface. He was able to breathe. He was carried by the current downstream for a while until the water finally deposited him safely on a riverbank some distance away. He was found on the riverbank, tired and wet, but very much alive. This extraordinary experience had a powerful effect on him and became a part of his teachings.

One of my yoga students, who has been rafting down the Colorado River, attested that the same instructions had been given to her prior to whitewater rafting through the Grand Canyon. The instructors had cautioned her group not to swim if they fell out of the raft; instead, their survival depended upon free-floating, feet first, down the river. In order to stop swimming in these dire predicaments, a leap of faith is required. One has to begin to trust in the flow of grace to carry them safely.

Where are you swimming? I find that I often get caught up in the daily struggle, and end up thrashing about, hoping to come up for air. It is only when I stop resisting, and allow the current of grace to carry me wherever it wants, that life becomes miraculous. This has been confirmed to me again and again. However, I am deeply humbled by my own resistance, because most of the time, I refuse to stop swimming.

I am filled with doubt and fear as to how things will go without my intervention. Grace is so much more intelligent and powerful than I am. When I insist on all this "swimming," I notice that I seem to be struggling against life itself rather than flowing with it. It can feel like I am drowning in all the challenges around me. When will I finally fully trust that grace has perfect timing, and that grace already knows the proper shore on which I should land? Perhaps God is the riverbank, or the river itself, or both. Perhaps flowing in the current of grace is what is meant by becoming one with Source. With this in mind, it is my prayer that I will trust myself to stop swimming.

> "You must live in the present, launch yourself on every wave, find your eternity in each moment."
>
> ~ Henry David Thoreau

You're Not Full of Holes, You Are Whole

Even though I hear it every week, today at church the word "holy" caught my attention. I began to meditate upon the meaning of this over-used yet "under-stood" word. Upon reflection, it came to me that the word "holy" really means "whole." Whole can be defined as entire, complete, total, intact. When we realize our wholeness, then we begin to fathom our sacredness. And we are whole. We spend so much time in life searching for the holes within ourselves that we fail to realize that we are whole, we are complete, just as we are. We are holy. In focusing on our "holes," our failures, and our mistakes, we miss out on our inherent wholeness. We spend so much time looking for cracks, defects, and what we perceive to be missing, our completeness is often missed entirely.

The only thing we are missing is the knowing that there is nothing missing, knowing that we are worthy. We have everything we need, and are everything already. God shortchanged no one, not even you. You are enough. You are entire, complete and intact just as you are. You are HOLY, not "hole-y!"

Furthermore, we make each other whole. We have different talents, different gifts. We are different pieces of the same puzzle. We are each whole in our own right, and each an important piece of the larger whole as well. With even one piece missing, the puzzle cannot be complete. Each one of us is sacred. It is only when we come together that we can see the big picture. If we spend our lives thinking we don't measure up, then we are not available to ourselves or to each other. It is in accepting that we were created whole from the beginning, and then owning and honoring our wholeness, rather than what we perceive to be missing, that our holy nature is revealed, and our holes are sealed. There is no need to search for what is already there. When we discover this, we are made whole.

Stop focusing on your holes and focus on your wholeness. From the beginning, you were created whole and holy.

New Moon, New You

In yoga and Ayurveda, nature is considered a powerful metaphor for our own existence. In fact, we too are part of the mystifying workings of nature. We only need to look to nature, divine creation, to discover eternal truths, natural laws, changeless values, and hidden answers.

The moon is a lovely metaphor for our own endless potential to start over. Approximately every 29 days, the moon begins a new cycle. The new moon is symbolic of new beginnings, and is said to be the optimal time to begin something new. Ancient in age, the moon reminds us that it is never too late to start anew or begin again. It fearlessly and repeatedly faces an ending and a new beginning every month. In our own lives, we too can observe a cycle of endings and new beginnings: births, marriages, careers, relationships, birthdays, anniversaries, deaths . . . All of these are part of this cycle of endings and new beginnings.

There is something exciting about a chance to start over, to try something new, to experience new experiences, and to fly to new heights. Like many people, I often approach new things with a bit of fear and trepidation. It is easy to stay cocooned in my little comfort zone. But without the possibility of renewal, life would lack zest and passion. We can stagnate within our fears, or move forward with enthusiasm! Often when I try something new, even though I am intimidated and unsure at first, once I begin, I find I enjoy learning, re-creating and being myself re-created. A new and different perspective emerges. New beginnings are ripe with possibility. Often, new beginnings require letting go of old ways of being. To start a new career, one must leave behind the previous job. To join into marriage, one must say goodbye to singlehood. It is only once we let go of what has been, that we can step into what is to come.

You can reinvent yourself! In yoga philosophy, human life has phases like the moon. We continually cycle through three phases: creation, sustaining, and transformation. *Creation* is the process of constructing something new in our lives. It takes time, energy and passion to create the life we want. *Sustaining* is a time when what we have created is being supported and maintained by our time, energy and dedication. *Transformation* inevitably comes. Sometimes it comes with ease, and other times it comes with struggle. Frequently we are resistant to transformation, because this process can seem scary, difficult or painful when we must let go of what we worked to create. Once the fire of transformation dies down, the phase of creation begins again. It is through this unending cycle that we are continually re-created in new and better ways, growing and evolving. When we understand that we too are a part of this natural process, we can watch our own lives move through these natural cycles. When viewed through this lens, we can simply relax and observe ourselves as we move from one phase to the next, and enjoy the passage, knowing that, like the moon, we too begin anew.

"Some changes look negative on the surface but you will soon realize that space is being created in your life for something new to emerge."

~ Eckhart Tolle

The Ebb and Flow

In reflecting upon a siege of appliance/car/home repairs, it becomes apparent nothing ever stays fixed, yet nothing remains forever broken! Why do these things always seem to happen at once? How it is that life can seem like feast or famine? I believe this is simply life's natural ebb and flow. Some days we are full of energy, and on others we are fatigued. We have times of joy and pleasure, and times of sadness and pain. We face both health and sickness. We have warm sunny days and cold gloomy days (especially here in Wisconsin). One week the stock market is up, the next week it is down. The price at the gas pumps climbs up and down. The bathroom scales move up and down. One week our back account is up, and the next it, too, is down. Some days we feel confident and know we can conquer anything, other days we feel small and unimportant. Creativity ebbs and flows, and we must seize the moments inspiration comes, or the next moment it may be evasive! Marriages have their ups and downs. Things at work seem to ebb and flow, chaotic one moment and quiet the next. One moment we feel appreciated and the next we can't seem to do enough, fast enough!

Our pulse is an ebb and flow. Our breath itself is ebb and flow. Once we breathe in, the lungs are full, but as we exhale, we create space for the next breath to return. It is those moments in life when we are emptied out which allow space for grace to flow in. It is in those moments of emptiness when the opportunity for wonderment occurs. These are the moments when potential is immense! These are the moments of anticipation, when life is getting ready to flow back in with freshness, novelty and possibility! In our moments of darkness, in the pause between the exhale and the next inhale, we are simply preparing to fill again. Once we become aware that these moments are necessary for life-force to work its magic, and to return to us with its fresh spirit and essence, we can rest in comfort. If the lungs did not contract, then they would never have the prospect of expanding. With this in mind, we do not have to allow ourselves to be pulled down by the strong undertow when pieces of our life are ebbing away. Look at it only as an opportunity for something better and fresher to flow in. We exhale out the old stale air which no longer serves us, only so we have space to absorb what the next breath holds. Don't let the ebbs in life cause you strife or panic. Trust that the return flow is on its way back in. For as we breathe life, life breathes us!

Breath
by Danna Faulds, *Go In and In*

Breath Breath, the mindful breath,
the rhythm, out and in,
the wave that washes
through our days, creating
space for stillness, sorrow,
joy, or exaltation. Full,
then empty, ebb and flow,
breath accompanies each
step into the unknown.
In the breath, the soul
finds an opportunity to
speak. Images or intuition,
poetry or wordless wisdom
come and go -- no effort but
to breathe and listen.

WHO?

For the past several weeks, I have been awakened at dawn by the voice of a nearby owl, hauntingly repeating the same question, "Who? Who? Who?" Over the weeks, I have begun to reflect and even meditate on this very question. The answer to the owl's question is one mankind has been seeking since the dawn of time: "Who, who, who am I?" This is a question which takes a lifetime to answer, perhaps longer, but the owl is there reminding us to continue asking, and to keep diving deeper into just who it is we are.

According to Native American tradition, particular animals will appear in our lives at specific times to bring us messages. The owl is said to be a bringer of wisdom, insight, perception and intuition. This is because the owl's eyes can penetrate the darkest night, seeing what no one else can. The owl can also turn its head completely upside down and almost entirely around, making it capable of seeing what no one else sees. The owl looks at things from a different perspective. The owl has the ability to see all that is there, and also what is not. Native Americans believe that if the voice of the owl is calling you, you are being encouraged to seek wisdom and truth, to open your eyes, ears, and mind to the wisdom hidden deep inside. It asks us to look into our own darkest places, seeing what is not so easily seen. It invites us to look at life and at ourselves from a different point of view. The owl's haunting question invites us to take a deeper look at who we truly are.

Perhaps there is something we need to see and hear deep within our hearts and souls. Perhaps that something is you. Take a moment to search into the darkness inside yourself, close your eyes and open your inner eyes, and discover who is there in the darkness. I would like to share what emerged as I began my own search for answers to the owl's persistent question . . .

Who you are not . . .

You are not your name, or the face in the mirror. You are not your dress size, or the number on the scales. You are not your money, or possessions, or your status. You are greater. You are not your job, your works, or your accomplishments. Those are only the surface.

Who you are lies beyond movement, chaos or noise. Who you truly are exists in silence and in stillness. When you put down the complexities of human existence for a moment, awareness emerges. In this awareness, who we are *not* falls away, and what we are left with is who we *are*, our truth and our self.

You are not your thoughts, you are knowing . . .

You are not your doings, you are being . . .

You are not your breath, you are awareness of that breath . . .

You are not your bones, muscles, flesh or blood; you are the spaciousness within them . . .

You are not contraction, you are expansion. You are evolution in progress from one moment to the next. You are not the same you whom you were 10 minutes ago, an hour ago, a year ago. As the breath fills the lungs and expands them, you too are ever expanding.

Who you are . . .

Who you are is NOW . . . You are not your past or your future. The real you exists only in the present. The real you is discovered again and again in each and every moment, and in each and every breath. The real you is only defined right here, right now.

Close your eyes. Settle into who you are at this very moment. Behind the darkness of your eyelids, bear witness to the light that shines within. Gaze into that light unashamed. That light is YOU!

This is what I'd like to say to you . . . stop being so hard on yourself. Stop beating yourself up for who you are not or who you used to be. Stop focusing on your imperfections. Focus on your truths, which are many, for that is the real you. Once you look beyond those unkind lies you have believed about yourself, the veil of darkness will fall, and you will begin to recognize that you are nothing but pure, glorious light.

Simply go inside and ask the question of the owl, "Who, who, who?" The truth will find you there.

Affirmation: "Help me to see through the veils of darkness into who I really am. Do not let me turn back or shy away from truth. Let my inner eyes perceive who is really there. I ask for the wisdom to know that on the journey into my darkest depths that my path will stay lit, guiding me towards the brilliant light who is: I am."

Who You Are
by Danna Faulds

Who you are is so much more
than what you do. The essence,
shining through heart, soul, and
center, the bare and bold truth
of you does not lie in your
to-do-list. You are not just
at the surface of your skin, not
just the impulse to arrange the
muscles of your face into a smile
or frown, not just boundless
energy, or bone wearying fatigue.
Delve deeper. You are divinity;
the vast and open sky of Spirit.
It's the light of God, the ember
at your core, the passion and the
presence, the timeless, deathless
essence of you that reaches out
and touches me. Who you are
transcends fear and turns
suffering into liberation.
Who you are is love.

Spring Back to Life

We are experiencing an awakening, a rebirth, a resurrection. Sap is beginning to flow in the trees. Lakes, streams and rivers have thawed, and the water is moving again. Birds have begun to chirp and flutter their wings. Plants are sprouting, and grass is greening and growing. Nature is emerging from months of hibernation, and as a part of nature, so are we. Spring is a time of revival, revitalization and new growth. It is as if an invisible life-force is pulsating through all of existence, as the natural world burgeons back to life. There is a frenzy of activity, energy and motion. In yoga, this mysterious force that animates all things is called *prana*.

Prana takes on different characteristics in each season. We all know the lazy, hazy days of summer, as the heat creates a sense of comfort and relaxation, helping us take life a little less seriously. In fall, we know the winter is coming. *Prana* is stirred up by the winds as they intensify, blowing leaves through the air. It is found in the frenzy of animals gathering their food. It is found in the movement of the birds flying south, and in the bees and insects in flurries of activity. But in winter, these activities come to a halt as *prana* subsides. Winter brings about quiet stillness as all of nature rests, seemingly frozen and lifeless. That sleeping *prana* bursts forth and rises with the advent of spring. How could Easter come at any other time of year? Nature shows us resurrection, as it embodies this potential returning to life before our very eyes . . .

Some of us reawaken in spring more effortlessly than others. Some of us need a little help getting our own "life-sap" moving again! In yoga, this is done through a *"prana* practice." A *prana* practice involves movement, energy and pulsation in the postures, encouraging our own bodies to pulse with the rhythm of life. Just as nature's energy surges in spring, we can also persuade our own life-force to move and flow again. By reawakening *prana*, it begins to rush through our own energy channels, much like water in the rivers and streams, and the sap rising in the trunks of trees. Natural movements help clear blockages and move stagnation left over from winter. This week I invite you to begin to bring movement into your yoga practice as if you are "thawing out" the poses. As nature thaws, so must we. As the sap in the trees warms and begins to move, it is important to warm and move our own life sap. "Spring" into action this week, and resurrect your own life force!

Inquiring Minds

I was born with an "inquiring mind." This has been both a blessing and a curse. At the age of three, I remember standing in the seat of a chair at the kitchen counter, "helping" my mother cook. On the counter there was an assortment of colorful peppers. As she left the kitchen for a moment, my mom warned me not to eat them, they were too hot! Well, she barely got out of the room before I had one of the hot peppers in my mouth. Inquiry got the best of me! She returned to shrieks and tears! It was in this moment that I learned that sometimes when you bite into inquiry, it bites back! Undeterred, this was only the beginning of my life of inquiry.

In elementary school, instead of reading children's books, I was checking out books from the library about archeology, ancient civilizations, UFOs, telekinesis, strange phenomena, psychics, Atlantis, the Bermuda triangle, and other ancient mysteries. (If only they'd had yoga books!) As a child, my favorite show was Leonard Nimoy's "In Search Of . . ." I could barely wait for each new episode and each week's mystery to unravel. In 4th-6th grade, I was determined to become an archaeologist and uncover ancient mysteries of my own. (That is, until I realized this involved digging with shovels in the hot sun.)

My high school years were also steeped in inquiry. I doubt I am alone when it comes to the inquiries of an adolescent . . . (I'll reveal those inquiries after both of my kids graduate!)

As an adult, my inquiry is body, mind and spirit. I am "in search of" the truth at the core of soul, spirit, God and self. At its' core, yoga is really about inquiry. In yoga philosophy, it is believed that direct perception alone is the path to truth. Generations of *gurus*, sages, and rishis spent their days exploring the sensations, benefits, and body/mind altering effects of postures, hand *mudras*, poses, pressure points, herbs, breathing techniques, and meditation practices. (They had plenty of time on their hands before the dawn of Facebook, Google and

Pinterest!) Some yogis even learned how to stop the heart and still the breath, as if no longer alive. Yoga was born out of inquiry! Yoga itself was developed from direct perception, trial and error. Over millennia of trial and error, yoga has evolved into a powerful practice of inner peace, healing and health. It is also a practice that leads us to our own inner truth.

Little did I know when tasting those hot peppers, that I was already destined for the path of yoga. I cannot imagine life without my inquisitive and curious nature! Where would we be without inquiry? If Galileo had failed to inquire into the solar system, we would still adhere to the notion that the earth was at the center of the universe! If Christopher Columbus hadn't set out to explore the planet, we'd still believe that Earth was flat! Can you imagine what technology would be like without the inquiring mind of Mr. Bill Gates? Inquiry leads to discovery, discovery leads to understanding, understanding leads to true knowledge, and true knowledge leads to evolution. Without inquiry, intelligence as we know it would standstill. It is inquiry or direct perception which keeps moving us forward. Nothing is more "enlightening" than actual experience!

What if we viewed life as more of an experiment rather than something to perform or perfect? Each of us can look back and see that we learned so much more from our own trials and errors than from following a script. Often we are closed off to trying something new. "What if I don't like it? What if I look stupid? What if it is a waste of time? What if it is a waste of money?" I think that the very worst thing that could happen is to NOT to have tried something new, and NEVER have had the chance to find out that I DID like it, I DIDN'T look stupid, and not only that it was NOT a waste of time, but it changed my life! What is it that you have been waiting to try, explore, or examine? Inquiring minds want to know!

The Path

It was a warm and sunny spring Sunday, the perfect kind of day for a casual walk. Except it is has not been in my repertoire to take a leisurely walk without an objective, destination or a workout in mind. Today something was different. The walk was just about the walk, and that was enough. For the first time, my walk became a meditation, rather than something else to accomplish. This was quite a new experience for a "recovering type A." In this spirit, the walk became magical and sacred.

I was not alone. My terrier, Bodhi, accompanied me, but on this walk I also felt accompanied by *buddhi*, the Sanskrit word for intuitive awareness or holy wisdom. As I headed down the trail, the first thing I noticed was how clearly defined the path before me was. There was no confusion as to where the borders of the path lay. I noticed I felt comfort in having a clearly defined journey. All I had to do was just put one foot in front of the other and move forward. Sometimes life unfolds that way too. It reminded me of times when my own life-path was remarkably distinct, and moving forward was easy and certain.

As I continued down the trail, I began to encounter small obstacles . . . a low hanging bough, a broken branch, a muddy dip, an overgrown tree, and even a fallen oak. Slowed only a little by the obstructions, my path was still clear. It reminded me of the times when obstacles have arisen in my walk through life, and how, despite those obstacles, I navigated my way around, over and through them, some with ease and others with struggle. But what mattered was that I continued forward on my path undeterred.

Then, I came to a place in the trail where another path circled out to the side, and reconnected farther up the trail. It was clear that taking that route was pointless and merely a distraction. Familiar with situations like these on my own life-path, I chose to stay the course, avoiding the pointless detours we can be tricked into taking in life.

Finally, I came to a clearing. The trail dissolved. There were no longer those safe, unambiguous boundaries to guide my feet. My dog Bodhi stopped, unsure of what to do next, and it became the task of *buddhi*, "inner wisdom," to now lead the way. I have come to these places in life too. Where the way forward became ambiguous, and my path became undefined. But *buddhi* said, "you know the way, you don't need a path, be free, be creative in how you get there . . ." So I knew that even when the path in life is unclear, that I must continue to move forward in what I know instinctively is the right direction, being creative, thinking out of the box, and not letting fear of the unknown slow me to a halt.

Eventually, we found our way to familiar ground, Bodhi, *buddhi*, and I, and we were back on a distinctive path. Not long after I found the path, I came upon a fork in the trail. One direction I knew would bring me home more quickly, and the other was the more scenic route. I chose splendor over speed, a novel approach for me. "Atta girl. You are learning," *buddhi* whispered. I felt the warmth of the sun on my skin as I moved forward along this stunning fork in the trail. It felt good just to observe the magnificence of nature and to be in that space . . . nowhere to go, nothing to do, no one to become. This newfound space brought out a sense of awe and reverence. Inhabiting this space was like being in a pocket of breath, beauty and freedom.

As I continued along the trail, I caught a glimpse of a place farther down the path which reminded me of a time in the past. Powerful feelings began to arise. This place brought up a time in my life when I felt caught in and oppressed by others' negativity, resentment and competition. It was a time when I had to struggle to shine my light. That time is behind me now, but the pain that rose still felt palpable. I didn't turn away from that reminder. I continued walking towards it with openness and inquiry. "Why was it this way?" I asked. "Why was this so?" And then I saw the people who caused my sorrow in the light of compassion. I knew it was only their fear that caused my pain . . . but it was that pain that moved me into action, and into a new direction, and as I turned the corner right before this reminder from the past, I forgave, and I moved forward.

Before I knew it, my path had come full circle, and what stood before me now was home. My journey was complete. My path this day had been a journey within, a walk on sacred ground.

> "To remain in a place of not knowing is profoundly uncomfortable, but ultimately rewarding. Use this time to look deeply within yourself in order to find your true north. Once the way is clear, trust the guidance you receive and do not fear to move in a whole new direction."
>
> ~ Danna Faulds

Sweetness

"Sweetness" is defined as the pleasant and delightful quality of some-one or something. The most commonly craved food is sweets, and we all know these cravings take on a life all of their own. Sometimes they are utterly irresistible! According to the ancient yogic healing science of Ayurveda, cravings themselves are a warning sign that an imbal-ance exists. They are your body's attempt at bringing itself back into balance. When our bodies are getting what they need, the cravings are always satisfied. Excessive or non-stop craving is a sign of a serious life-style or dietary imbalance.

Why do most of us crave sweets? Is it because our bodies need more sugar? Sweet cravings can result from low energy reserves, and low *prana* or life-force, which often arises from excessive exercise, over-work, too little sleep, excessive anxiety or worry, or being overly driven in one's ambitions. Very often, sweet cravings arise from the lack of "sweetness" in our way of life. Perhaps you are in a pattern of putting yourself last, being too hard on yourself, putting up with a job you hate, over-scheduling your time, or a bickering or stressful family life. The lack of "sweetness" in your life can send you seeking sweetness from your pantry and refrigerator.

How often do we miss out on the opportunity to embrace sweetness and delight in our day-to-day lives? Instead, we fill our minds with the negativity of the evening news, prime-time TV, or internet. Instead of sweetness, we endure hard-core workouts, beating ourselves up. We spend extended hours at the office, or become buried under our to-do lists. Where is the sweetness? Often, we are too guilty to indulge our-selves in the sweetness life has to offer, only to settle for the sweetness which comes inside of a wrapper. We think who am I to deserve joy? Our lives lack simple pleasures like a leisurely walk, time in nature, a warm and fragrant bath, or a quiet cup of tea. Without moments of delight in our daily lives, all we have left is the false sense of sweetness found in a pint of ice cream or a soda can. This kinds of sweetness is here one minute and gone the next, and changes nothing. This kind of sweetness is empty — empty calories and empty to our souls.

When sweet cravings arise, these signal a need for sweetness in our existence. Examine your life and discover how you can allow more "sweetness" to naturally flow. Give yourself the "sweetness" you are truly craving. This kind of sweetness doesn't come in a bar or a cone. Don't be afraid to practice self-compassion and self-care. Be sweet to yourself in as many ways as you can, and watch your sweet tooth fade. In what ways can you bring sweetness into your life without the cookies, cakes and candies? How can we expect to have more sweetness in our world, if we won't even give sweetness a place in our lives?

Without Space, There is
No Room for Grace!

For Valentine's Day my husband gave me a ring. Upon it was supposed to be inscribed the word "BELIEVE," inspired by the intention I set for this year, "Believe in yourself in 2012." However, upon opening it, we were both shocked to find the word "PERSEVERE." This is not really the word you want to receive from your spouse on Valentine's Day . . . There's nothing romantic about the word "persevere." I told him I didn't want it! I could see he was really disappointed by the mistake. Then, I stepped back, paused, and thought for a moment, and it hit me. Persevere may not have been the word I *wanted*, but indeed it was the word I needed. This became a moment of grace. I slipped the ring on my pinky finger, and there it remains!

For over a year, I have been working tirelessly on my book *40 Days to Enlightened Eating*. Trying to break through in the publishing industry has been even more difficult! Writing the book was the easy part! I could have missed, ignored or refused to hear the message that I was given, but I have learned to make space for grace in my life. I will "persevere."

The movie *Matrix* is popular in our house. One part which sticks with me is when the "Oracle" tells Neo that he is not "the one." Later in the film, Neo discovers that indeed he *is* "the one." He asks the "Oracle" why she lied. She replies, "I told you what you needed to hear."
If we only listen, grace provides us with exactly what we need to understand at that moment in time. However, very often, we miss out on the grace which awaits us. There is no room for it to emerge when our lives are filled to the brim and our minds are overloaded with noise. Most of us find ourselves bombarded by the constant chatter of the TV or iPod, iPhone, iPad and anything else beginning with an "i." When there is no room for open thought or spaciousness in the mind, there is no room for inspiration or grace to surface.

There is no space for grace when we are over-scheduled, and our lives are over-crowded without a moment to spare. By cluttering our lives and our minds so completely, there is no space for grace to whisper its subtle messages and unveil the hidden truth. How many moments of illumination are you missing out on?

Grace speaks through thoughts, dreams, songs, images, words, chance encounters, *déjà-vu*, intuitions, coincidences, and synchronicities. It comes unexpectedly, but by invitation only. If we leave no opportunity open in which to encounter grace, it stays at arm's length. How many times has grace passed you by, without even a sliver of your time or attention for it to slip through? Where in your life can you make space for grace?

Personally, I've learned to schedule moments of silence and stillness into my day. I leave off the background noise of the TV. I give myself space to be. This is not something that comes naturally to me as a "type-A"; but it is vital. The classes I create each week and the weekly blogs I write come to me through moments of pure grace. Grace flows in, trickle by trickle, if there is room otherwise it flows quietly by. Is there an opening in your life, in your day, in your mind, through which the stream of grace can flow? When you make enough space, your life will overflow with grace.

Is Yoga Evil???

This weekend I had the pleasure of teaching a kids' yoga class for one student's birthday party! It was lots of fun! We all laughed, giggled and had fun except for one little girl. This little girl's mother told her she was not allowed to do yoga at the party, just watch, because yoga of course can ruin your soul. The little girl sat back and watched us play, laugh and giggle in the poses, clearly trying to figure out what it was about what we were doing that was so awful. As she watched I could tell she wanted to participate so badly. My heart went out to her. She finally burst into tears, sad and confused and clearly feeling like she was missing out on all the fun. I felt in that moment that her emotions had more power to damage her soul than yoga possibly could.

As a practicing Catholic Christian, a long time yogi, and yoga instructor, I continue to be perplexed by the idea preached by some well-meaning but misguided pastors that yoga is evil. How could something that brings about improved health, calm, a relaxed mind, inner peace and overall well-being be evil? Isn't that what God wants for all of us? I remember my dad saying that his grandmother believed that dancing and playing cards were of the devil. It seems to me that yoga is perhaps getting the same rap today as dancing or cards once did.

Is yoga spiritual? Absolutely. For me, yoga quiets my mind so that I can experience God. Yoga has only deepened my own faith. I have studied yoga extensively, its' history, its' philosophy, and its' practice. Yoga has been a great complement to my own faith! I have never felt that one is in conflict with the other. Both of my children are my own yoga students in my kids' yoga and teen yoga classes. In light of this recent experience, I asked them what yoga means to them. My 10 year old said that to him, "Yoga is about inner peace and connecting with God." I asked my 14 year old what yoga means to her, and she said, "It is about going within yourself to find light, and detoxifying your body from the foods you eat, but also detoxifying your mind from the stress of the week." Clearly, yoga isn't doing my children harm, for how could something that does that for them be bad!

In Matthew 12:25-27, after the Pharisees called him a devil for casting out an evil spirit, Jesus himself stated that Satan doesn't work against Satan, because a kingdom divided against itself cannot stand. If yoga brings people inner peace and helps them connect with God, heal their bodies, minds and spirits, then this certainly can't be working in the devil's favor. Yoga also teaches ten ethical principles as a part of the practice, which in essence are the Ten Commandments phrased in slightly different ways. There is non-stealing or *asteya*, truthfulness or *satya*, non-harming or *ahimsa*, chastity or *bhramacharya*, non-coveting/ non-greed or *aparigaha*, purity or *saucha*, contentment or *santosha*, spiritual self-education or *svadhyaya*, self-discipline or *tapas*, and surrender to God or *ishvara pranidhana*. Following these ethical principles alone would pit Satan against himself!

It is fear, illness, depression, anxiety, worry, harm and self-destruction which are the things evil seeks, and yoga couldn't be further from that goal. Sadly, many people have been misinformed about yoga by people who have never even practiced a single pose. Yoga is a beautiful practice which has only enhanced the well-being of my own spirit. I am someone who came to yoga amidst a stress-induced illness. I cannot imagine God preferring the old stressed-out pre-yoga version of me! I think of yoga in my life as a precious gift from God, a gift which I am passionate about sharing with others. I can't think of many other things further evil from than that!

A translation of Yoga Sutra 1:21 is, "Whatever your faith, practice it with all of your heart."

Releasing the "Should" Out of the Shoulders

As a former classroom teacher, I am accustomed to writing out lesson plans. My professors would be proud to know that I still use this methodology even when teaching yoga! The other day, as I was composing a class, I was writing the word shoulders. I ran out of space and ironically I was left with the word "should." This was a "light bulb" moment. The word "should" is contained in the word shoulders! How fitting! It made me think of my own tight shoulders and all of the "shoulds" that I carry in them. No wonder my shoulders are stiff and tight and often sore. I doubt I am alone with my shoulders weighted down with "shoulds." How many "shoulds" are you carrying in your shoulders? How heavy have your shoulders become under the weight of all the "shoulds"?

Maybe it is time to set down some of the shoulds. Perhaps now is the time to let some of them go. Imagine how free your shoulders will feel. How do you know if you have too many shoulds to carry along? If you are feeling tension, pain or stress in the shoulders, neck or back, you are suffering from the excess weight of too many shoulds. Which ones can you set aside for a while? Which ones can you release permanently? How many shoulds do we need to keep carrying with us? When we get rid of the shoulds we don't want, and the shoulds that we don't need, we are left with the person we could be.

When carrying too much, we certainly don't have the strength or energy to go as far or navigate the twists and turns of life with ease. In fact these shoulds make it much more difficult to do the things we are here in the world to do. Carrying too many shoulds saps our creativity, our passion, our empathy, our joy, and our zest for life. Too many shoulds stands in the way of our full potential. Some of us even buckle under the weight of too many shoulds. They affect our health, mood, emotional balance, and vitality. In thinking we are doing ourselves a favor by carrying around all of those shoulds, what we are really doing is weighing ourselves down, and holding ourselves back.

Elise Cantrell

Let go of the guilt, and let go of the shoulds. Are you carrying more than your share of shoulds? Just ask your shoulders!

Pressing the "Pause Button" in Your Life

Yesterday some of the electronics in our home took on a life of their own. The computer wouldn't stop printing until it ran out of ink and paper. The DVR wouldn't stop rewinding no matter what I did until I finally had to shut off the TV! Earlier in the week, the coffee machine was overfilling and overflowing the cups until it went kaput! It seemed these items were speeding along until they inevitably crashed!

Isn't that what we often do to ourselves? We plow along so fast, never pausing to see where we are going. We often fail to take a moment to gain insight, perspective, joy or even needed rest. These mysterious incidents caused me to take pause and reflect on my own speeding through my day-to-day tasks, without pause. Like the printer, if we keep going non-stop, we will become depleted, not of paper and ink of course, but of our own life-force.

Americans have an outstanding work ethic. Having lived outside the country and witnessed another point of view, I am not sure whether this is a blessing or a curse. My friend, Elaine, told me the story of her father. He worked hard year after year, and saved for his retirement. His dream was to purchase a small seaside home when he retired, and live out the rest of his years with his beloved wife in their home on the beach. At age 65, he finally retired, and purchased the home he dreamt of. He and his wife settled in and enjoyed their new life for 3 months before he died of a heart attack. His story saddens me because he waited his whole life to have his dream, but the waiting made it too late. He was like my printer, going until he just ran out. *Carpe diem.*

It makes me wonder why we wait till we retire to rest, have fun, and relax. We squander away our best years working towards the opportunity to enjoy life. Why not now? Like my friend Elaine's dad, we may have spent the opportunities we had to live our dream working and saving for the right day or time, failing to pause and enjoy the here and now. It is said that all we really have is now. The only reality that exists is now, the past and the future exist only in our minds.

Several times daily, press the "pause button" on your life. Take time out to reflect, to live, to be, to enjoy, to dream, to love, and to rest. Do it NOW. If ink cartridges and paper can become depleted from going and going for too long, how much more so can we? If you find yourself caught up in a frenzy of going and doing, press the pause button on your life, for if not now, when?

Blissed Out

Something we all are searching for in life is a little more bliss. This search has led to all sorts of things in our society. Experimenting with drugs, alcohol, voracious consumerism, achieving, winning, acquiring, conquering, doing more and more, faster and faster, with bliss ever eluding us, staying just out of reach. What we don't realize is that bliss is already there within us. But it is only accessible when we clear all the other murk out of the way. Bliss is our true natural state. It is all the wanting, striving, reaching, and grasping for the external which makes the bliss that exists as our true nature within impossible to reach.

What is bliss? It is easier for me to answer that question first with what bliss is not. Bliss is not wanting, but it is appreciating what you already have. Bliss is gratitude for what is. Bliss is not striving and achieving, but knowing you are already enough, just as you are. Bliss is not running from task to task, errand to errand, chore to chore, but it is there within the stillness. Bliss is not in words or sounds, radio or TV, bliss is waiting there in the silence. Bliss is not achieved through artificial means like alcohol or drugs, but through living in harmony with yourself. Bliss is not looking outwardly for what you do not have, but looking inwardly and discovering all that you do have.

Bliss is not as elusive as we think. It is there waiting underneath all our "stuff." It is not unlike my teenage daughter's closet. Somewhere, underneath all the towels, clothes, and shoes, is that perfect pair of comfortable jeans she has been searching for, but just can't seem to find.

Let go of searching for bliss, and allow the swirling and commotion around you to settle like ripples on the water. Suddenly, in the stillness, everything becomes crystal clear, and the beauty of what is already there appears right before you, as a beautiful reflection of who you really are . . . inside this very moment, bliss reveals its hidden treasure!

Yoga is Unity

"Existence feels empty in separation."

~ Deepak Chopra

There are many folks practicing yoga who do not understand what "yoga" really means. There are many others who *don't* practice yoga who are confused or even fearful as to what yoga really is. The word "yoga" comes from the root word "*yuj*" meaning to join, yoke or unite. At its most basic level, this is what yoga is truly about: unity. According to yoga philosophy, separation is an illusion. In separation, there is nothing but fear and emptiness. Disconnected we are broken, but in unity we are made whole. The intention at the root of yoga is to return us to our wholeness. Yoga works to piece us back together, like a broken vase. In the modern era, we have become disconnected and separated from each other, the natural world, God and our own selves. We have become very fragmented in the modern age, and need unity now more than ever.

The first illusion of separateness we as human beings experience is separation of ourselves from others. This sense of separateness is an illusion of the *ahamkara* or ego consciousness. The ego is what creates the sense of "I," and identifies the self as autonomous. The ego is merely a thought process rather than a reality. It is the mental process behind thoughts such as "I am Elise." "I am a yoga instructor." "I am from the south." Ego provides us with an internal system of classification which gives us a sense of identity, however, it is not who we truly are. When we see ourselves as separate and alone, we are small and powerless. When we see through the veil of the ego we begin to awaken to our belonging, to our interconnectedness rather than to separation. As human beings, we are each pieces of the same puzzle, we are patches of the same quilt, we are shards of the same vase. It is only in our wholeness and connection that life makes sense. Albert Einstein put it like this:

"A human being is a part of the whole, called by us the "universe," a part limited in time and space. He experiences himself, his thoughts and feelings as something separated from the rest — a kind of optical delusion of his consciousness. This delusion is a kind of prison for us, restricting us to our personal desires and to affection for a few persons nearest to us. Our task must be to free ourselves from this prison by widening our circle of compassion to embrace all living creatures and the whole of nature in its beauty."

Caught in the delusion of the ego, we have also lost our connection to the natural world. Long ago there was reverence for life, nature, and all beings. Mankind previously lived in complete dependence on the fruits of the earth. What was once revered and respected has become something to use and to exploit in order to serve the "I," the *aham-kara* or ego self. Nature, even human life itself, has somehow become disposable! We believe we have mastered nature, or won the imagined battle between man and nature, but nature has yet to have its last word.

We are conditioned to believe we are separated from God. That he is "up there," and we are "down here," and that occasionally we can get his attention, but at other times he amuses himself by toying with our lives. Nothing could be further from the truth. Meditation is the part of yoga where we experience unity with God. Meditation allows us to experience God, to feel the presence, to understand the peace that is ours for the taking. It is through meditation that we gain a knowing that God dwells not far away up in heaven, but with us and within us. We have been told that our bodies are a temple, but it is through meditation that can we experience this for ourselves. Meditation is yoga of the mind. When we "un-mind the mind," our souls are opened. It is through the openness of the soul that one experiences the proximity of God. Here, there is a deep knowing of his existence within you and you within him. This is unity, and this is "home." The body is nourished by food, but the soul is nourished by the presence of God's light.

Yoga is ultimately about uniting the self. Unless we are fully integrated into the self — mind, body and spirit — we are not capable of understanding or finding unity with others, nature, or God. It is not difficult to recognize someone who is in discord. According to Gandhi,

"Happiness is when what you say, what you think and what you do are in harmony." Yoga begins to create unity by first working through the physical body. Yoga postures are a series of exercises designed to work the muscles, bones, joints and energy meridians in unison. Weight-lifting for example, isolates one group of muscles, and places emphasis on that alone, oftentimes putting excessive torque on the joints. Yoga works the body as a complete unit, the way it was designed to move and flow. Yoga removes the energy blockages created by stiff, tense muscles or tight, rigid joints. When energy flows through the body properly we feel invigorated, and health and vitality are the natural result. Yoga releases tension from the muscles rather than creating tension as many modern forms of exercise do. When we release tension from the body, the mind begins to relax. When the mind is relaxed, we see things more clearly. As rigidity is removed from the body, the rigidity of the mind dissipates. A more harmonious relationship is created between the body and mind; they are no longer at odds with each other. When the body and mind are in harmony, the soul feels at home. Giving our soul a hospitable abode allows it to prosper and flourish. It is only then when we experience the merging together of mind, body and spirit. This union is yoga.

> "Yoga means union — the union of body with consciousness, and consciousness with the soul. Yoga cultivates the ways of maintaining a balanced attitude in day-to-day life, and endows skill in the performance of one's actions."
>
> ~ B.K.S. Iyengar

Get Unstuck

Are you craving a change? Do you sense there is something more to life, but you feel stuck where you are? Are you ready for your soul to break free? Are you ready to rise to the next level? It doesn't matter if you don't know how you are stuck, why you are stuck or what is keeping you where you are. YOU have the power to move things along, release whatever is holding you, and get to where you are going. Try this advice to get unstuck!

Learn to unlearn. Very often we get stuck in our own "knowing," like a fly caught in a spider's web. Our minds become closed by preconceptions, biases, judgments, foregone conclusions, shoulds, unconscious patterns, habits and conditioning. We get so trapped in the way we have always done things, and seeing things as we have always seen them, that we fail to see that it is time to change. We let our knowing block the doorway to possibility! "Unlearning" is when we consciously stop clinging to past conditioning, old programming and learned behavior. To get unstuck, weed out old behaviors, beliefs, habits, ideas and ways of doing things that stand in the way between you and your highest self. Become open to new ideas, higher truths and greater wisdom. "When I let go of who I am, I become who I might be." ~ Lao Tzu

Break old patterns. Yoga helps undo and counter the habitual patterns of moving the body in predictable ways: sitting, hunching, contracting and tensing up . . . patterns that adversely affect our health. For example, backbends and lengthening the spine undo slouching and hunching, hip openers counteract patterns created by spending hours in a chair, stretching the muscles counters tensing them up, and inversions reverse the effects of gravity. By consciously using yoga postures to break up patterns in the muscles, bones, joints and spine, you can redirect energies through the body in new ways, which promote health and longevity. Yoga practice not only develops new patterns in the physical body, but new patterns in the mind. When you consciously undo habitual patterns in the body, you create new neural pathways in

the mind. Changing the body changes the mind. Just as you consciously counter physical patterns in the body with yoga postures, you can do
the same with the mind. Meditation, silent stillness, resting, and spending time in nature all get you off the hamster wheel of life and allow
you to break free and look at things differently. When you give yourself time and space to recharge and renew, you begin to notice what
is not working for you. "Choice. Chance. Change. You must make a
choice, take a chance, or your life will never change." ~ unknown

Get comfortable with the uncomfortable. Get comfortable with
criticism, get comfortable with being judged, get comfortable with being misunderstood, get comfortable with being a misfit, get comfort-
able with saying "no", get comfortable with saying "yes", get comfort-
able with not knowing the answers, get comfortable with stepping into
the unknown, get comfortable with not knowing what is ahead, get
comfortable with fear, get comfortable with doubt. If you back away
from the discomfort of any of these things, you stay stuck right where
you are. Can you risk being vulnerable enough to show up in the world
exactly as you are . . . unmasked and unedited? Too many people sacrifice their true identity to fit in with the crowd. True courage is about
standing up to the world and saying, "You can judge me, and you can
criticize me, but you cannot shut me down. I WILL let the light of my
own soul be seen. " Allowing your True Self to be seen is the highest
form of courage there is. You will never step into your own greatness
if you don't get comfortable with being You! "There is only one way
to avoid criticism: do nothing, say nothing and be nothing." ~ Aristotle

Stop following the herd and blaze your own trail. You will never
be a leader if you just follow the crowd. To get unstuck it is essential
that we accept and appreciate our own special gifts and embrace the
beauty of our uniqueness! Stop fearing rejection. We all have special
work to do here, and if we get too caught up in following the herd
instead of following our heart, we are rejecting our own soul! Are you
being held hostage by what you THINK others think? The greatest
teachers in history were nonconformists and rebels. Jesus, Buddha and
Lao Tzu blazed their own trail amidst doubters, critics and detractors.
They lived what they knew was right in their hearts despite popular
opinion, and changed the world in their own special ways! They are not

alone in this; you can do it too! The holocaust is probably one of the greatest examples of people following the herd against their own truth and their own heart. "If you do not change direction, you may end up where you are heading." ~ Lao Tzu

Speak up for yourself. Ask for what you want, and be prepared to receive it. Ask for help, guidance, opportunities, and support. Stop being afraid to ask for what you need or want. Your voice is your power. When Jesus said, "Ask and you shall receive", I don't think he was referring to some magical power that we just haven't been able to tap into. I think he was trying to teach us how to use the power of our own voice and our own words on the journey of life to get where we are trying to go. Indeed asking for what we want is one of the most overlooked gifts we have! Nine times out of ten, when my kids ask me for something, they get it, unless it is something completely unreasonable. And honestly, sometimes they get unreasonable things too, just because they ask! Somewhere along the way, we adults we have lost the power to speak up for ourselves and ask for what we want. Speak from your heart! When your heart says "no", then your mouth should say "no" too! When your heart says "Yes, please!", then let the word "yes" roll from the tip of your tongue! If you can't speak your truth, and ask for what you want, you will never get unstuck!

Receive. Help, hope and change often come in very unexpected ways and from unexpected sources. If we don't remain open to receiving the unexpected, in unforeseen ways, then we miss out and stay stuck right where we are. There is a story about a man caught in a flood who climbed to the roof of his house as the floodwaters rose. He prayed for help and waited. A helicopter came by and dropped a ladder to him. He said, "No thanks, God is going to save me." Then a boat came by and offered to rescue him as the waters rose higher. Again the man declined, expecting God to save him. As the floodwaters rose above the roof of the house, the man drowned. When he got to heaven, he asked God, "Why didn't you save me?" God answered, "I sent a helicopter and a boat!" Where are you unknowingly declining help from God, the universe, or from other people? We must learn to receive help in order to get to where we are headed. "In the end, it's not so much from one's own effort, but from becoming a vessel that is capable of receiving." ~ Swami

Step out of the story. The story we tell ourselves about who we are sets the intention for the life that will unfold before us. What stories have you been telling yourself about YOU? "I'm too old to go back to school." "It's too late to change my career." "I'm not smart enough to be a success." "I never have enough money." "I have no self -discipline when it comes to . . . " What story line are you living and affirming daily in your life? Your life will unfold just like that story unless you change the story line! When we get stuck in our stories, we stop seeing the unlimited possibilities and the infinite number of plot lines our life can take on! You are the author of your own life! Why not create a new story with a fairy tale ending? What obstacles will you overcome? How will you be the hero? What is your "happily ever after?"

Get creative. Creativity is undervalued and underrated in our culture. Often mistakenly considered a waste of time, creativity is a portal to move forward! I find that when I do something creative, whether it is writing a poem, cooking, or making something with my hands, that my creative juices begin to flow in many other ways and in all directions! When I get my creative juices flowing, I get fresh new ideas and in-sights and inspirations about how to do the things that really matter in new creative ways. I perceive fresh, innovative ways around obstacles. I am able to look at things from a different perspective. I am always amazed at how one creative act unlocks the doorway to moving forward in countless ways.

Take action. Taking just one step at a time is better than remaining still. Many folks get so overwhelmed by the list of things they perceive are necessary to move forward that they stay frozen and stuck right where they are. Others get stuck, fretting over the "right" first step to take. There is no one "right" step to get started. Just start! Just take one step . . . a step at a time, one day at a time. The most beautiful and celebrated works of architecture in the world were built one stone at a time. They simply started with one stone. Stone by stone, day by day, the Taj Mahal was built. It took years. Building a life also takes an archi-tect and a builder, and that architect and builder is you. The Taj Mahal couldn't have designed and built itself. Envision the life you want, and then start building, one day at a time and one small action at a time. Over time, these small action steps will produce profound results. The Buddha taught that "An entire pitcher is eventually filled by many tiny drops." Action, no matter how small, moves stagnation and gets us unstuck! "Any action is often better than no action, especially if you have been stuck in an unhappy situation for a long time. If it is a mistake, at least you learn something, in which case it's no longer a mistake. If you remain stuck, you learn nothing." ~Eckhart Tolle

Get unstuck. Take one routine or pattern in your life and change it up. For example, I changed the route I use to walk my dog. For my personal yoga practice, I moved the position of my yoga mat to face a window and get a different view!

Starting Over

The most wonderful thing happens on January 1 of every year. We give ourselves permission to start over! We put the past behind us and begin again! The New Year is a gift! It reminds us that it is always OK to start anew, and to try as many times as it takes to get life just "right." I suggest you seize the opportunity for transformation now! You can begin by asking yourself some thought provoking questions:

1. What would I like to be different about this year?

2. How do I want to spend my time?

3. What relationships do I want to nurture, build or improve?

4. What do I want to accomplish this year?

5. What would I like to develop in myself?

6. What would I like to create?

7. What do I want to learn?

8. What are some things that haven't been working in my favor that need to go?

9. What do I want this year to be about?

10. What is my theme for this year?

11. What is my passion, and how can I nurture that part of me in the coming year?

12. What would I be disappointed about not doing or completing in the coming year?

13. What will give my life more meaning this year?

Ponder these questions, and even write down your answers. Don't let the opportunity to fully receive the gift of "starting over" pass you by!

> "We will open the book. Its pages are blank. We are going to put words on them ourselves. The book is called Opportunity and its first chapter is New Year's Day."
>
> ~ Edith Lovejoy Pierce

Eight Stepping Stones to
Manifesting Your Intentions

Intentions are powerful, however few of us realize the potency of our own intentions, and even fewer of us actually attempt to harness intention to create the life we desire. This is the year to wake up to your full potential and make your deepest longings and aspirations a reality! Intention is defined as stretching or bending the mind toward an object, goal or desire. It is "fixedness" of attention, earnestness, will, purpose, aspiration and highest vision. Dr. Wayne Dyer says that "Our intention creates our reality." And according to Dr. Deepak Chopra, "Your intention is the most powerful tool at your disposal."

Intentions are often likened to planting seeds. Seeds themselves are metaphors of pure intention or pure potential. If seeds are planted and nurtured in fertile soil, there is little doubt they will become what they are destined to be! A Chinese proverb assures: "From intention springs the deed, from the deed springs the habits, from the habits grows the character, from the character develops the destiny." With this in mind, how do we sow seeds of intention?

Step 1 — Awareness. It is essential to first know that we have the power to manifest the life we desire. It has always been so, and we already have everything we need in order to make it so. In order to tap into the potential that is already there, we must become aware of this truth. You were the creator of the life you already have, whether you were aware of it or not. With awareness, you can create the life you want to have. We have the power to write our own stories; we have the power to create our own lives. We must understand that thoughts, words and visions form our reality. The life we currently have is a result of our past thoughts and visions, whether conscious or unconscious. By bringing conscious awareness to our thoughts and imagining, we can begin to root out deep-seated intentions of which we are unaware. It is not uncommon to be unaware of our deepest desires. Many people don't know what it is that they really want, and this causes them to flounder rather than move forward. Our own illusions or disillusions may be interfering with us having the life we want and deserve. By looking within, we can bring awareness to innermost desires buried deep within us, longing to be discovered! Too often we haven't searched within ourselves deeply enough to understand what is hidden there. Our own inner truths go unspoken and unheard by our own being. Once we perceive and recognize our unconscious thoughts on a conscious level, we can gain direction and mastery over our thinking. Carl Jung put it like this: "What we think, we become." What are the stories you have been telling yourself? Take a moment to become aware of the beliefs you hold about yourself and about your life. What is it that you really desire? What is hidden away deeply within you? What wants to come out?

Step 2 — Resolve. Get out of your own way. So often, consciously or unconsciously, we set intentions based on what we think we deserve rather than based on what we really want. Often what we think we deserve is distorted by our own feelings of unworthiness and self-doubt rather than based on any reality. It is we who hold ourselves back from the life we truly desire. Your intentions should not be based on the life you think you deserve, but on the life you really want. Don't stand in the way of how high you can go. As Zig Ziglar said, "If you aim at nothing, then you will hit it every time." Those who dare to dream big are those who achieve great things. Your life can be no bigger than your highest aspirations. You will only rise as high as you envision. If your expectations are low, then that is exactly what you will receive. Be aware that intentions are limitless, and that your intentions are limited only if you let them. It is important not to let others set your intentions for you. Don't let others limit you or define who you are or who you will become! Most often however, YOU are your biggest obstacle in manifesting the life you want! This is the year that you leave your judgments of yourself behind, and step out of your own way! Do not deny yourself your dreams, desires or your deepest longings for another year! As Rabbi Hillel asked, "If not now, when?" There is no guilt allowed in intention setting. We were all created to be great, so do not shy away from living in your greatness. Do not shrink yourself, but be willing to grow into who you were created to become!

Step 3 — Envision. Once the light of awareness has shined on the hidden aspects of who we are, and what is holding us back, we begin to understand what it is we really want. Take time to envision what it is you want. Meditate on it. Observe what comes. Allow it to play out in your mind. Make space for the intention to become centered within you. Let the end results of this intention unfold in your mind's eye. Will this make you happy? What are your motives? Is this something that will contribute to your greater good? Will it contribute to your soul's development? Will it add to the world as a whole in some way? Take time to clarify your intentions in your conscious mind. According to Dr. Deepak Chopra, "The starting point of any journey is having a clear intention." I suggest you use this process to create intentions for all aspects of your life: personal, career, finance, family, health, fitness, relationships/marriage, and spiritually.

Step 4 — Verbalize. Take your intention out of your imagination and put it into clear and detailed words. It is very important to language the intention in positive words, verbalizing it optimistically in the affirmative. Secondly, word it as if it has already happened. This creates great potency. Once you have the intention in words, write it down precisely as you would like the intention to unfold. Be very specific in your wording. Words bring structure and form to thoughts and dreams. After all, it is recorded in the scriptures of many faiths that it was through words that God "spoke" the universe into being.

> "Just what is meant by **your word**? It means your conscious intention, your conscious direction, your conscious faith and acceptance that, because of what you are doing, the Power of Spirit will flow through your word in the direction you give it."
>
> ~ Ernest Holmes

Step 5 — Surrender. Release your intentions to God or the Universe. Let go and trust that the right thing will unfold. This concept of surrender is called detachment. You have sown the seeds of intention; now let God or the universe take care of the rest. Remember, seeds grow not with force, but with tenderness and nurturing. Seeds need care and tending, but if they are overwatered they wither. Also know that a cucumber seed will not grow tomatoes. The seed you planted will grow into exactly what it is destined to become.

"Once you make a decision, the universe conspires to make it happen."

~ Ralph Waldo Emerson

Step 6 — Open. Be open to grace. Remain open to how your intentions unfold. Allow them to take their own form. Let go of expectations. Don't place judgments, precepts or perimeters on the way things develop and come into being. Trust that your intention will manifest in just the way that it should.

> "A good traveler has no fixed plans and is not intent upon arriving. A good artist lets his intuition lead him wherever it wants. A good scientist has freed himself of concepts and keeps his mind open to what is."
>
> ~ *Tao Te Ching* 27, translated by Steven Mitchell

Step 7 — Believe. Have faith. Trust that all seeds flower into what they are destined to become. It has often been said that, "If you don't believe, you won't receive." Trust that potentiality leads to actuality, which becomes reality. BELIEVE!

Step 8 — Create. Now it is time to create a vision of what it is you would like for your year to hold. It is this final step in which you bring your intentions out of the mental field and into the physical realm. Taking your thoughts and ideas into the material world gives your intentions substance and form. For these to unfold in our reality, it is necessary to make them visual and real. Creating a vision board collage can be as simple or as complex as you care to make it. I suggest starting with the background. The background can simply be a solid color, one that you really like; or it can be a large photograph or magazine picture of a place or setting that you resonate with. Next, peruse magazines to find pictures and words to add to your collage which embody the intentions that you wish to set. Cut and paste them onto your background in a way that appeals to you. If you are unable to find some of the words or pictures that you wish to add, feel free to write, draw or paint them into the space. Only you will know when your collage is complete. When making your intentions for the year, remember that:

> "A journey of one thousand miles begins with just a single step."
>
> ~ Buddha

My Year of *Karma* and "CAR-ma"

2011 started out like any other year, Wisconsin winter in full swing. But very early on it seemed we were repairing one thing after another: broken appliances, broken pets, broken kids, but particularly broken cars. By no fault of our own, our cars were in three collisions. They also went into the shop for odd, unexpected repairs, flat tires, you name it! In good humor, I began to refer to 2011 as our year of "CAR"ma!

Although I knew what *karma* meant, I began to study it in more depth as a part of my Ayurveda training. I always thought of it as sort of "reaping what you sow" or "that which goes around comes around," which is certainly true . . . But what did I do to deserve this year's "CAR-ma"?

As I studied, I learned that *karma* is really nothing more complicated than the law of cause and effect. Nothing exists that is uncaused, and like causes produces like effects. Because of this law of cause and effect, we see justice in the world. Every action we take, whether positive or negative, is a cause. The result of that action is always similar in nature. If we are hateful, we will be hated. If we are lovable, we will be loved. We ourselves are responsible for most of the circumstances in our own lives, good or bad. If we push ourselves too hard, the result is illness or injury. If we over-eat, or eat a poor diet, we become overweight and suffer from disease. If we are cranky and unkind to people, we suffer from loneliness.

This year I was able to watch *karma* unfold as my best friend's cruel and unbearable boss finally met his fate. I watched *karma* unfold again as an unethical yoga instructor I know of had teaching certification and credentials revoked. *Karma* is real.

Incredibly, what this means is that we have control over our life to a great degree! The good news is that just as cars can be repaired, we can repair our own *karma*, and thus repair our lives! There are reasons for everything that happens, and if we uncover the reasons, we can take action to reverse them. To reverse the effects of our causes, we simply apply corrective actions of the opposite nature. Change eating for the better, and watch health and weight be restored. Change a crummy attitude, and friendships begin to develop.

Interestingly, this year, each time we had our cars repaired, they came back even better than before. The car repair people seemed happy to fix this or that additional little thing they found. The scratches from the kids' bikes were gone. The paint was shiny and new. The little dings on the bumper, erased! The inside was cleaned and vacuumed! Here is where I started to understand that when you start repairing your own *karma*, other unexpected things are also mended and restored in the process! The power to change our lives and our world rests with us, not with some mysterious thing called "fate." The law of *karma* is simply one of cause and effect. What we have damaged we can heal, and eventually improve beyond measure. This is yoga, and this is what I have learned from a year of "CAR-ma."

Is Exploring Your Lunar Side Lunacy???

The glorious full moon and today's lunar eclipse remind us to stay connected to our own lunar side. *Hatha* yoga is all about creating the right balance of the solar and lunar aspects of life and of the self. "*Ha*" translates as sun, and "*tha*" as moon. These concepts are also most often recognized as the "*yin*" and the "*yang*." These two forces are said to coexist within us. According to yoga philosophy, our solar or *yang* side is dominant on the right side of the body. It represents daytime, and the heating, energizing, aggressive, fast, hard, and masculine side of who we are. Our lunar side is dominant on the left side of the body. It represents nighttime, along with the cooling, mysterious, soft, calming, yielding, passive, feminine side of our inner being.

Modern society tends to accentuate and favor the *yang* or solar side over the *yin* or cooling side. In our culture, we are conditioned to be aggressive, dominant, competitive, striving, and goal oriented. These are all heating aspects of existence. The problem is that too much heat can lead to "burnout!" And "burnout" is all too common in this day and age!

What *hatha* yoga attempts to do is to bring balance and harmony between the sun and the moon aspects within us. It is important not to lose sight of our lunar side in this fast-paced era. It is important to temper the heat with the cooling lunar facet of who we are. It is important to practice slowing down, moving with grace, and allowing things to flow, rather than always pushing or forcing them along.

It is these two parts of ourselves that make us whole. One cannot exist without the other. However, we cannot live in deference to one over the other and still live in harmony and peace. Day cannot exist without night, heat cannot exist without cold, light cannot exist without darkness, and the masculine cannot exist without the feminine.

Let the full moon and the lunar eclipse that occurred today be a re-minder to give equal consideration to your lunar side, remembering to cool down and slow down so as not to "burn out." Keep in mind it is OK to be a little "loony" sometimes!

Weeding Out Your Life

We have all weeded gardens at one time or another. Pulling weeds is necessary in order to keep a garden thriving and healthy. Weeds are insidious plant forms which are capable of "choking out" or stealing away the life force from other vegetation. Weeds keep the preferred plants from prospering and flourishing. If left unattended, eventually weeds can take over the entire garden.

Just like a garden, our lives need continuous weeding, and you are the gardener of your own life. Only you can remove the weeds. The weeds that keep you from prospering and thriving are those same weeds that can eventually take over your life. If left in place, they can eventually choke out the beauty and joy that is you in full bloom. As this year comes to a close, resolve to seek out the weeds in your life. Is there something or someone around you that drains the life out of you, choking out your energy or joy? What is keeping you from "growing"? What is preventing you from opening up into "full bloom"? What stands in the way of you thriving? Take time to examine your life for weeds. Have the courage to pluck them out.

Maybe the weeds are simply household clutter getting in the way of you fully enjoying the comfort of your home. Anything in your home that you don't use or love is a "weed," crowding out the beauty of your personal garden. Maybe the weeds are schedules or routines which need tending or abandoning all together. Are you over-scheduled? Is your schedule crowding out the space you need in which to live joy-fully, to learn and grow? The weeds may be unproductive or harmful habits. How are you eating? Are you getting enough rest? Are you feeding your mind with negative images, ideas, television programs, or literature? Are you "fertilizing" the garden of your mind-body system or treating it like a garbage dump? Are there things in your life which deplete your spirit? What keeps your spirit from blossoming into the most radiant version of you?

The weeds may be that awful boss or job that is robbing you of happiness. The weeds may be those nagging health issues that need taking care of. They could be excess food or drink, or medications. The weeds could be those unwanted pounds you've only wished away, but done nothing about. The weeds may be negative people around you who are bringing you down with hurtful, unconstructive actions or words. You may recognize people in your life whose negative energy is sucking the life out of you, like a weed to a flower. The weeds in your life could be unnecessary or unwanted expenses and debt that drain your bank account. Perhaps the weeds are the negative thoughts you keep thinking, personally beating yourself up or putting yourself down. The weeds may be negative perceptions you have about yourself. They may be unproductive or destructive habits. Perhaps there are aspects of yourself which are in need of removal.

Now is the time to take action and root out the weeds! Before the year is out, determine where the weeds are in your life. Sometimes it is difficult to tell a weed from a plant. Some weeds are "copycats" and try to mimic plants in how they look and behave, but they can never produce the same fruits or beautiful blooms as the real plant! Once you have identified weeds, decide how they will be removed. Will you dig them up, pull them out, or spray them? Most important is to make sure to get them out, seeds, roots and all. Otherwise, they will just come back.

Returning Home to Yourself

When traveling back to my hometown for Thanksgiving each year, I experience a true coming home. I return to southern accents, home cooking, old friends, schoolmates, and familiar shops and restaurants which bring back memories. I travel down familiar roads, pass by my old schools, and see loved ones who have known me since I was "knee high to a grasshopper!" How nice it is to be able to come home!

However, it occurs to me that to really come home, we must return home to ourselves. We must take time to return to the essence of who we really are. One of the most profound statements of all time is Nietzsche's, "Know thyself." Isn't the true journey in life just that? Self-knowledge, self-understanding, self-unfolding, and peeling back the layers until you get to the core of who you are. So many folks travel down life's path never knowing or understanding who they really are, never diving deeper, never even peeking beneath the surface! So many people fear so deeply what they will find that they remain ignorant of their true nature for a lifetime. Many people use the stimulation of the outer world to distract them from getting to know their inner self. Most people spend their lifetimes "above water," only seeing the tip of the iceberg of who they really are.

What is it we fear? Ancient Chinese sage Lao Tzu says, "Knowing others is wisdom; knowing yourself is enlightenment." According to yoga philosophy, self-knowledge is the foundation for all other forms of knowledge. Through knowing the self, everything else is known. Reality is uncovered. We begin to understand the natural world and the laws of the universe, because those same laws exist within us. It amazes me that people will climb the tallest mountain, parachute from great altitudes, explore dangerous jungles, all in search of something, but what they fear more is searching within.

How do we go about returning home to ourselves? Stop running from yourself! Spend time with yourself. Don't smother yourself with so many obligations and activities that you never get the chance to meet the real you. Stop allowing the sensory input of the outside world to distract you from who you are. We are more than our activities, we are more than our actions, we are more than our accomplishments, we are more than our experiences. Take time to meditate. Your true self is often unveiled spontaneously through formless meditation. You are your life-long companion; shouldn't you know yourself better than anyone else?

What are you drawn to? Returning home to yourself comes by actively following that which moves you, that which ignites your passions. Give yourself time for what is important to you. Stop judging yourself. Coming home to yourself is learning to truly take care of yourself, love yourself, and forgive yourself. Returning home to yourself is simply asking the question "Who am I?" and patiently waiting for the answer to arise . . .

> We are the mirror as well as the face in it.
> We are tasting the taste this minute of eternity.
> We are pain and what cures pain.
> We are the sweet cold water and the jar that pours.
>
> ~ Rumi

Shape Shifting

In yoga practice, it is amusing how quickly we can shift from one pose to the next. One moment we are a tree, and the next we can be a rabbit, a tortoise, a fish or a frog! When we are in these poses, we take on some of the physical characteristics of these life forms. Each pose is different, and each pose is temporary.

Life is the same. Life situations are also temporary. As life changes, you change with it. I find I shift and change many times throughout the day: parent, employee, teacher, chauffeur, referee, chef! We get to try on so many shapes and characters and sizes in life. We begin as tiny embryos, then we crawl on all fours, during adolescence our shapes change quite suddenly, even from one day to the next. I remember how much my shape shifted when I was pregnant with my children! And as we continue to age, we continue to change shape.

In yoga, we can choose which posture comes next. We can choose which shape we want to be. What pose feels right in this moment? What is the body asking for next? We can also make conscious choices as to what form our own lives will take on next! We have the power to shape-shift our lives! We have the power to transform. If we can change into a lizard, a dragon, a cat, a camel and a plow on the small plane of a yoga mat, think of the possibilities of changes we can make in the much larger plane of our lives!

Simply choose the shape you want your life to take next. You will know in your heart if it feels right! Like the phoenix, you can rise up out of the ashes and become who you are destined to be! What shape will your life take on next?

> Let go of perfection,
> There are no mistakes,
> Only learning.
> Accept where you are,

embrace your resistance,
and be open to growth through experience.
Honor your humanity,
and learn from all teachers.

~ Lao Tzu

Come on to Your Mat as Little Children

I think children have much to teach us "grown-ups" about yoga. I have had the absolute privilege to teach kids' yoga for the last 6 weeks. Even though I am the teacher, I have learned so much more from them! They come in with so much openness and curiosity. They have no expectations. They come with "beginner's mind," and they are willing to try, and they are willing to fail! They love to let the Sanskrit names of the postures roll off their tongues, and they don't shy away from trying to say them. They don't compete with one another, and they don't give up just because they don't get the pose the first time. There is no judgment . . . They honestly don't care what they look like, they care how they feel! They are able to let go and just play on the yoga mat. To them, yoga is another way to play. For this reason they are so joyful and full of laughter. Kids get yoga! Kids are born already yogis. It is we adults who try to overcomplicate it, and take ourselves too seriously.

My brother recently emailed me a photo of my 4 year old nephew in headstand on the living room sofa! I remember noticing my son Christian was also born doing yoga poses! Without having ever seen mom practice yoga, he'd transition from up dog to down dog, and from cat to cow pose. He went in to full splits with ease, and could recline back into full saddle pose. He loved attempting tripod or plow pose on the floor in front of the TV. I was amazed at how naturally he went into random yoga positions and poses, with the ease of BKS Iyengar himself!

I think we all are born doing yoga and thinking like yogis . . . I don't know when it is that we stop, but it seems that before we reach adulthood our inner yogi gets lost! No wonder our bodies become rigid, and our minds quickly follow suit! We begin to strive and compete, and we leave behind doing things just for pleasure's sake. We approach all that we do with expectations, and consequently wind up full of disappointment. We come into all that we do judging ourselves and judging those around us. When do we ever just approach things with openness and curiosity, with the innocence of a child?

What if we looked at life itself upside down as if in a headstand? Think of how amazing the world would be if we sometimes took a moment and looked at things upside down, in a different way, and in a different context than the usual. How magical the world could be! What if we just approached new things without any expectations? I wonder what we would discover . . . I wonder what we'd achieve . . .

In the words of my 3rd grade yoga student Rachael M., as she taught her younger brother tree pose: "Jake, yoga is peaceful and healthy for you!" Somehow kids just get yoga! It is they who should be our teachers!

Peeling Away the Layers

Human beings are not unlike onions, according to yoga philosophy. Like an onion, the innermost "juicy" part of ourselves is covered in layers of protective skin. It is believed that our soul is encased in five layers, or sheaths, called the *Pancha Koshas*. What is revealed when we peel back these layers?

The **first layer** is called the *Annamaya Kosha*. This literally translates as the "food body" because the physical body is composed entirely from the foods we eat. The brain itself, as an organ of the body, is also composed entirely from the foods we ingest. The physical body is how our internal souls are able to interact with the physical world and allow it to interrelate with us. The "food body" makes it possible for our spirit to be incarnated into a physical existence. Our sensory organs and organs of action make it possible for us to give from ourselves and take in to ourselves worldly things of matter and form. This is our vehicle in which to travel through life, but it is not who we are.

The **second layer** is the *Pranamaya Kosha*. This is the "breath sheath" or the *prana* body. It is this layer which is responsible for animating us and giving us life and energy. *Prana* literally means "life-force." It is responsible for our breathing and for movement throughout the entire body. Life-force is responsible for health and vitality. This layer is life itself, for without the breath we cannot live.

> "Inhale, and God approaches you. Hold the inhalation, and God remains with you. Exhale, and you approach God. Hold the exhalation, and surrender to God."   ~ Krishnamacharya

The **third layer** is the *Manomaya Kosha*. This is the layer of the mind, thought, memory and emotions. It is composed of the conscious and unconscious mind. Note that the brain is not the mind. The brain is an organ of the physical body. The "mental sheath" is present throughout the entire body because information is perceived through the intelligence of all the organs and senses. The mental body is composed of thoughts, impressions, memories and emotions, whether conscious or unconscious. Memories and emotions can be stored anywhere in the body, not only in the brain. This is why it is not uncommon in a yoga class to sense emotional release during poses and postures of any kind. It is the mental body that processes sensory input, thoughts and impressions received from the physical body's interactions with the outside world. Thoughts, moods and emotions can swirl, shift and fluctuate. The mental body is not static; it is ever changing. This process can be observed as continual waves of thought and emotion in the mental field, referred to as *chitta vritti*.

The **fourth layer** is *Vijnanamaya Kosha*. This is the "wisdom sheath." This sheath is composed of conscious awareness. We are not our thoughts, we are not our moods, we are not our emotions, we are the witness of these. When we are able to transcend the chatter of our minds, then we are left with pure awareness and pure consciousness. The *vijnandamaya kosha* is the inner witness ... The witness does not react or judge, it simply observes. It is in this sheath that wisdom, insight and intuition arise. Here is where our deepest inner knowing exists. It is our inner voice, the wisdom of our hearts. This sheath does not exist in any other animal. It is only present in the human being.

When the other layers are peeled away, we encounter the most delicate of all the layers, the **fifth layer**, or the *Anandamaya Kosha*. This is the "bliss sheath." When all of the layers are peeled away, only bliss is left. At this level, only bliss exists. Bliss is the highest state of consciousness. Bliss is beyond body, emotions, thoughts and awareness. The bliss *kosha* is where we give and receive bliss. Bliss is pure light and pure essence. Bliss comes from alignment with and connection to God. It is here where we understand our interconnectedness with all of existence, and where we sense that we are a part of something greater. At the same time, we experience freedom and liberation. It is only through nurturing and fully developing all of the other layers that we can enter this deepest layer of human experience.

Beneath all layers, our souls exist, protected by these five sheaths. The soul is constantly interacting with each sheath, and is subject to the strength or weakness of each of them. If the physical sheath is not well cared for, then each layer beneath it is also weakened. Thus the soul is subject to and bound by the weaknesses or strengths of the sheaths which encase it. If the layers of an onion are strong and supple, the onion inside is juicy and sweet. Unprotected by its healthy sheaths, an onion is subject to rot and decay. Beneath the five *koshas*, is your own "onion" juicy and sweet?

The Remover of Obstacles

A few nights ago I had a dream which continued to haunt me in my waking hours. I was on a bus in India heading for a city, the name of which evades me now. The driver, a suspicious-looking, overweight, sweaty, unattractive, hairy, middle-aged Indian man told me, "You may never reach your destination." In the seat beside me was a thin, teen-aged Indian boy, around 14 years of age. This boy told me, "You will reach your destination, I am going there too, and I will help you." While still dreaming, something intuitively told me to trust the boy rather than the man, even though the man was the one actually in the driver's seat. Then I awoke. What did this dream mean?

The next day I spent time pondering and meditating on the meaning, and I knew immediately when I had come to the right conclusion. The driver was my own "self-doubt," and the boy was "self-belief." For years, I have let self-doubt be the driver, and I have let him deter me from reaching my destiny. Self-doubt is middle-aged, like I am. Apparently, he has matured right along with me; however, he is not very likable, reliable or attractive. The boy was idealistic, enthusiastic, unassuming, awkward and naive, just like my own self-belief, which was likely left behind since my early adolescence.

In the dream, I had unexpectedly chosen to listen to the seemingly improbable advice from self-belief, and I had dismissed the discouraging words of the older, but not wiser, self-doubt. What a revelation! For so long, I have let the flawed advice of "self-doubt" drive my life. Unexpectedly, I should have relied on the advice of "self-belief" all along. I now realize he is the one who can actually be trusted to get me to my destination on life's journey. On the road to my destiny, I have allowed "self-doubt" to be an obstacle. Once I identified him as such, I was able to see though his deceit! Only I have the power to remove him from the driver's seat.

In yoga and Ayurveda, it is known that energy can become stuck in areas in the body, when it hits internal obstacles, blockages, tightness, or tension. When this *chi* or *prana* hits an obstacle within us, it cannot reach its destination, and the energy stagnates in the body. If it doesn't move, eventually disease sets in. When we find ourselves running into a road-block or an obstacle to our dreams, desires, plans or goals we also stagnate, and this too causes "dis-ease" in our lives. There is no difference; they are both life-force energy, only one is internal and the other external. No one can begin to move the stuck energy in our bodies but we ourselves. Practices like yoga, *tai chi*, and acupuncture are specifically designed to help remove energy blockages from the body, through releasing areas of stagnation, thereby restoring proper energy flow.

I firmly believe that it is we who create our own obstacles in life, and thus it is only we who can remove them. It is we who block our own way! How? It is we who set our intentions whether we are aware of them or not. It is we ourselves who get stuck in habitual patterns, and it is we who, out of fear, often chose not to act at all. We believe the stories others have been telling us and the ones we've been telling ourselves — that we aren't good enough, or smart enough or attractive enough. Somehow we believe we just aren't enough . . . We believe this so firmly that we create our own blockages and our own stagnation! We are the creators of our own realities, and we are the ones who can change them.

Know that you already are enough just as you are. You were created to reach your destiny in life. No, you haven't been short-changed. You have been given more than enough to live the life for which you are destined! You just have to believe. BELIEVE that you are enough! Is "self-doubt" driving the bus to your destiny? Who do you trust to lead you to where you're going? Have you trusted the wrong driver to lead the way all along? It is never too late to change drivers and remove obstacles! Now is the time to let "self-belief" lead the way!

"Don't let the noise of others' opinions drown out your own inner voice. And most important, have the courage to follow your heart and intuition . . . Everything else is secondary."

~ Steve Jobs

"Believe and act as if it were impossible to fail."

~ Charles Kettering

Riding the Winds of Change

Fall is a season of transition, a time of change. There is no mistaking this, because Mother Nature makes the changes so apparent! The air becomes cool and crisp. The trees illuminate with brilliant color before they shed their leaves. Birds begin their journeys southward, insects and spiders sneak their way indoors, and creatures of all kinds make preparations for winter "shut-down."

According to the ancient science of Ayurveda, fall is governed by wind or *vata*. Wind is erratic, sometimes blowing, sometimes still, and always changing directions without any prior notice. Wind is full of movement, shifting the air, shaking the leaves, bending tree branches and causing us to shiver. Nature becomes animated by the energy of the wind! As a part of nature, we ourselves are affected by the cool, dry, moving character of the wind. During the autumn, we frequently find ourselves scurrying about erratically. Often we begin to notice increased dryness of our skin and hair, and even dry mouths. Frequently the influence of the seasonal wind expresses itself in us as a dry cough. Have you noticed all the coughing lately? Physically, we are influenced by the moving nature of wind, and begin to move faster, and often we become harried and erratic in our daily routines. We may notice our energy levels and moods take on the erratic qualities of wind, up one minute and down the next, completely still yet a moment later!

Mentally, we are also affected by the autumn winds. Our thoughts become scattered, and begin to circulate and swirl around the mind, shifting quickly from thought to thought. Due to the wind qualities of autumn, we may notice more nervousness, restlessness, and even agitation arising in the mind due the accumulating windy qualities of the season. Many people note a change in sleep patterns in the fall, such as difficulty sleeping, or waking in the night. These patterns accompany a sharp increase in *vata*, the wind's qualities present within us, which become provoked by the external wind present in nature!

There are several actions we can take to help balance some of the excess *vata* or wind qualities when they become aggravated. Soups and cooked vegetables warm the body and replenish moisture sapped by the dry, cooling aspects of wind. Heating spices such as black pepper, ginger and cinnamon warm the body, and soothing teas calm the mind while replenishing needed moisture and heat. Root vegetables bring about a sense of groundedness, which is often lost in the blowing winds of the mind, body and external world. Slowing down the body, making movements more soft, smooth and deliberate, can help counter the agitated qualities of wind. Slowing down the mind through yoga, relaxing, and meditating can often help. This is a great time to spring for a massage, or surrender to the longing for a nap!

Transitioning through the changes of autumn does not have to be uncomfortable. We just have to set our sails! We can harness this wind quality, and allow it to move us forward. We can take advantage of this extra energy and movement of the mind and body by getting things done, and accomplishing our goals. We can honor our erratic energy levels by resting when we feel depleted, and by sailing forward when we feel energized! Just as the trees begin to shed their leaves, we too can begin to shed things which no longer serve us. Instead of struggling against the winds of change, ride them along! An old proverb says, "It is not the towering sails, but the unseen wind that moves the ship." And in the words of the legendary Bob Dylan, "The answer my friend is blowin' in the wind, the answer is blowin' in the wind."

"Bee" Inspired!

As the days grow shorter, and the air chills off, it seems the bees come out to work and to play! They know somehow to "seize the day" and make the most of the remnants of temperate weather. It is inspiring to observe the bees this time of year. They move from flower to flower, absorbing the nectar each flower has to offer, before carrying it away, and storing it to sustain themselves and their "family" during times of hardship.

Like the bees, we buzz from moment to moment and from task to task. How many of us forget to take with us the "nectar" from each encounter, interaction and undertaking? Are we just going through the motions, or are we finding meaning, beauty and sustenance in each moment? If we are buzzing around too quickly, without being present to our routines, even our most mundane activities, we may be leaving behind the most important and vital aspect of living, that of being unaware of the nectar in the present moment. In each life experience, it is possible to draw some "sweetness" from it and take it with us.

Bees not only take nectar with them as they leave each flower, but they also leave something of themselves behind. It is the bees who actually pollinate the flowers. Because of the bee's encounter with the flower, the flower now too has the opportunity to flourish and proliferate. It seems that the bee leaves behind a precious gift in each place it lands, yet it takes along the nectar and sweetness from each encounter as well.

The bee then takes this nectar back to its home, the hive, and makes something amazing from it. The honey that the bees make is a miraculous substance! It feeds the bees' larva, it sustains the bees during the winter, and there seems to be plenty to share with us! Honey has amazing healing and nourishing properties, it never spoils, and it contains a magnificent sweetness. We too should know that if we take a bit of nectar with us from each occurrence in life, and leave a little something life-giving behind, we too will be healed and bring nourishing sweetness to sustain ourselves and the others in our "hive." "Bee"lieve!

The bee can inspire us to draw the sweetness, the nectar out of each chore, task, encounter, interaction or destination in which we happen to land. Let it "bee" your reminder to soak up the nectar we need to sustain each life experience. Leave a little something special and life-enhancing behind in each conversation, in each task, in each interaction. This is *karma* . . . paying it forward. When we do this, we will be sustained. How can we not "bee" inspired?!

> "Aerodynamically the bumble bee shouldn't be able to fly, but it doesn't know it so the bumble bee goes on flying anyway."
> ~ Mary Kaye Ash

Polishing Your Inner Jewel

"*Om mani padme hum*" is perhaps the most sacred and revered Tibetan *mantra* through the ages. This *mantra* best translates as: "The jewel of the lotus lies within." It is said that once a student discovers the true meaning of this *mantra*, they become enlightened.

Perhaps the magic of this *mantra* is that it takes on its own meaning for each individual. For me, it shines a light on the fact that we often forget to focus on the part of ourselves which is really valuable. It isn't the home we live in, the clothes we wear, the car we drive, the color of our eyes, or having a long list of accomplishments which makes us valuable beyond measure. Who we are within, underneath the designer jeans, small-talk, accomplishment and awards, is our greatest treasure.

Our country and the world have faced "hard times" over recent years. Perhaps for the first time in ages we are beginning to appreciate our inner treasure more so than outer signs of wealth and prestige. Perhaps we are starting to see beyond what initially meets the eye, not only in others, but in ourselves. One thing that remains unchanged, whether we are in times of affluence or times of strife, is who we are. I am not my clothes, my home, my car, or even the physical embodiment of myself. My soul lies underneath all of those external things. What really matters is whether the beauty of my inner jewel shines through. Who am I beyond all of that which surrounds me? Where lies real value in the being that I am?

Some people feel that they have nothing more to offer than their outer selves. They become all "show and blow," hoping others can see their great worth, and perhaps proving their value to themselves. Some people have never thought to look inside to find their greatest wealth. Instead their inner jewel remains "buried treasure" underneath all that they have in the worldly realm.

In yoga, this is true of our practice as well. Many yogis seek to tweak each and every bone and muscle into the perfect external expression of the pose, and sometimes they achieve just that. Yet their practice remains so empty and so fixated on the external manifestation of the pose that they have never in fact practiced "yoga." The most important aspect of yoga practice is not how the pose appears on the surface externally, but what you are experiencing within. If someone finds the perfect alignment in the pose, but is not aligned within themselves, then they are performing gymnastics or "Cirque du Soleil," but they are not practicing yoga. I have seen students take the most basic variation of a pose, and find the pose so deeply from within themselves, that their yoga practice is profound. This embodies the essence of yoga. The external expression of the pose, and the external manifestation of ourselves, does not come close to embodying the light, brilliance, worth and beauty of the jewel that lies within.

Stillness Amidst the Storm

In the late summer, one tropical storm after another swirls around in the Atlantic Ocean. These storms are chaotic, with swirling winds, dark rolling clouds, churning, turbulent seas, driving rains, and walls of water. The turmoil of these storms is not unlike our own daily lives. We, too, swirl around from task to task, scattered like the wind. We are hurried like the driving rains, and pressured like the churning seas. We rise up to each and every challenge like the walls of water and forceful waves breaking on the shore.

Ironically, right in the midst of the most powerful storms on earth, there is a place of stillness. In the "eye" of the storm, the central point, there is perfect calm. The winds are quiet, the waters are tranquil and serene, and the sky is bright and sunny, all while the storm rages around it. Without this "eye," the storm would dissipate, and loose its strength. It is paradoxical that the place of stillness at the center is what holds the whole storm together!

We, too, require a place of stillness to hold us together in the chaos of modern life. That place of stillness is found right in our own center. We can go there any time to retreat from our tumultuous and turbulent daily lives. We can find this place through meditation, moments of silence, walks in nature, a quiet cup of tea, a soothing bath, a massage, or a yoga class. It is important to nurture that place of inner stillness in order to maintain our own momentum and strength. Give yourself permission to restore and strengthen your own place of inner stillness. Give yourself the gift of taking mini-breaks throughout the day to go to that place of inner calm. Nourish yourself there in the silence. Find points of stillness through which to gather your strength to transcend the storms of life . . . at least until you "make landfall" at the end of the day, crashing into the tranquility of your own bed, and dissipating into the silence of sleep . . . At least until the silence is pierced anew by the sound of your alarm . . .

"If water derives its lucidity from stillness, how much more the faculties of the mind! The mind of the sage in repose becomes the mirror of the universe."

~ Chuang Tzu

Letter from an Open Soul

Many people wait until they are dying before they try to figure out how to live. Intuitively, their souls have known these truths all along, but they have refused to see them or believe them. When someone is looking death in the eyes, their soul opens up profoundly, and finally the truth becomes visible. I am not dying. I am alive and thriving, but I am writing from the openness of my soul about how I have learned to live. Not all of these lessons came with ease, many were hard-learned, and I am *still* learning. Yet, I'd like to share with you the lessons life has taught me so far, because I wish someone had shared these lessons with me . . .

Let your heart space be expansive . . . do not hold back anything of who you are, of your love, or of your light. It is yours to share. Do not fear the rejection of your love and light, let it flow freely. Let it be your gift to give. It will flow back to you many fold.

Give yourself space . . . space to be, to feel, to dance, to sit, to rest, to laugh, to love, and to grow. If you do, you will be supported.

God has your back. Do not move out of fear, but move organically. Let your soul move you. If you move from the soul, you will be moving with grace, power, strength, authenticity, love, and light. You will not fall. You are being supported by forces more powerful than your wildest imaginings . . . forces of love, peace, and light.

All will be well. No need to struggle, no need to fix. Relax. All will be well on its own. We try way too hard, always struggling and striving. The things we are really supposed to do just come naturally and flow organically. Release the struggle.

Let go . . . Let go of that which pulls away your light, love or peace. Clear it away to have room to fully blossom into who and what you are created to be. You are radiant; you are luminous, ephemeral, iridescent, and light. Leave behind that which stands in the way of spreading your light.

Grace will rain on you all the days of your life. It is there for you without fail. Just ask and you will receive, for it already belongs to you.

Simplify. Get out the clutter that crowds and confuses your mind, your body and your space. Allow spaciousness to surround you, and your soul will have room to expand and grow.

Take care of you. Be kind to yourself. Be compassionate with yourself. You are as precious as any other being, and you deserve your own love as much as anyone else. Do unto yourself as you would do unto others. Play, sleep, relax and eat well . . . Care for yourself properly without the slightest twinge of guilt.

Take time to get to know yourself. You are your own best companion, your own best friend, your own best advisor, advocate and guide. You may be surprised at how much you like hanging out with you! You may be surprised at how much you have to teach yourself.

Do not fear the power of your own light. Do not be afraid of your own magnificence. Do not hold it back, let it out and let it fully shine. Shining your light is why you are here.

Believe. Believe in yourself. You will never let yourself down. Believe in something bigger . . . God, universal love, underlying peace, our soul's interconnectedness. Just believe that there is something greater loving us, supporting us, protecting us, listening to us, and rooting for us to succeed in this life. Believe.

Do what you like. Do what you feel powerfully drawn to. You are drawn to things for a reason. Trust that. These are your gifts. Do the things that you love, and share them with us all! This is why you are here.

Meditate . . . every day, if even for just a few minutes. It will change your life! Meditation feeds your spirit, like food feeds your body, and air feeds your breath. Meditation replenishes you in ways nothing else can. It nourishes your whole being.

Pray . . . every day, for those you love, and for those you don't. Pray for yourself, pray for your family, your country, and your planet. Pray for people whom you know need help, and for those who need help whom you don't know. Pray for strangers, and pray for all who are suffering. Our prayers can change lives and can change the world.

Don't be afraid of the difficulties that arise in life. They are there to help you transform. Don't be afraid of transformation. Remember, gold must be put through the fire to become pure enough to shine. Charcoal must be placed under powerful pressure for a diamond to be created. When you travel through difficult times, you are a diamond in the making . . .

Receive these ancient words from Lao Tzu: "When I let go of who I am, I become who I might be." Let these words awaken who you are destined to become.

Pancha Mahabhutani:
Balancing the Five Elements Within

According to the sciences of yoga and Ayurveda, all of nature, including the human being, is composed of the *pancha mahabhutani,* or five natural elements: earth, water, fire, air, and ether. It is in the fusion and varying combinations and ratios of these elements that all things in the natural world exist. When these elements are in balance and harmony, the natural world itself is in harmony and so are we. Imbalances or excesses of these elements in nature result in things like hurricanes, floods, tsunamis, tornadoes, forest fires, extreme temperatures, and other natural disasters. It is also paramount to our own state of harmony and well-being that these five elements remain in balance within us.

Earth is the element of cohesion and substance. Its qualities are solidity, stability, and substance. The bones, muscles, skin, hair, nails, and bodily tissues are composed of earth qualities. Too much earth element results in excess tissues such as tumors or obesity. Too little earth element within us results in emaciation. Earth governs our sense of stability, on both mental and physical levels. It helps us to feel grounded and secure. It enables us to stand and move through life with stability. Its grounding force helps us to maintain stable moods and emotions. Is the earth element in balance within you? Are you grounded? Do you feel stable and secure? Are your moods and emotions stable? Are you over- or under-weight?

Water is the primordial substance of life and creation. Water is the element from which all of life on earth emerged. Babies are nourished in the womb in amniotic fluid. Water continues to nourish life on all levels. We can only survive without water for 3 days. The human body itself is composed of 70-80% water. Blood, plasma, urine, saliva, phlegm, mucus, synovial fluid, sweat and other secretions are the manifestation of water within us. Water carries with it the qualities of liquidity, fluid motion, and creative potential. Water governs our ability to "go with the flow" in life. It is the force that enables us to flow over and around our obstacles. Water is behind our own ability to create things in life. Too little water leaves us dehydrated and feeling dried out. Our hair, skin and nails become dry. Our bodily fluids begin to evaporate. Our creativity also dries up. Too much water can leave us bloated, swollen, heavy, lethargic, and "wishy-washy" on a mental level. Is the water element in balance within you? Are you left stagnant by the obstacles you encounter, or can you flow around them? Are you able to go with the flow in life, or are you rigid and inflexible? How well does your creativity flow? Do your thoughts flow freely?

Fire is the element of heat and light. Fire is heating and consuming, yet it is illuminating. Fire has the power to purify and to transform. In our own bodies, fire governs the digestion of food and its transformation into energy. It helps us regulate our core temperature and metabolism. Fire also governs our ability to digest thoughts and impressions on a mental level. Fire is responsible for fueling our passions, our inspirations, our will-power and our ability for inner transformation. Too much fire element can lead to indigestion, fevers, hot flashes, inflammation, and even mental or physical "burnout." Too little fire leaves us feeling chilled, pale, and with a sluggish digestion and metabolism. Is your fire element in balance? Do you feel inspired? Do you feel a passion for whatever it is that you do? Do you enjoy a zest for life? Are you strengthened by your will-power? Do you feel clarity, focus and determination? Do you enjoy good digestion? How is your metabolism? Is it sluggish or slow? Is your skin vibrant and glowing, or pale and dull?

Air is a more subtle element; neither seen nor heard, it is essential to life. Air is contained in our breath, the atmosphere, and the wind. Air governs the qualities of respiration, energy, movement, and life-force itself. Air is necessary for our breathing, cellular respiration, and all movements of the body, even the pulse and the movement of food through the digestive system. Air is the source of chi, *prana*, or life-force within us. Excess air element leaves us nervous and shaky, gassy and is often responsible for insomnia. Too little air element leaves us dull and lethargic, lacking sufficient *prana* or life-force. Is your air element in balance? How is your energy, your life-force? How do you move, with lightness and ease, or are your movements heavy, sluggish and dull? How is your breath, deep and invigorating, or light and shallow? Are you calm and relaxed, or nervous and fretful?

Ether is the most subtle of the five elements. Ether is the element of space. It carries the qualities of spaciousness, expansion, liberation, harmony, interconnectedness, and self-expression. Ether governs the emotions and mental qualities. It rules the mind, senses, and the nervous system. In our bodies, ether inhabits the cranial cavity, the head. It is responsible for free self-expression and expansion of consciousness. Excess ether could result in one being a bit "spacey" and disconnected. Too little ether leaves one fixed in their ways, closed to new ideas, unwilling to try new things, and unable to freely express who they are. Is your own ether quality in balance? Do you feel free to express yourself, the real you? Do you give yourself space and freedom in life? Are you open to new ideas, thoughts and experiences, or are you fixed and limited and closed? Is your mood and emotional state calm and harmonious? Do you feel in harmony with others, with life and with nature? Do you feel in harmony with your own mind, body and spirit?

The five elements or *pancha mahabhutani* are always at play within us. Once you are aware of this, you can observe the roles they play in maintaining health and balance on mental, physical, and emotional levels. You can also observe when one of them comes out of balance. Human beings are but a part of nature, and nature's own elements are alive within us, whether balanced or imbalanced. These elements brilliantly balance and harmonize each other. It is like a continuous game of "rock, paper, scissors" inside of us. Excess water element is dried up by adding more air. Excess earth is balanced by ether's space and weightlessness. Water extinguishes fire. Fire is increased with air. Excess air and ether are weighted down by water and earth. Amazingly, the five elements help to keep each other in check, to help keep you and Mother Nature in balance. It is only when these elements are way off balance that a hurricane results . . .

Knowing When to Cry Uncle

In my early 20s, just out of graduate school, I landed my first teaching job, in the so-called "worst" high school in one of the largest school districts in the country. After being ecstatic to achieve my dream of being a high school art teacher, it didn't take long for me to face some pretty challenging circumstances. I remember the first class on the first day of school; 40 students came into my classroom . . . We only had 35 seats. It is difficult teaching art with students sitting on the floor. It was certainly not the best start! Throughout the 3 years I taught there, I faced violence, arson, theft, drugs, guns, knives, life-threats, fights, and many other difficult situations they never prepare you for when you are studying to be an art teacher! I felt more like a "cop" than the teacher that I had studied to become. Anyone who knows me knows that I do not have a "cop" persona! Stubbornly, despite the pleading of my husband, I refused to quit. Instead, I suffered from stress and anxiety, difficulty sleeping, and total disillusionment with my career choice. Fortunately, God got me out of a situation I had no business being in when my husband was transferred to Texas. We moved to a small town where there were no art teaching positions open, so I began teaching art privately in my home. This change was transforming. Away from my previous situation, I realized how incredibly unhappy and stressed I had been over those 3 years. My husband said I was like a different person. To this day, I still occasionally have nightmares in which I am back in that classroom! The problem was I did not know when to cry "uncle!"

I have been reminded of this theme again over the last couple weeks. Knowing when to cry "uncle" is an art, one that I constantly have to practice and hone. It takes courage and a sense of balance to know when to cry "uncle." Just recently, I had to call on these skills. I had planned to complete a 10-day yoga teacher training module in August. I am also writing a book, which is one of the hardest things I've ever done (besides my first teaching job) . . . not to mention I have two active kids out of school for the summer! I realized it was time to cry "uncle" and postpone my training module until the next time it was offered. How relieved I felt when I made this decision, and I am confident I did the right thing. Since then, my book writing has gone much smoother without the added pressure!

How different my yoga students are from the high school art students I taught long ago! However, practicing yoga is also all about knowing when to cry "uncle." It is about knowing when it is time to come out of a pose and take care of yourself. It about knowing when to bow out of a situation that isn't serving you. Like in my first job, so many of us suffer needlessly, on the yoga mat and in life, because we stubbornly refuse to come out of the pose. There are situations when life demands the wisdom and the courage to cry "uncle!"

Free To Be You

In anticipation of celebrating of our country's freedom, we can be reminded to take a look at our own sense of freedom. From a personal standpoint, I have to keep learning, over and over again, that it is usually me who is the one holding me back from being fully free! As a "recovering type A" personality, I still tend to keep myself pretty tightly scheduled, and always have a list of "to-dos." One day, not long ago, I realized that I do not give myself enough space . . . enough freedom. It's sort of like a smothering mother or boyfriend, only I am the one smothering myself! Ironically, since it is me doing the smothering, you'd think it would be easy to remedy, but old patterns are very hard to break!

A quote from the Sufi poet, Rumi, really hit home, "You were born with wings, why prefer to crawl through life?" There is something that holds each of us back from fully spreading our wings! I think many of us, including myself, have a "fear of flying!" We actually fear experiencing the magnitude of our own freedom, so we keep ourselves in chains. Somehow we end up forgetting that freedom is in our own hands. By keeping ourselves bound up, we are missing out on many aspects of ourselves, and on the many treasures life has waiting for us! Chains are heavy, freedom is weightless and boundless. What is it that you need to be freed of to fully experience the being that you are? What do you need to free yourself of to be more comfortable in your own skin and in your own life?

Personally, I used to fear what other people thought of me. I remember while I was living in France, I tried so hard to speak French with the "perfect" accent, ashamed to be speaking my southern-American-accented French. That was until a French gentleman at the local *Monoprix* (a grocery store) told me how lovely my American accent sounded. What a revelation! After that I quit trying for that textbook accent, and I was amazed at how easily my French speaking was able to flow once it was unedited!

This became a life lesson for me too. I began to stop editing myself, period! Yes, I am a little artsy, a bit of a hippy, a tad bit quirky, part intellectual, and part airhead. Yes, I'm a health nut, a yoga geek, and I'm also a committed Catholic. I no longer try to be who I think others want me to be, I simply am who I am. This in itself has been so freeing! Just like my French, life flows so much more smoothly unedited!

In the words of the late Dr. Seuss, "Be who you are and say what you feel because those who mind don't matter, and those who matter don't mind." In honor of the freedom we are celebrating in the coming days, don't forget to be free to be you!!!

Repair, Rebuild, Restore, Renew

For some reason this has been a year of fixing things for the Cantrell family . . . We've had to repair both cars. We've repaired the dishwasher, the washing machine, the refrigerator, and the toilet. The house is getting painted next week, and even the family cat has been in for "repairs" with kidney stones!!!

It occurred to me there must be a message in all the repairing we've done this year . . . and of course there is! The message is that if appliances, cars, homes and cats need repairing, how much more so do we as human beings! Of course a little preventative maintenance goes a long way, but sometimes we need an overhaul to be restored back to our wholeness, our completeness, and our former glory!

Here is where yoga comes in. If we practice in the right manner, yoga has the incredible power to repair, rebuild, restore, and renew the mind, body and spirit simultaneously. Does your yoga practice restore you, or does it tear you down? Do you come away feeling renewed, or just plain exhausted? It is all in how you are practicing. Are you really practicing yoga, or just doing a workout camouflaged as yoga?

A well-balanced yoga practice heals in a way that repairs the body. It rebuilds by strengthening not only the muscles, joints and bones, but the mind as well. A well-balanced yoga practice restores the mind, body and spirit back into harmony with one another. A true yoga practice renews because each time you return to your yoga mat, you have the opportunity to return home to yourself.

How do you approach yoga? As a work out for the physical body only, or as a way to reunite with yourself, mind, body and spirit?

Next time you find yourself amidst a laundry list of home, appliance, car, or even cat repairs, check in with yourself and observe whether you could use some repairing yourself!

Aparigraha: The Art of Letting Go

Anyone who owns a cat knows that the more you want to lavish it with attention, the more elusive the cat becomes . . . but when you are busy and want nothing to do with the cat, it is drawn to you almost magnetically! When you are not seeking it, the cat comes right to you! The universal law of attraction works the same way. The more we grasp, and covet, cling and claw for something we want, the more we repel it. The energy created by grasping is not the energy of attraction! For example, nothing scares off a potential mate more than a stalker!

Aparigraha is the 5th *Yama* or ethical observance in the yoga system. It translates as non-clinging, non-coveting, non-attachment, and non-hoarding. *Aparigraha* is the art of letting go . . . It is about letting go of our attachments to expectations and outcomes; letting go of things in life which no longer serve us; letting go of our burdens and giving them to God; letting go of "have to's," "should's," and "what if's."

Letting go creates space in our lives for new things to emerge. A couple of months ago, I decided to purge my formal living room/dining room area of all the furniture, rugs, drapes, etc. It was the most expensive room in the house, but the least used! Letting go of the pricey furnishings was a little difficult at first . . . But by letting go, I opened up the space for my own in-home yoga studio! Since that time, I have spent countless hours in the space practicing yoga, meditating, and teaching classes and private students. I am finally using the space that was always there. This "letting go" taught me a lot. Some times the price of opening up space for something new to come in is simply the cost of letting go. My letting go made no sense on a financial level, and it certainly wasn't the "cool" or popular thing to do. But I let go anyway, and I have no regrets!

Just as our homes are sometimes cluttered with old belongings, sometimes our minds are cluttered with old thoughts, old ideas, old ways of doing, and old ways of being. When we clear out the clutter of the mind, we make space for learning, discovering, exploring, and creating. When we let go, things immediately begin to open up. Barriers are removed.

In yoga, my struggle was with handstand. It took me 7 years of yoga practice to finally achieve a handstand. The more I sought out this pose, like the family cat, the more elusive it became. Each week I'd tell myself, this is the week I'll get into a handstand. Each week I came away more frustrated. Finally, I gave myself "permission" to *not* get into handstand. I realized I could still enjoy practicing yoga throughout my life without ever standing on my hands. I let go . . . Not surprisingly, it was then that the posture came to me. When I let go of "having to," the struggle was gone, and it happened with ease. When we let go of the preoccupations we have with wanting, having, keeping, grasping, "should-ing" . . . that is when new opportunities will seek us out . . . just like the family cat.

Beat to Your Own Drum

From the age of five, when I was the only little ballerina in the recital out of synch with all the other little ballerinas, I knew I beat to my own drum. Becoming a yoga instructor in the conservative Midwest further demonstrated my willingness to follow my own path. I'd be much more "accepted" here if I just joined the bowling league, drank beer, ate sausages, and figured out how to get rid of my strong southern accent. However, I stink at bowling, I prefer wine, I don't eat meat, and, at age 45, I've realized this accent isn't going anywhere! According to Swami Kripalu, "Yoga is the courage to be yourself."

It saddened me the other day when my teenaged daughter came home and told me about an encounter with a boy in her class. He was listening to his iPod in study hall, and she noticed he was listening to Trace Atkins. She tapped him on the shoulder and said, "I see you like country music too." He said in reply, "I don't like country, and I'm not listening to country music." She said, "I saw you were listening to Trace Atkins, and I know who he is, he's a country singer!" He shrugged nervously and said, "Well don't tell anybody I like country. The guys will all make fun of me if they find out."

We adults also fear people finding out who we really are. Isn't that what the financial melt-down was all about? Adults were trying to keep up the illusion of wealth and success instead of being ok with who they were. This house of cards literally collapsed. I recently read a Chinese proverb: "Tension is who you think you should be; relaxation is who you are." I believe we are at a time in our evolution when we can freely celebrate who we are in our own individuality. I believe we are at a point in history in which we can honor others just as *they* are, appreciating the beauty of their uniqueness. An original is much more valuable than a carbon copy!

The *Bhagavad Gita* teaches that it is "Better to follow one's own *dharma* (life path) though imperfectly carried out, than the *dharma* of another carried out perfectly." I was recently privileged to enjoy listening to a group of about ten live drummers. Each had their own sort of drum, and seemingly played to their own beat. How beautifully it all came together. It was here where I realized that if we each beat to our own drum, we will make beautiful music together.

The Power of Words

Growing up, I remember children chanting the phrase "Sticks and stones can break my bones, but words can never hurt me." For a long time I thought this was true, until I read about Dr. Masaru Emoto, a Japanese physicist. Dr. Emoto has done extensive studies concerning the effects of words on the structure of water and food. One of his studies involved filling glasses of water from the same source. Some of these water samples were spoken to with positive words such as "thank you," "I love you," and "peace." Other samples of water were told "I hate you," "I want to kill you," and "war." Subsequently, the water was frozen, and then examined under a microscope. Amazingly, the water samples subjected to positive words had formed beautiful crystalline structures which looked like snowflakes under the microscope. The water samples which were subjected to the negative words looked like ugly "splats" under the microscope. Positive and negative words and phrases actually changed the structure of water! When we take into account that human beings are composed of 70-80% water, Dr. Emoto's studies become significant. Words can actually affect people and things energetically!

How is this possible? Dr. Emoto's experiments tap into the realm of quantum physics. This science has proven that everything in the universe vibrates at certain frequencies, including our thoughts and speech. Positive thoughts and words vibrate at high frequencies, and negative thoughts and words vibrate at low frequencies. When these vibrations are directed at something or someone, the receiver's energetic vibrations are also affected, thus changing its vibrational frequency. Thoughts and words carry with them tangible energetic vibrations which influence the world around us. This is a fact of quantum physics.

Understanding this fact, how often do we chastise ourselves, calling ourselves "old," "fat," "ugly," or "stupid"? What do these words do to us energetically? How does this affect our own life-force, our inner being? Think of the times we have berated our children. How has this affected their own internal structures, their very souls? I think of how some bosses lead their employees by fear, intimidation, and "brow-beating" in order to get results. Is this really going to get the wanted results, or is it going to further weaken, diminish and break down the employees, handicapping them energetically?

Dr. Emoto has gone on to do numerous experiments on water and food and the effects of positive and negative words. He has also studied the effects of curses and prayers. The results have continued to show how powerfully words and phrases affect the energy and structure for better or for worse. Interestingly, in the studies, distance had no effect on the power of the words. The results remained the same even from very far away, as long as the words were directed towards the particular sample. Written words were found to have as powerful an effect on samples as spoken words. Also of note, the more positive words were spoken to the samples, the more complex and beautiful their structures became. The converse was true with negative words.

We have incredible power right at the tip of our tongues. What if we harnessed and used it to create a better self, a better life, and even a better world? What would happen if we used our words to build up not only people, but to literally change the life-force of all things for the better? Something as simple as positive thoughts, words, phrases, labels, and prayers has the power to change this world for the better. That change can begin now . . . with just a word!

> "Kind words are a creative force, a power that concurs in the building up of all that is good, and energy that showers blessings upon the world."
>
> ~ Lawrence Lovasik

> "Words — so innocent and powerless as they are, standing in a dictionary, how potent for good and evil they become in the hands of one who knows how to combine them."
>
> ~ Nathaniel Hawthorne

Thawing Out Your Mind, Body, and Spirit

In the upper Midwest, things are just now starting to thaw out. The snow and ice are slowly melting, and the ice cover on the lake behind my house is growing thinner and thinner. Thawing out is a process. It involves warmth, melting and liquid movement. When things thaw, they become soft and supple, losing the rigidity and density of their frozen form. How often are our yoga postures hard and frozen, with our faces determined, hard and fixed? How too can our minds be rigid, unyielding and dense, letting in nothing new? How much can our spirits benefit from renewed warmth and softness?

My 9 year old son has been practicing karate since age 5. Although he still loves the art, he became stagnated and frustrated with a grumpy and rigid *sensei* (teacher). He began to dread each visit to the *dojo*. He was on his fifth belt, couldn't seem to progress further, and lost the heart and the passion he once had for the practice. For weeks, my husband and I suggested trying a different martial art, at a different *dojo*. My son stubbornly refused because he did not want to start over as a white belt. Finally, with a big push, he decided to give the new *dojo* a try. He walked in fearful and timid, his shoulders rigid and drawn in. Not long after he started class, a smile returned to his face. His shoulders softened. He loved it. It was different, it was new, and he was good at it! The *sensei* was warm and encouraging, which was just what he needed. I watched my son "thaw out" that day. As soon as he was done, he came to me with a radiant face and said, "I want to keep doing this, it was great! I loved it!" The rigidity of being the expert melted away, and my son started anew. His unbending attachment to his belt, and to his former *dojo* which no longer served him, now yielded like the melting snow. His lost joy in the martial arts was renewed, just as nature is renewed in the spring thaw.

When the mind thaws, the body thaws too. I watched my son's posture soften, as if thawing out. In this more relaxed state he was better able to learn and enjoy something new. When the mind and body thaw, the spirit thaws too. The radiance so obvious on my son's face was the light of his spirit rekindled, and warm again.

How often does rigidity hold us back as adults? We can be single-minded, unmoving, obstinate, unyielding and inflexible in our own lives. Does this really serve us? As we set the intention to "thaw out" our yoga practice this week by remaining open, soft, warm, pliable and flexible, we can mirror that intention in our lives. Thaw out rigid thinking, and watch your body soften and relax as tension melts away. Thaw out old thinking and fixed attitudes, and give your spirit new space to illuminate and glow. Just as thawing out and melting in nature invites the renewal that is spring, we too can allow the same thawing to happen in ourselves. This thawing is the catalyst for our own renewal.

"The flexible overcome the adamant, the yielding overcomes the forceful."

~ Lao Tzu

Shine Your Light

During a recent conversation with a dear friend and yoga instructor, we began to discuss "the essence of shine." There are those people we meet in life who have a luminous essence about them. They have a certain "glow." They have found their inner light. It is detectable to the discerning eye. There is just something about them.

I have been taking a mindfulness meditation class, and today was the last meeting. One of the students in the class is a school janitor in her mid-50s. When I first met her in class, she had a plain appearance and a pleasant but melancholy demeanor. Over the weeks, I began to see a change in everyone in the room. There was a new softness and peace about them. But this school janitor showed the most profound change of all. During the last class, I looked at her, and saw a radiant glow. There was a discernible vibrancy about her that wasn't there before. She had found her inner light. It wasn't her job, or her looks, or her material belongings. What made her glow came from within. I saw her light and was deeply touched because I knew she had discovered it too.

We all have a light. Some of us are afraid to let it shine. Often we stand in our own way! Sometimes it is others who try to suppress and even steal our light. "Light robbers" are people who are filled with fear that you will "out-shine" them. They stop at nothing to try to steal or dim the light of others. What they do not realize is that inner light can't be had by stealing or smothering the light in others. In fact this very act only dims their own light. Inner light is already there in each of us. We only need to go within and discover it waiting there. Once you find it, let it out!

My friend put it like this, "The essence of shine: Those who have it . . . glow with it. You can see it, you can feel it. When a person has it, they walk into a room, and their essence fills up the space as they step into it. It is a radiance that is so powerful, people stop to sense that something has shifted. Many can't figure out what has happened, but they know something is different in a way words can't grasp. But a dangerous few seek to steal it, stop it, destroy it . . . for they are unable to find it in themselves. They lack their very soul." Marie also said, "I do know that I am blessed to have surrounded myself with those who glow! They walk next to me and guide me through this maze called life! They are my family and friends!"

Don't be afraid to shine your light! Walk with those who shine theirs! Don't be afraid of the "light robbers" in your life. They can only take your light if you give it to them! Uncover your light, and let it shine! If we all do this, this world will glow!

"You are the star in your own life, don't be afraid to shine."
~ Marilyn Monroe

Sacred Rest

We live in a culture where the answer to fatigue and exhaustion is an energy drink or a trip to Starbucks. We are rather proud of the fact that we can just "suck it up" when we are sick or tired. Instead of taking a day of rest when we are ill, we swallow down tablets and pills which mask our symptoms so we can soldier on! When the body aches from a long day of work, the response is to push even harder. If muscles are fatigued and sore from yesterday's "punishing" workout that just means we need to "dig a little deeper." We feel guilty if we aren't doing, striving, endeavoring, or accomplishing, even for a brief moment! God forbid, we would never, ever listen to our body and do what it is begging us to do: REST!

We have lost touch with the power of sacred rest! Rest is a GIFT, yet we refuse to receive it and open it! Rest is a cure to all that ails us, body, mind and spirit, according to Ayurveda. Rest is so essential that it was included in the "top ten list" for human good, handed down by God himself in the "Ten Commandments." This is one commandment that humans as a whole seem to find trivial and pointless. What could God have been thinking? Who needs rest when we can force our mind and body to do more, push harder, endure, tolerate, persevere, dig deeper, persist, soldier-on and withstand?

We are not machines, and our bodies weren't created to motor-on endlessly. The majority of us live in a state of "rest deficit!" There is no Olympic metal for exhaustion! It is no wonder that chronic fatigue, adrenal fatigue, hypothyroidism, hormone imbalance, heart disease, cancer and inflammatory disease are the plagues of our times. We are chronically rest-deprived and depleted.

The irony of life is that many a person loses their heath to make more money, only to spend their fortune in order to regain their health. Sickness is your soul's way of informing you that you are out of balance and harmony. When we restore balance and harmony, we restore health. One way we all fall out of balance in our culture is our resistance to rest . . . not just sleep, REST! Rest and sleep are two different states of consciousness.

Paradoxically, rest does not automatically make us unproductive, lazy and idle. It actually helps us become more vibrant, energetic and enlivened! It spares us our heath and youthfulness. It enhances the well-being of body, mind and soul. Fatigue is counter-productive, and rest is SACRED!

Here are a few suggestions to incorporate more "sacred rest" into your life.

1. Unplug from electronics. Go off-line for a few hours each day. Electronics are over-stimulating to the mind-body system. Give yourself a deadline in the evening, after which there are no more emails, phone calls, texts, Twittering or Facebook!

2. Take a 20-30 minute *savasana* every day. *Savasana* is a practice of silent stillness which is done lying on the floor comfortably on the back.

3. Take a 1 hour *savasana* once a week.

4. Meditate on a daily basis, giving the mind a "time-out."

5. Take a "mental health" day periodically. A day of ease and self-care when you nurture yourself and give yourself whatever your mind, body and soul are asking for.

6. Take a vacation, sabbatical, hiatus . . . even a "stay-cation."

7. Set aside time to practice just "being" on a daily basis . . . a period of time when you have no requirements to do, strive, learn, accomplish, or complete anything!

8. Do not fling yourself out of bed in the morning, rushing into the day with recklessness! Give yourself space to awaken, appreciate, and embrace a new day. Start your morning in stillness, peace and gratitude for a restful night's sleep! Say a prayer or set a positive intention for the day!

9. Spend time in nature. Nature is "soul-nourishing." It is grounding and reconnects us to who we are and where we came from, as we are part of nature.

Some of my favorite ways to incorporate rest into my own life are: restorative yoga, *yoga nidra*, meditation, a prolonged *savasana*, a warm aromatherapy sea salt bath with essential oils, reading by the fire, spending time in nature or relaxing to soft music, lying down meditation, and vacation.

How vibrant we all would be if we received the rest we are craving! Is your body, mind or soul crying out for needed rest? Nourish, replenish and empower yourself NOW. Rest is a natural part of divine order. Rest is sacred!

Affirmation: "It is natural and necessary to rest and renew. I am tender, kind and compassionate with myself. I allow myself to receive the benefits of sacred rest. "

> "Man surprised me most about humanity. Because he sacrifices his health in order to make money. Then he sacrifices money to recuperate his health. And then he is so anxious about the future that he does not enjoy the present; the result being that he does not live in the present or the future; he lives as if he is never going to die, and then dies having never really lived."
>
> ~ Dalai Lama XIV

The Healing Power of Beauty

While enjoying my vacation on the beautiful Island of Saint Kitts, West Indies, I was reminded of the amazing effects of spending time in a place of beauty. According to the healing science of Ayurveda, beauty has profound healing effects on the entire mind-body system. In Ayurveda, we actually prescribe spending time with beauty because it is inherently healing. I could not help but feel the effects of this first-hand while surrounded by the natural beauty of the mountains, flowers, lush tropical greenery, sky and sea. We can intentionally tap into the healing power of beauty on an everyday basis as a part of our own wellness maintenance regime! Here are a few suggestions!

1. Cultivate beautiful thoughts. Choose your thoughts carefully. Keep them positive, peaceful, full of love and light. Let your imagination wander to beautiful places. Consciously steer your thoughts away from fear, anger, resentment, guilt or other dark, ugly places. Have beautiful daydreams, and watch your nightly dreams be filled with beauty too!

2. Consciously surround yourself with beauty. De-clutter your home and office, and opt to make your living space neat, clean, positive and friendly. Decorate in a way that brings you JOY and uplifts your senses. Choose pictures, plants, paintings, pillows, and rugs with the intention of surrounding yourself with beauty. Use paint colors that make you feel happy and calm. Let the sounds in your home be cheerful and harmonious. Play melodious, uplifting music, or place a trickling fountain in your home, rather than having a blaring TV be your background noise! Dinner always tastes better on a beautiful plate, and tea always tastes better in a beautiful cup! Make your surroundings therapeutic!

3. Beautify yourself. When I am feeling down or sick, I notice I immediately feel better when I shower and take the time to beautify myself by fixing my hair, and putting on makeup and a splash of perfume.

Everyone feels beautiful after a trip to the salon for a new haircut, pedicure, or facial. Beautifying yourself on the outside sets the intention of feeling beautiful on the inside!

4. Feed your mind with beauty. Carefully choose your books, music, movies, and TV programs. The sounds, thoughts, suggestions and images you take in through the five senses have a profound effect on the mind. The mind digests everything we feed it. If you want beautiful, harmonious thoughts, then be selective as to what you feed your mind!

5. Feed your body with beauty. The body-mind system instantly responds to the food we eat. Natural foods that vibrate with beauty, health, vitality, and life-force energy impart this same beauty and vitality into us. Foods that are heavy, lifeless or chemically contaminated confuse, pollute and weigh down the body and the mind. By choosing foods that vibrate with life and beauty, you are choosing life and beauty for yourself!

6. Beauty is as beauty does. Let your actions spring from kindness, compassion, forgiveness and love. When you act from the beauty of these intentions, your entire life becomes a work of beauty. My mom always said, "Beauty is as beauty does."

7. Draw in the beauty of nature. Being in nature is innately healing. There we are able to draw upon the healing sounds, scents and colors of the water, wind, grass, birds, trees and flowers. We can soak in the healing rays of the sun (not to mention some vitamin D!). We become harmonized, grounded, and tranquil when we reconnect with nature. Humans are a part of nature and humankind actually began in the "sacred garden." It is important to return to the garden from which we came, and reconnect with who we really are. Spend time in the beauty of nature: by a pond, in the woods, in the mountains, or by the ocean. You don't have to "do" anything but allow the beauty surrounding you to do its powerful healing work. The healing effects from the beauty of nature are well documented and quite profound.

8. Connect with the powers of flowers. Each species of flower is known to have its own specific healing energy and essence. Many flowers' essential oils are used in aromatherapy. Flower remedies also draw from the healing nectar and essences of flowers, each flower essence unique in its healing effect. Just being in the presence of and gazing at flowers is known to be curative, restorative and healing. Flower gazing is a delightful form of meditation, which is also prescribed for the treatment of various ailments in the healing science of Ayurveda. In the modern age we have often lost touch with the powerful healing effect of the beauty of flowers. Bring the healing beauty of nature into your home or office by placing fresh flowers on display in a prominent location where you see them often. Choose colors and blooms that you naturally feel drawn to, trusting that you intuitively know what you need. Gaze at them often and draw in their beautiful healing aroma. There is a reason we send flowers to people who are sick or infirm! Flowers are inherently healing to the body, mind and soul!

Beauty is divinely created and deeply healing! When we lose touch with the beauty around us, we lose touch with the beauty within. Beauty is to be cultivated, appreciated and embraced. Fill your life with healing beauty now!

The Message of the Snow

The scene out of my back window looks like a post card: frozen lake, trees blanketed in snow, boughs bending gracefully under the weight of heavy whiteness. The sun sparkles and glistens even brighter, catching the crystalline flakes. There is a stillness out there that seems at odds with the hustle and bustle of the holiday season. The snow seems to muffle all sound and quiet the landscape.

The snow also slows us down. Schools are delayed. One must drive slowly and mindfully. It takes longer to put on the right gear before we get out and about. Driveways need shoveling.

It's as if nature is sending us a message, during this holiday rush: "Shhhhhh, be quiet, and slow down." Will we listen???

Letting Go . . .

There is a story which Jon Kabat-Zinn writes about in his book, *Full Catastrophe Living*, which describes the cunning art of catching monkeys in India. Hunters will cut a hole in a coconut, big enough for a monkey to put its hand through. On the other side of the coconut, they will drill two smaller holes and wire it to a tree. A banana is placed inside the coconut. Then the hunter hides and waits. A monkey will crawl down from the tree, put its hand inside the coconut, and seize the banana in its fist. The hole is just wide enough for the monkey's hand to go in, but the fist is too wide and cannot get out. If the monkey simply "lets go" of the banana, it could slide its hand out, and it would be free, but monkeys do not "let go" and hence they are trapped.

Our human minds ensnare us in similar ways. We are trapped when we find ourselves "stuck" right where we are, unable to move forward in life. What are you holding on to like a monkey in a trap? Like the monkey, our holding on tight keeps us from obtaining something we want even more, namely our freedom. Often letting go is the only way to free ourselves.

When we let go of expectations, outdated goals, unsupportive life-styles, and habits which weigh us down, we are suddenly free to experience the miracle of exciting possibilities, answered prayers, new outcomes, unfolding dreams, and spectacular transformations.

This week, set the intention to "let go" of whatever it is that is keeping you from the life you want. What is your banana? Let go of schedules that do not serve! Let go of clutter in your home. Let go of what people might think about you! Let go of old outdated plans! By letting go, you are the catalyst for a fresh and alternate future, holding the magic of the unexpected. Sogyal Rinpoche reminds us, "Although we have been made to believe that if we let go, we will end up with nothing, life reveals just the opposite: that letting go is the real path to freedom."

Let go, and step into your future. It is already there waiting for you! In the words of Raman Maharishi, "Let what comes, come; let what goes go. Find out what remains . . ."

Inner Strength for Life's Obstacles

Salmon season is rather spectacular to watch here in the upper Midwest. These rather large fish are swimming up-stream, against the current, towards their destiny. They swim with fierce determination to get back "home."

One Sunday I took my children to the dam to watch the salmon amazingly leap up over the waterfall and dam, swimming against a powerful current in their journey back to the sea. Seeing a rather large fish leaping 15 feet into the air with a powerful current working against it is simply amazing! It became clear how much inner power, strength and energy these creatures have to muster from within to accomplish this amazing, seemingly impossible, feat! But with a strong resolve, these fish tap into their internal power source, to overcome a great obstacle, in order to continue on their way.

Watching this, I realized that if a fish has everything within that it needs to succeed in overcoming the seemingly impossible obstacle in its path, then so do we. Just like the salmon, we already have everything we need for our journey. When we encounter the obstacles that crop up in the journey of life, we only need to tap into that river of strength and power that lives there within us. If we remember it is there, then we too can do the impossible!

What is Coming Between
You and Living Your Dream?

How is it that some people live their dreams seemingly with ease, while others just observe in wonder? Too often we dismiss our power to create our dreams by saying that other people are somehow unfairly lucky, blessed, smarter, richer, or have very good *karma*. We talk ourselves out of what is really ours. We rob ourselves of our own destiny by imprisoning ourselves in our own set of ideas about the way things are and how life works. By clinging to this old conditioning as if it was TRUTH, we stay locked behind our own self-created bars, shackled to our present life, longing for something different. We helplessly dream of a different life, not realizing that it is only we ourselves who hold the keys to our own dreams and the doorway is not even locked! Stop coming between you and living your dreams.

Reject your inner critic. Very often we hold ourselves prisoner with judgment, fear of failure, and self-doubt. On the other side of fear, doubt and judgment is an alternate reality. The keys to this doorway are courage, trust, faith and change. This reality already exists right there within in you. The wall of fear, doubt and judgment is an illusion. When you walk through the wall, you will meet your dreams on the other side! Affirm: "I am enough, exactly as I am, to get to where I am headed."

Own what you have within. When we live from within, instead of without, everything changes! Outward focus on accumulating, appearances, achievements, impressing, material possessions, and people-pleasing is a fatal distraction to dream realization. We can quickly become prisoner of these things because they keep our focus directed away from our true desires and longings. When we look within ourselves, we uncover our deepest yearnings and the intuition, inspiration, insight, power, courage, confidence and creativity to own our dreams. Within us are the only tools we will ever need to make our dreams come true. Anything you are looking for on the outside already exists on the inside waiting to be discovered, accessed, opened and exposed. Don't get distracted by the external; the way to your dreams is the inner path. Affirm: "I already have everything I need."

Discard the thought "I can't." "Can't" is a lie! Yes, you can! Many people are held prisoner by this false belief for a lifetime! You can put as much belief in "can" as you do in "can't!" Whichever one you put your belief in will determine the final outcome. I remember one of my teen yoga students saying "I can't" every time we learned a new pose. She believed this false STORY, that somehow she lacked what everyone else in the room had. Over and over, I showed her that indeed she could! Impossible is only a concept, it is not a reality! "Can't" is a self-imposed obstacle to your dreams! If impossible were true and real, a certain clumsy, un-athletic, stiff, un-flexible middle-aged southern woman would never be a yoga instructor and author! We get to the field of pure potentiality by sailing through the river of faith! The key to the doorway of this magical place is to believe in any and every possibility! Affirm: "I can and I will."

Cast off perfection. Perfection can be one of the slyest obstacles on the path to the realization of our dreams. Perfection is an illusion. Perfection is not balance; it is not freedom; and it is not real. Refuse to be imprisoned by the illusion of perfection. Perfection does not exist in nature or in ourselves. We often get so caught up in doing things "perfectly" that we enslave ourselves to a mirage of perfection instead of freeing ourselves to live our dreams. Give yourself permission to be messy, to make mistakes, to look like a fool. Let goofing up be a sign that you are moving forward and are no longer stuck behind the false wall of perfection! Have faith that if nature survives its imperfections, so can you! Affirm: "Perfection is an illusion, my dreams are real."

Stop focusing on "how." Oftentimes we get so focused on "how" we can achieve our dreams, that we lose focus on our dream! Where attention goes, energy flows. "How" is a waste of time and energy. The "hows" happen on their own if we stay focused on what we really want. If we get stuck on "how," we fail to move forward. You don't HAVE to know the "hows". The "hows" do not matter, they are just clutter. The "hows" get in the way and take our dreams out of focus. Trust that there are an infinite number of ", not just one! Concentrating your energy on "how" rather than on the dream itself blocks the flow of grace. When we trust in grace rather than "how", that is when magic and miracles happen. There are higher ways and greater forces beyond our limited human knowledge of "how." In the space beyond the "hows," that is where miracles exist! Don't "spin your wheels" chasing the "hows," chase the dream itself! We become our dreams in each moment just by being entirely ourselves at exactly where we are. Affirm: "I am the way to realizing my dreams."

Trust that what you want already exists. According to quantum physics, every outcome already exists in the field of possibility! It is up to you to go in and get it! Ideas, insights, signs, signals . . . Follow the "rabbit" into the "rabbit hole." You have to go into the field of possibility to access your dreams. You have to follow them as they call to you. Follow them inwardly and then outwardly, even if you don't know where they will take you and how they will get you there. Go and follow! What you are seeking is seeking you! It is drawn to you in equal measure, and is moving toward you at the same speed you are moving towards it. Like two ends of a magnet, you and your desires are drawn together. This is nature. This is physics! Affirm: "As I move towards my dreams they move towards me."

Don't ignore and miss the signs and messages. Signs are like bread crumbs leading you down the path to your destiny. Signs come from expected and unexpected sources. Follow each one completely, seeing it through to its final destination, where you will receive another sign. Following your dreams is fun, like a treasure hunt! Signs may appear as hunches, coincidences or moments of synchronicity. They can come from nature, a wise soul, lyrics of a song, a poem, or a quote, or they may arise through prayer and meditation. Affirm: "I am continuously receiving divine guidance and wisdom. I trust and I follow."

Take action. God helps those who help themselves. Action + grace = momentum. Action and grace brought together create a powerful force. Fusion of these two things is magical. Apart they do little; together they can accomplish anything! Action + grace + momentum =

manifestation. This is the alchemic formula for making the impossible possible! You can't just make a grocery list of things you need at the store and expect those things to appear in your refrigerator without going to go get them. You must decide what it is you want and then go get it and bring it home. By taking action, you can manifest everything you wanted on the grocery list. All things work this way. Affirm: "I am my dreams, my dreams are me."

Only YOU can make your dreams come true. Only you come between where you are now and what it is you want. The dream is already is yours! Go get it! This forgotten knowledge is to own our true POWER and step into our true FREEDOM to live out our GREAT-EST DREAMS!

Are You Breaking Your Own Heart?

Last week in my Teen Yoga class, a student came into class crying. Thinking something horrible must have happened, I asked what was wrong. The answer surprised me . . . a bad grade on a test. Teens are so hard on themselves. And who are they are learning this from? Us adults! We model this self-flagellating behavior almost daily. I was very hard on myself as a teen and young adult. It has taken me years of practice to "undo" the pattern of being my own harshest critic, meanest boss, and merciless judge. I am still a work in progress.

We are born into this world joyful, free and at peace, but somewhere along the line, we forget who we really are. We learn to insult ourselves, bully ourselves, and judge ourselves; but we forget how to LOVE ourselves. As humans, we seem to be addicted to inflicting our own suffering. According to Ayurveda theory, if you are feeling unloved, it is because you are not adequately loving yourself.

I am not here to tell you that you need to learn to love other people more; I am here to tell you to give your heart back to yourself. The compassion and kindness we have for ourselves is directly proportional to the kindness and compassion we show to others. We cannot give what we do not already have!

Silence your inner critic. Stop rejecting your own Self, the very essence of your soul. Stop breaking your own heart. Stop betraying yourself. YOU are exactly the being your soul chose to experience incarnate! You are extraordinarily special! Accept yourself, love yourself, and appreciate yourself just as you are without condition. Become your own dearest friend and your own best mother. Give yourself permission to make YOU a priority, to live joyfully a life you love. Don't see failures or weaknesses as flaws, see them as lessons or teachings, as parts of you that just need more nurturing and growth. Whoever you are, however you are, right now is enough. Love yourself NOW instead of waiting for perfection, because perfection doesn't exist! Choose to see the radiant soul that you already are!

Elise Cantrell

"Dear God, help us to believe the truth about ourselves no matter how beautiful it is."

~ Dr. Christiane Northrup

"My beloved child, break your heart no longer. Each time you judge yourself, you break your own heart;
You stop feeding on the love, which is the wellspring of your vitality.
The time has come. Your time to live, to celebrate.
You my child are pure. You are sublimely free, and you are always perfectly safe.
Do not fight the dark, just turn on the light.
Let go and breathe into the goodness that you are."

~ Swami Kripalu

Affirmation: "I love myself completely and unconditionally. I am worthy. I am enough just as I am."

"If you live the life you love, you will receive shelter and blessings. Sometimes the great famine of blessings in and around us derives from the fact that we are not living the life we love; rather, we are living the life that is expected of us. We have fallen out of rhythm with the secret signature and light of our own nature."

~ John O'Donohue

Make Your Yoga Practice a Mini-Vacation

While practicing yoga during my recent vacation, it occurred to me that yoga itself is a "vacation!" While practicing, it seemed I was even taking a vacation from my vacation! Going within during our yoga practice takes us to a different place, and time seems to pass in a magical way. We come away rested, refreshed, and renewed, in a relatively short span. The great thing about a yoga practice is that you can bring it with you anytime, anywhere and allow it to last as long or short as your time allows!

The Dali Lama has said that "Going faster and faster is the sickness of our times." A recent article in *Yoga Journal* by Jenn Shreve discussed how saturated we are with technology, social networks, smart phones, text messages, email, etc. It's as if we are constantly available, continuously distracted, and find ourselves working or networking in restaurants, waiting rooms, airplanes, hair appointments, and other places where we would have once found respite. The article emphasizes that research on the effects of computer use on human health has shown that it is anxiety inducing, and can even cause the human psyche to go into a state of fight-or-flight.

Here is where yoga practice comes in. It shifts your mind from without, and brings your mind to its inner vacation place. Yoga practice slows the breath, slows down our multitasking mind, and reminds us what it feels like to focus on only one thing at a time. It keeps us in the present moment, simultaneously uniting body, mind, spirit and breath. We become connected to ourselves once again.

I often urge my students to take moments of stillness during their days, taking their yoga "off the mat" and into their lives. These are "mini" vacations from the business of our days. Perhaps it's a quiet cup of tea while sitting comfortably looking out the window. It could be taking a few stretches and mindful breaths at your desk. It could be a quiet walk in nature. If we hit the "pause button" in our lives, we will be calmer and more focused when we return from our mini-vacation. Take as many of these moments as you need each day for as long as you can, without the least twinge of guilt, knowing that you are taking care of your mental and physical health. Approaching yoga practice as a mini-vacation from the hustle and bustle of life, and returning to that same state of mind often during the day, is where balance, peace, and contentment exist.

Shifting Momentum in Your Life

Sometimes we feel we have no control, as if we are just passengers on a wayward roller coaster called "Life." We feel helpless and unsure, as if we are merely being pushed and shoved around by the forces that surround us. We become dazed and uncertain when we land in unknown territory. Although we feel powerless, what if I told you we have much more control than most of us realize? What if I told you we have the potential to shift the momentum in our lives towards the outcomes we desire?

Momentum is energy. It is the force of movement and its velocity. In the martial arts, the master uses his opponent's own momentum to defeat him. By pulling him in the direction he is already moving, he can be easily taken to the ground. Even a smaller opponent has the potential to overcome someone much larger if he masters the skill of timing and momentum.

How can we shift momentum in our favor? We too can become masters of timing and momentum, if we stop spinning our wheels and use momentum in our favor. We can shift the momentum of our lives in the desired direction just by harnessing simple forces that exist around us.

1. Intention. The practice of setting intentions is powerful. Unconsciously we are setting intentions all of the time . . . "I'm no good at bowling." "I always mess things up." "I can't lose weight." These little messages are heard by every cell of our being! Whether intentions are set consciously or unconsciously, the mind creates a belief system around them. When belief systems are set, the mind holds fast. When we set intentions consciously or unconsciously, the mind focuses on them.

Where the mind focuses, energy follows. Where energy flows, action results. Actions bring intentions into being.

If we let them, other people can set intentions for us. "You will never amount to anything." "You're no good at X, Y, or Z." We have all had people in our lives try to tell us who and what we are. However, we have the power to consciously set our own intentions, moving thought into energy, energy into action, and action into results.

What do you want to happen? What is your dream? To set an intention, speak your desired result in the present tense as if it has already happened. "I weigh the same as I did in high school." "I am writing my own book." "I have the job of my dreams." Whatever it is that you desire, speak it into being. Then, write it down, place it somewhere in view, and re-read it often. This, alone, launches momentum.

> "From intention springs the deed, from the deed springs the habits. From the habits grows the character, from the character develops the destiny."
>
> ~ Chinese proverb

2. Conscious action. Action is energy. Conscious action is energy used skillfully. If you are playing chess, you have to make a move. To win the game of chess, it must be a skillful move. A conscious action is taking an intention and making a move in a tangible, concrete, and intelligent way. Conscious action is awakening, taking charge, and creating change. Taking conscious action moves stagnation, and breaks up old patterns. Conscious action begins with the mind as the catalyst, but then moves into the physical realm. It is a concrete "doing." It is an action which formally breaks with the past, and brings about the energy of new momentum. Conscious action is really *kinetic energy* which is the energy possessed by virtue of being in motion. Combining skill with being in motion creates the right action behind our desires, which is powerful momentum.

3. Prayer and blessings. Prayer is the alignment of our own energy, actions, and intentions with God or the divine. Prayer unites human power and momentum with a higher force. This force powerfully directs energy and momentum on our behalf towards that which is best for us. Never underestimate the power of prayer to shift momentum in your direction. Don't be afraid to ask for what it is that you want. It is written, "Ask and you shall receive, knock and the door shall be opened for you." Volumes have been written on the miracles associated with prayer.

Blessings also carry divine energy. A blessing is asking for God's favor and protection over someone, something, or some act. With divine assistance and protection, how can momentum not move for your favor? There are mighty forces, more powerful than ourselves, waiting lovingly for us to ask for assistance and guidance.

4. Positivity. According to quantum physics and the law of attraction, "like" attracts "like." Knowing this truth, why not use this law in your favor? If you want positive things to happen in your life, then you must put out "positive" energy in order to attract it back to you. Positivity is a choice. It does not happen by its self. By choosing to focus on the positive and send positivity out into the world around you, you will be amazed at what you receive in return. Positivity will be drawn into your life almost magnetically, increasing the momentum for your life to shift in a positive direction. Identify ways you can put more positivity out into the world. Just a smile or a kind word creates a ripple effect around us! The more positivity you are willing to project into the world, the more positivity you will receive in return!

5. Letting go. In tug of war, when two people are grasping onto a rope and pulling in different directions with equal energy, nothing happens . . . stalemate. The tugging can go on and on. But what happens when one person lets go? The second person is toppled by the force of their own pull. Sometimes we are pulling so hard against the forces that be that we end up in a fruitless struggle. We can't go anywhere until we let go! I have a dear friend who had been trying to sell her high-end home for over 4 years in the current real estate crisis. She had gone from feeling stressed and overwhelmed, to feeling frustrated and desperate, but finally she let go. When she let go, she could develop a different plan, a way to keep the home as a vacation home until she and her husband retired. She set things into action (conscious action), and hired movers to move in sufficient furniture for vacations, and planned to take the home off the market as soon as her realtor contract expired. Ironically, it was when she finally let go, and created a new plan, that the phone began to ring. Only weeks after she let go of having to sell, she had a signed contract on her home! This was after over 4 years of straining, and holding on to "the rope." When we struggle against the powers that be, sometimes the only way to win is to let go!

6. Rituals or sacred acts. Performing rituals or sacred acts are another way to shift momentum. This is a physical, concrete way of setting an intention. It brings the desired concept or idea into the physical realm. After I was married, I placed our wedding announcement inside my Bible, and there it remains today after 18 years. Some people light candles as a symbol of their ongoing prayers for someone or something. During the depths of the recession, I bought bamboo plants, which are symbolic of prosperity, for my home. I even went as far as keeping the doors of our bathrooms closed, a *feng shui* ritual to prevent financial loss! A common ritual is to bury a St. Joseph statue in the yard in order to sell a home. The idea is the same, an intention is set in a "real" and physical way. This act alone is "birthing" the idea or intention into the material world, into reality, and into being. This "birthing act" creates the momentum of the actualization of an idea, dream or concept.

7. Getting out of your own way! More often than we realize, it is really we ourselves who are standing in the way of our own success and happiness! Perhaps we feel we do not deserve it. Perhaps we are afraid of the changes success will bring. Perhaps we fear the unknown. More often than not, we are the obstacle, holding ourselves back. Being an obstacle, we create our own friction against forward moving momentum! We often unconsciously sabotage the momentum we have moving towards our ideal self. Often, deep down, there is fear of the expectations that come along with achieving our goals. For example, overweight people often sabotage their efforts to lose weight for fear of returning to dating, of making their friends jealous, or of the work that is required to maintain healthy weight. For most people, being in your own way shows up as just being "wishy-washy" about obtaining your desires. When there is something you want in life, being indecisive scatters energy and spins wheels, but gets you nowhere. To get what we want, we have to be purposeful and resolute. Being hesitant and indeterminate only creates stagnation and paralysis. Stagnation has no momentum. Once you are aware that you are the only one in your way, then it becomes apparent that it is all up to you. This in itself can be scary. Be aware of this fear. With this awareness, you can make new choices, and create new patterns and ways of being which serve you on the path to your destiny. If you notice that it is really you who is standing in your way, then you have the power to step aside, and then move forward towards your greatness.

8. Hope. Hope is aspiration, confidence and expectancy. Hope is pure *potential energy*. Potential energy in physics is defined as energy derived from position or condition, rather than motion. Hope is the powerful stored-up energy of positivity and optimism, just waiting to be unleashed! Hope doesn't need "hows" or "whys" to back it up, it defies explanation, and exists independently of logic. Hope carries with it a confidence that things can change despite the circumstances. Hope is the assurance the future will be better. The positive energy of hope attracts positive energy to us. Hope is also considered a virtue. This is because it involves the confidence that divine forces for which there are no obstacles are working on our behalf towards a positive outcome. Hope is the opposite energy of despair, which carries with it the energy of dullness, torpor and stagnation. Despair carries no momentum. It is hope that propels us forward. With the virtual potential energy of hope behind your intentions and actions, momentum is magnified exponentially.

9. Taking a leap of faith. Faith carries powerful momentum. Someone once told me that faith is like a crystal bridge across a deep canyon. You can't see it, but it is necessary to take it to get to the other side! Often, to shift momentum in your life and get to the other side, walking forward into the unknown is required, with nothing else but the faith that things will all work out. An attorney friend of ours was miserable in his corporate job. He went to work each day with a deep sense of dread. The recession was in full swing, and he felt he had no choice but to grind it out, and stay where he was. He felt that he should just be thankful he had a job. But, one day he had enough. He took a leap of faith, submitted his resignation, and joined an attorney friend to form their own firm. He resolved for his family to live frugally on savings until they made a go of things. It wasn't long before business was booming, and financially he was doing much better than in his former job! Had he not made that leap of faith, he'd still be miserable in his same position. Today he is prospering and happy, but it took a leap of faith to get him to a better place!

Everything in life has energy behind it, the good, the bad and the ugly. However, not only can you *choose* your energy, and your direction, but you can *create* powerful momentum, which can be life changing. Eventually momentum will take you to that moment of transformation, where intention, action, prayers, and hope merge to form a new reality. The only thing in the way is you!

Relaxing the Grasp

After reading a magazine article on *feng shui* and decluttering, I was inspired to purge my home of everything I neither use, need nor want. This was easier said than done! I don't want to add more garbage to the local landfill, so I really had to put thought into who could use each item, or decide if it was even usable at all. One of the most difficult places to purge was my "tea drawer." I have a collection of over 50 kinds of tea, so there were numerous open, half-used boxes of tea that just had to go. But to whom? They certainly cannot be donated! It is hard to let things go, even if we don't use them, need them, or want them.

Over the past few weeks, as I've confronted the challenge of detaching myself from the numerous items from all corners of the house, that I don't need or use, it has really brought to the surface for me the 5th *Yama* or ethical observance in the yoga system: *aparigraha*. *Aparigraha* translates as non-grasping, non-clinging, non-coveting, and non-hoarding. We all struggle with this in some way, my "teas" are a small example.

Throughout the recent "great recession," the best has been brought out in some people, while the worst has been brought out in others. Most of us know someone, or have ourselves, lost jobs, homes, incomes, retirement or health benefits, and possibly even marriages during this difficult time. In many instances, this has brought out the human predisposition to grasp, to cling, or to "claw" if you will, to get or keep something we want. Like a dog with a bone, growling and showing his teeth to anyone who gets close, this behavior has been brought out in the human animal during these trying times. I've noticed people in business have turned to "finger-pointing," throwing others "under the bus," ducking personal blame, and seeking to edge others out, for fear of losing their jobs. I've recently noticed more false advertising than ever before, in which people and businesses have resorted to outright lies in order to achieve financial gain. However, these acts of desperation, will in the end, most likely have the opposite results.

Aparigraha is about letting go. The universal law of attraction tells us that the more we grasp, cling and clutch onto something, the more we repel it! There is no better way to scare off a date than to desperately want a date! Stalkers push away, rather than attract the victim of their attentions. The converse is true as well. When we let go, things immediately begin to open up. Barriers are removed. I know of several couples who, after years of desperately trying to conceive a child, turned to adoption. It was then, when they had let go, that they actually conceived.

In yoga, my struggle was handstand. It took me 7 years of yoga practice to get into a handstand. The more I struggled with this pose, the more elusive it became. Each week I'd tell myself, "This is the week I'll get into a handstand." Each week I came away more frustrated. Finally, I gave myself "permission" to *not* get into handstand. I realized I could still enjoy practicing yoga throughout my life without ever standing on my hands, and I let go of the struggle . . . Not surprisingly, it was then that the posture came to me.

If ever you discover yourself clinging or grasping at something, whether it is a job, a material object, a person, or a yoga pose, practice *aparigraha.* The act of relaxing the grasp, allows whatever it is to come to you.

Unwrap Your Radiance

The brightness of the summer sun is a daily reminder of our own inner radiance. It sparkles and shines, it warms, lights, and seemingly glows. It is the radiance of the sun that really brings things to life. But how many of us keep our own radiance cloaked and under wraps, afraid of unleashing our own brilliance and splendor?

In elementary school, I remember being the last girl picked for teams in gym, whether it was kickball, baseball, basketball, volleyball or something else. I admit I was pretty uncoordinated then, but I felt like a loser when it came to sports! I carried this insecurity with me throughout high school, refusing to try out for a single sport, being afraid of reliving the rejection I felt when I was younger. Instead, I focused on art and academics, where knew I could succeed. What I didn't know until years later was that, as I had matured, at some point my coordination had developed, but I had never given it a chance. If I had continued to hide behind my fears as an adult, I would never have attended my first yoga class, and I'd never have found my passion, my calling, which is teaching yoga.

Are you keeping your own radiance cloaked? Are you hiding in the shadows of yourself, afraid to come out and shine? Are you afraid of failure, rejection, or feeling like a loser? You are not alone! We have all let something or someone stand in the way and shadow our passions, desires, talents, and dreams. Very often that someone or something is ourself! We are all, each one of us, afraid that we are not good enough, big enough, strong enough or special enough, so we hold ourselves back from truly manifesting our magnificence! What if I told you that you are enough just as you are? There is nothing to change, no one to try to be, no more you have to do to arrive. Your radiance is already there, hidden within you. Unwrap your radiance! Let it out! We're all here to shine!

Swami Kripalu was quoted as saying,

"My beloved child, break your heart no longer. Each time you judge yourself, you break your own heart. You stop feeding on the love which is the wellspring of your vitality. The time has come. Your time. To live, to celebrate, and to see the goodness that you are. Do not fight the dark, just turn on your light, let go and breathe into the goodness that you are."

~ Swami Kripalu

"When you observe the warmth and light of the summer sun, do not end your search for light and radiance there. Go within and unleash your own radiance.

Ask not what the world needs. Ask what makes you come alive, then go do it, because what the world needs is people who have come alive."

~ Howard Thurman

Index

A

Acknowledgements 6

Affirmations to Heal and Harmonize the *Chakras* 37

Am I On the Right Path? 44

Aparigraha: The Art of Letting Go 243

A Prescription for Self-Care 49

Are You Addicted to "Busy?" 22

Are You Awakening? 16

Are You Being Kind Enough to Yourself? 81

Are You Breaking Your Own Heart? 267

Are You Listening to Your Intuition? 27

A Walk Among the Dead 114

B

Balancing Life 130

Beat to Your Own Drum 245

"Bee" Inspired! 226

Be Kinder . . . to You 159

Blissed Out 191

C

Christmas in July? 149

Come on to Your Mat as Little Children 216

Conversation: Speaking Skillfully 145

Creating Space for Grace 91

Cultivating Courage 151

D

Don't Do Yoga, BE Yoga 56

E

Eight Stepping Stones to Manifesting Your Intentions 202

Eight Ways to Refill Your Tank 132

Enough 120

Experiments in Love 74

F

Finding Your Tribe 20

Flowing in the Current of Grace 163

Flowing Water Never Decays 64

Free To Be You 240

Free Yourself 100

G

Get Unstuck 195

H

Hidden Treasure 144

How to Do What You Love, Succeed and Thrive! 97

I

Inner Strength for Life's Obstacles 262

Inquiring Minds 176

Introduction 7

Is Exploring Your Lunar Side Lunacy??? 208

Is Yoga Evil??? 185

K

Knowing When to Cry Uncle 238

L

Letter from an Open Soul 232

Let the Real You Come Out to Play 84

Letting Go . . . 260

Letting Go to Set Yourself Free 40

Life is a Playground 76

Life is Like a Yellow Brick Road 140

Life Lessons I Learned from Writing a Book 110

Life Lessons I Wish I Could Go Back and Teach My Younger Self 32

Living with Paradox 103

M

Make Your Yoga Practice a Mini-Vacation 269

My Year of Karma and "CAR-ma" 206

N

New Moon, New You 167

Non-Striving: Life is Like a Cat 122

P

Packing Guide for the Journey of Life 69

Pancha Mahabhutani: Balancing the Five Elements Within 235

Paradise 73

Peeling Away the Layers 218

Polishing Your Inner Jewel 228

Pressing the "Pause Button" in Your Life 189

R

Relaxing the Grasp 277

Releasing the "Should" Out of the Shoulders 187

Repair, Rebuild, Restore, Renew 242

Returning Home to Yourself 212

Riding the Winds of Change 224

S

Sacred Geometry: The Power of the Triangle 95

Sacred Rest 253

Seven Things Thriving People Do Differently 46

Shape Shifting 214

Shifting Momentum in Your Life 270

Shine Your Light 251

Simplify Your Life 29

Spring Back to Life 174

Starting Over 200

Staying Balanced and Grounded During Times of Transition 106

Step into Your Light and Shine 53

Stillness amidst the Storm 230

Sweetness 181

T

Taking Your Vacation Back with You into Your Life 78

Thawing Out Your Mind, Body, and Spirit 249

The Art of Balancing Effort with Surrender 136

The Ebb and Flow 169

The Healing Power of Beauty 256

The Law of Expansion and Contraction 118

The Message of the Snow 259

The Path 178

The Power of Words 247

The Remover of Obstacles 221

The Seven Doors 66

The Sound of Silence 156

Transformation 161

Trying vs. Being 60

Turning Your Thinking Upside Down 125

U

Uncloaking Joy 127

Unplugged! 117

Unwrap Your Radiance 279

Unwrap Your Spiritual Gifts 34

W

Weeding Out Your Life 210

Weekend Review 89

What Can Dogs Teach Us about Stress? 62

What is Coming between YOU and JOY? 24

What is the Significance of 108? 14

What is Your Personal Mission Statement? 58

What Stands between You and Feeling Free? 154

WHO? 171

Without Space, There is No Room for Grace! 183

Y

Yoga is Unity 192

You're Not Full of Holes, You are Whole 165

About the Author:

Elise holds a Master's Degree in Education from The University of South Carolina. Formerly a high school art teacher, Elise combines her background in teaching with her passion for body, mind and spirit wellness. Elise is a student and teacher in the classroom of life. Elise received her 200 hour YTT certification from White Lotus Institute in Santa Barbara, California, and her 500 hour level Certification at Kripalu Center for Yoga and Health. Elise is a certified Ayurvedic Life-style Counselor via the American Institute of Vedic Studies in Santa Fe, NM. Elise is a Reiki practitioner, a Certified Relax and Renew TM, restorative yoga instructor, and a spiritual intuitive.

Elise is currently the owner of Shining Lotus Yoga and Wellness in Kohler, Wisconsin. She is a happily married mother of 2 teenage children. Among her favorite classes to teach are Aligning with the True Self and 40 Days to Enlightened Eating. Elise is also passionate about cooking and eating natural foods, and has developed an eating plan inspired by the sciences of Yoga and Ayurveda. She has authored a book based on this plan entitled *40 Days to Enlightened Eating* released November 2012.

This book/material is possible because of the wisdom of my guides, teachers, numerous authors, and experts in the field of Yoga, Mindfulness and Ayurveda as well as my students, family and friends. I am constantly reading yet also learning from my own experiences. There are so many insights and inspirations, which have come about over the years that it would be impossible for me to acknowledge or remember where they all came from. If I have inadvertently herein articulated a concept as my own, as if from my own thoughts, when in fact they are someone else's, I express my sincere apology. I am deeply appreciative of the transmission of this wisdom, and will happily correct any misperception to honor authentic authorship. It is only my intent to empower, encourage, inspire and enlighten others like me, who thirst for soul-growth.

To all who have played a role in the creation of this book, I honor the light and the teacher within you which has inspired the light and the teacher within me.

Nameste,

Elise Cantrell

"Reinvigorate your metabolism, optimize your weight, awaken your energy and enliven your spirit."

www.40DaystoEnlightenedEating.com